MHCC WITHDRAWN

DS 830 .C6913 1984
Courdy, Jean Claude.
The Japanese   9108

DATE DUE		
NOV 1 1985 DEC 1 0 93		
MAR 1 4 1986 JUN 3 94		
MAY 9 1986 MAR 1 0 1995		
JUN 5 1987		
FEB 1 2 1988		
JUN 3 1988		
MAR 1 0 1989		
OCT 2 8 1989		
NOV 2 0 1989		
DEC 8 1989		
JUL 0 4 1989		

MT. HOOD COMMUNIT
Gresham

D0955890

THE JAPANESE

THE JAPANESE

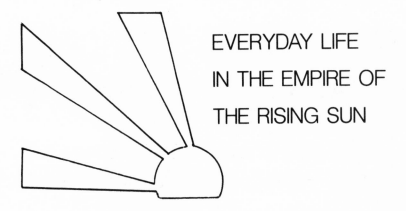

EVERYDAY LIFE
IN THE EMPIRE OF
THE RISING SUN

by Jean-Claude Courdy

Translated from the French
by Raymond Rosenthal

HARPER & ROW, PUBLISHERS

New York, Cambridge, Philadelphia, San Francisco,
London, Mexico City, São Paulo, Sydney *1817*

This work was first published in France under the title *Les Japon-ais: La Vie de Tous les Jours dans l'Empire du Soleil Levant.*
© Belfond, 1979.

THE JAPANESE. English translation copyright © 1984 by Harper &
Row, Publishers, Inc. All rights reserved. Printed in the United
States of America. No part of this book may be used or reproduced in any manner whatsoever without written permission except in the case of brief quotations embodied in critical articles
and reviews. For information address Harper & Row, Publishers,
Inc., 10 East 53rd Street, New York, N.Y. 10022. Published
simultaneously in Canada by Fitzhenry & Whiteside Limited,
Toronto.

FIRST EDITION

Designed by Ruth Bornschlegel

Library of Congress Cataloging in Publication Data

Courdy, Jean-Claude.
    The Japanese.

    Translation of: Les Japonais.
    Includes index.
    1. National characteristics, Japanese.   2. Japan—
Civilization.   I. Title.
DS830.C6913   1984   952.04   80–5775
ISBN 0–06–038010–1   AACR2

84 85 86 87 88 10 9 8 7 6 5 4 3 2 1

Contents

Preface

I had been having a fifteen-year flirtation with journalism when I learned in May 1963 that I had a chance to be named permanent representative of the French Radio-Television Bureau in the Far East, with Tokyo as my base of operations. I was living in the euphoria of the Cannes Film Festival; the uncertain weather, or actually the constant downpour of rain, favored an exotic reverie. I had already decided to make the journey by boat, and had boned up on it: Marseilles to Yokohama, a thirty-two-day voyage, with a number of ports of call—Port Said, Cairo, Aden, Bombay, Colombo, Singapore, Saigon, Hong Kong, Kobe. . . .

I thought of other cities, included in my territory: Seoul, Manila, Peking. . . . But I am a realist; I did not have too many illusions about my chances of hitting the front page often. After my arrival at Tokyo, this impression was confirmed. Paris had very little interest in Japan.

As it turned out, radio would soak up most of my output. Television would broadcast about four hundred items in seven years, of which some 70 percent would have as their theme the American involvement in Asia, Korea, China, and Vietnam. Among Japanese events in Japan, the student revolts would arouse some interest—for example, the boarding of a commercial plane at saber points by five members of the "Red Army" terrorist group. But with few exceptions, my journalistic life there would prove to be pure frustration.

The years passed. I quit Japan after being there for seven of them. I got married. The first years of my children's lives slipped by. I was happy. Yet I still had the feeling, on my return to Paris, that I had been unable to reveal a great country and a great people to my friends.

The first part of this book, "Meetings," is the story of my infatuations and revulsions vis-à-vis the Japanese as I have seen them, trying to forget my prejudices, my education, what people had told me about Japan, and the clichés I myself harbored. On reflection, I wanted to go beyond my meetings, and I discovered those "dualities" which are the subject of the book's second part. History and civilization have produced the permanent coexistence of myth and reality, tradition and modernism, East and West. Perhaps the reader will be better prepared than I was initially to tackle the "realities" of contemporary Japan, of the Japanese at home, in society, and in his business world. One's consideration of everyday life in the Empire of the Rising Sun could stop right there if the Japanese did not have an umbilical cord that ties each individual to his country, to Japan's soil. So, in order to explain what the Japanese feel, one must evoke the ground swells which threaten them: the challenges of foreign bodies, which must be either assimilated or rejected; the challenges of demons from the past which are at odds with demons of the present, and of today's demons which want to annihilate those of yesterday; the challenges of systems trying to pass themselves off as values.

This book does not fit any clear-cut classification. My task was to report on the life of the Japanese people almost from day to day and, through this view of the quotidian, help people to understand other people.

Does this book come at the right moment? I trust so, if I can judge from Japan's penetration into our daily lives, by the place it has gained through objects as familiar as radios, televisions, high-fidelity phonographs, calculators, and now, family computers, not to mention automobiles. My aim in writing has been to overcome my frustration and to provide the curious with some of the indispensable perspectives that may lead to new horizons. I must therefore express my gratitude to those who facilitated my landing and my acclimatization on the planet Japan:

Anne-Marie, my wife, an expert researcher and a lover of Japan, a country we arrived in separately. One fine day, she agreed to accompany me to the French consul, Reginald Austin, and to bind her life with mine, in the presence of Jean Dhouc and Henri Deguichi, our witnesses and friends.

My colleagues whose teachings I have tried to remember, with special mention for Jacques Jacquet-Francillon of *Figaro*, Robert Guillain of *Le Monde*, Marcel Giuglaris of *France-Soir*, Bernie Krisher of *Newsweek*, the Italian writer Fosco Maraini, as well as the British composer-musicologist Dorothy Britton.

My *sensei* professors: James Morley, director of the Asian Institute at Columbia University, whose teaching gave me a sense of history; Mike Oksemberg, one of the perspicacious American Sinologists who clarified for me the context of Chinese-Japanese relations; Zbigniew Brzezinski, encountered in the corridors of Columbia University and at seminars on Japan, whose incisive criticism helped me to qualify and add nuance to certain judgments.

The French in Japan, the *tatamisés*, those who could not live elsewhere, such as the Buddhist René de Berval, the banker Roger Denoual, the geographer Jacques Pezeu-Massabiau, and Father Valade, the missionary and correspondent of Abbé Pierre.

The French diplomats and experts on Japanese history and culture: André Brunet, Michel Huriet, and Jean Perrin.

French ambassador Louis de Guiringuaud, who occupied the post at Tokyo before going to the United Nations and then becoming France's minister of foreign affairs.

U.S. ambassador David Osborne.

Japanese ambassadors Fujiyama, Kagami, Kitahara, Motono, and Nakayama.

Professors of political science Inoki, Kosaka, and Mushakoji; professor of constitutional law Miyazawa; professor of letters Ko Iwase; former governor of the Bank of Japan Sumita Satoshi; administrator of the newspaper *Asahi* Takeo Enna; artist and philosopher Taro Okamoto; composer, orchestra conductor, and writer Ikuma Dan; and my friend Takashi Suzuki.

I am also indebted to the staffs of the embassies of Japan in France and France in Japan, to the Foreign Press Center in Tokyo, and to the Japanese minister of foreign affairs who opened numerous doors for me. I also want to thank the Franco-Japanese Economic Bureau and the Office of French Documentation, whose staffs have always been able to track down a date, statistic, or document that was not in my files.

Modernity is not only the art of paradoxically assuming the responsibility of technical know-how and of discovering in it a kind of profundity, but it is also the art of assuming the essential mobility that characterizes the act of virtuosity.

—VLADIMIR JANKELEVITCH,
Liszt and the Rhapsody: An Essay on Virtuosity

Introduction

Many Japanese are overtaken by a feeling of vertigo and discomfort when they visit the palace at Versailles. The extremely symmetrical garden plots, paths, and fountains seem to them too artificial. This is affirmed by Kinhide Mushakoji, professor of political science at the University of Sophia in Tokyo. They are upset by the vanity of those who want to subject nature to man, who is not its master. How can man think of imposing his will on nature, when our problem as human beings is essentially that of adaptation to and coexistence with our environment? In this there is an aesthetic choice closely related to the Japanese concern not to be confined intellectually to a geometric concept. Here the Japanese are closer to Pascal than to Descartes. The Japanese state is of course a model of organization. But as Professor Mushakoji has observed, "There are plans and plans." He mentions the case of the architect and urbanist Kisho Kurokawa, who during a visit to Brasília was struck not by "the empty and inhuman city in its geometric beauty but rather by the shantytown, constructed without a plan, by Brasília's workers."

It was there that the Japanese architect discovered the most evident harmony between man and his environment, because, as Kurokawa said, "When one builds one must take into account the rhythm of destruction of the component parts with which one builds. Man and nature are complementaries in the same system." One cannot visit Japan without being struck by this evident fact.

Professor Takeshi Muramatsu cites two eloquent manifestations of this: the permanence of the Shinto religion, as it appears in Shugendo, or mountain shamanism, a nature religion par excellence which goes back to the origins of Japan; and the cultivation of rice in a northern country, whose acclimatization over the centuries demanded a superhuman effort from the Japanese peasant, creator of an exceptional bond between earth and man. Such harmony has its repercussions in the relations of each Japanese with his neighbor. Moreover, a Japanese cannot assume that he is essentially opposed to another Japanese; hence, perhaps, the idea that individualism does not exist in Japan. Yet the "individualist" experience finds a marvelous arena in which to unfold, and it is in accordance with this criterion that Japanese youth strives to express itself today. But when individualism is felt as alienation, the Japanese abandon the confrontation of oneself with another and the quest for harmony is resumed.

This attitude confers on Japan an appearance of pluralism different from the liberalism of the West, where each person thinks he has a lien on the truth. There is competition in all Western pluralism; in Japan, there is cooperation. In the West, truth must triumph; in Japan, one must choose what best serves the society in which one lives and must never sacrifice human relations to the truth. Love of one's neighbor comes before love of truth. This is in part the message of the writer Shusaku Endo in his book *The Silence of God,* an adaptation of which was presented at the Cannes Film Festival in 1974. The priest who sees his followers tortured one by one is convinced that Christ would have disavowed himself in order to save a Christian being put to death because of Him. For a Christian, this is heresy. Western philosophy is not immune to "let justice be done and the world perish," whatever its absurdity. Vladimir Jankelevitch has explained this very well: "Beyond what seems to us to be the truth, there is another, profounder truth, all of whose elements we do not possess."

The Japanese, in their uncertainty, feel obliged to employ the metaphor of a house of two stories, one story entirely Japanese, the other entirely Western, with a continuous coming and going between the two, which translates into a permanent inability to be clear-cut. Should one see in this a respect for complexity or an enigmatic habit of thought that is intended to deceive? Is it true that the Japanese are unable to choose between black and white because they prefer gray? Is it true that in opinion polls the Japanese beat all records for those who reply "No opinion," which could imply ignorance but instead reveals embarrassment when confronted by a question that demands a simple yes or no?

How then can their fanaticism and violence be explained? Japan's history has never been lacking in bloody episodes that reflect extremist positions, decisions coldly acted on, hesitations swept aside, deliberate choices. To the indecision expressed into everyday language by *shikashi . . . ga,* "however . . . but," can be opposed the determination represented by the headband a man ties around his forehead to show everyone that he means to proceed to the bitter end. "This bitter-endism" is the obverse of the coin whose other side is "weighing the pros and cons," all of which casts doubt on the real nature of the coin.

Social behavior springs from this double heritage: the heritage of violence in the country's geography, history, and people, and the heritage of stoic impassivity acquired in order to survive in a society subject to severe shocks. Ruth Benedict, the American writer whose pertinent observations people saw fit to praise although she had not yet visited Japan, spoke of a "civilization of shame" in conflict with a "civilization of sin." This is only how it appears, even though the vocabulary of elaborate apology dominates Japanese usage.

During the years of vertiginous growth, countless small and middle-size businesses failed, and these failures increased even more strikingly after the 1972 crisis. Each time, the same ceremony was repeated. At a special meeting of the stockholders, each member of the management staff publicly confessed his shortcomings and, bowing, asked to be forgiven for having caused the business to fail. In the Diet, a particular politician, let us say the prime minister, is caught out on a promise he has not kept, or on an obvious failure of his policy. He immediately presents his apologies to his colleagues and to the entire nation before handing in his resignation. This attitude carries over into everyday human relations. . . .

At two in the morning, Tokyo is deserted. Dinner at the house of the French cultural attaché has ended late; I offer to drive another guest back to his hotel—the historian Albert Soboul, an authority on the French Revolution and a member of the Central Committee of the French Communist party. I take a shortcut down a street between two rows of small wooden stores, intersected at the end by another street. I enter the intersection without looking either right or left, and have almost crossed it when we feel a violent shock in the right rear of the car. Our car spins around and comes to a stop. Four young men jump out of a car facing us. They are aggrieved. All of us bow and offer reciprocal apologies. We have both been careless—I for having entered the intersection without looking, they for having exceeded the speed limit. I am sure that deep down, the four Japanese whose car is now a wreck have only one desire—to beat my brains in. Inwardly they curse me, just as inwardly I call them alcoholic bastards. Can one identify so profound an emotion as shame with what is merely a code of coexistence imposed by conditions of life in a society different from ours?

When a society imposes such severe constraints, it is essential to provide escape valves for the collective release of repressed emotion. Thus public displays of violence are an expression of *vox populi*, which is normally stifled by good manners. But the release of repressed emotion also functions on the individual level.

In Tokyo it is still dark. Six o'clock in the morning. In Setagaya Street, the sound of footsteps. It is too early for the trash to be collected, and one doesn't hear the characteristic whirring sound of the crusher slowly digesting garbage. Noises are still muted. Some light rattling indicates that people are closing the exterior sliding doors at the foot of small gardens. Shadows flit by, heading for the nearest subway entrance, railroad station, or bus stop. They are all under twenty-five and belong to a *dojo*, a club devoted to the martial arts. Judo, karate, aikido, and kendo are the escape valves for individual repression, for young people who physically are victims of living conditions on an overpopulated archipelago and morally are unable to achieve the ideal embodied in the virtues that autarchic Japan bequeathed them.

Arimasa Mori, professor of philosophy, declares: "We are being dragged along on the rails of European ideas." The observation carries a certain nuance of regret that Japan has no way of attaining a modern society other than by borrowing an alien mode of thought. This means that "Western ideas are not only effective but also contain a certain truth and universal validity." Here one finds a Japanese specificity opposed to Western universality. But Mori hastens to add that these ideas, which reduce everything to a "numerical and quantitative" proposition, stifle "what is directly and profoundly human." Is this ambiguity or duality? The Japanese concept of human relations creates a kind of intense privacy, while the Western concept always runs the risk of depersonalization. Those Japanese who question their identity should in fact be reassured. They are closer than Westerners to answering the question: Who are we?

Coming from Europe, I was upset, full of apprehension at finding myself in the midst of a crowd. Getting off at the Ginza at six in the evening, I realized I would never again be afraid of crowds. Summer on Sukiyabashi Square at the moment when the traffic lights switch to green for pedestrians coming out of the Mitsukoshi-Ginza is an unfurling of white short-sleeved shirts. You are hemmed in on all sides, and yet you can move quite easily. If it rains, a forest of umbrellas grazes you, and suddenly, in the middle of this tide, behold an incongruous blotch: the "American-jin," who may also be French, identifiable by his sports clothes or his raincoat. The Japanese never wear raincoats. It is not fashionable. Zabo, a French caricaturist who has exercised his verve and etching needle at the expense of the Chinese, Indians, and Japanese, had an interesting experience one day. He put on a rice grower's hat and wore the two straw panels, front and back, that peasants wear in the rice paddies in bad weather. Thus rigged out, Zabo crossed the Ginza, back and forth, while a camera followed his movements from afar. The reactions of the crowd as seen on the film were astonishing. Only two schoolboys of thirteen or fourteen whispered to each other and choked back their laughter at the sight of Zabo, who looks not at all like a Japanese peasant. The crowd paid no attention to this brute.

I have never felt ill at ease. You can look right into the girls' faces. The smile with which they answer your glance is almost an invitation. The store windows are filled with everything that can attract the eye, and you never stop dreaming up cravings and imagining how you will transform your apartment into a bazaar of bric-a-brac and gadgets. The theater and movie posters are unusually large; a helicopter breaks the monotony of the noises; the subway mouths disgorge and swallow; the crowd is like a perfumed bath. Night falls quickly, the neon signs switch on, and the street is transformed into an immense Luna Park. You never feel like going to sleep, you are so attracted by little things: the horoscope at the street corner; a plateful of noodles held out to you by a vendor of o'soba; the small bistro à la Japonaise where ten customers, not one more, have the honor of tasting the tempura (fried fish), the yakitori (skewered meat), and sashimi (raw fish), or the sushi (raw fish wrapped in rice held together by a frond of seaweed). Without fear, you can go in anywhere, to be greeted by a thunderous "Hirashaimase" (You are very welcome). Whoever you may be, you are the kingly customer.

I go from astonishment to astonishment. At Hiroshima, a "child of the bomb" explains to me that the Americans are her friends. At Nagasaki, in the marvelous basin that encircles the bay, making it look like an immense theater in which the port is the stage, I come to know the cult of Puccini, who created *Madame Butterfly* without ever setting foot in Japan. Today no one knows whether Madame Butterfly's house was rebuilt according to Puccini's description or whether he, by some gift of telepathy, dreamed a reality from the back of beyond. At Ebussuki, two thousand people are bathing together in the midst of gigantic plastic cactuses. People go once a year to the nearby peninsula of Shimokita to commune with the spirits of the dead. At Happo-En, in the setting of an ultramodern resort, some hundred yards from a four-star restaurant you enter a modest thatched cottage; you are then led to the bank of a river that runs past the kitchens, where they have set up a fish pond. Here you can catch a carp or a trout, which, for a few hundred yen, is cooked right in front of you. You can still find some hotels in the Gion in Kyoto that rent their rooms by the hour but will allow you to stay after ten o'clock at night, until eight o'clock in the morning if, as often happens, you cannot find anything in the normal circuit provided by the Japan Travel Bureau. At Dotombori, Osaka's amusement quarter, you are given a lesson in anatomy in the guise of a striptease. The newspapers print several million copies every day. Typewriters have no fewer than two thousand keys. At the University of Tokyo, the students study Provençal and read Mistral in the original. Hundred-year-old pine trees grow only one foot tall. On the No stage, the actor takes twenty steps and pronounces twenty words in the course of two hours. The perfumed bath continues. . . .

This first phase of the encounter distills euphoria. Certain perpetually grudging individuals never know it, repelled as they are by the incomprehensible world surrounding them. How can one live without street names, with taxi drivers who are ignorant or nasty, in the midst of a stifling crowd, with humorless people who wear a look of consternation when you laugh and who laugh when there's truly nothing to laugh about? One can't even console oneself with the cuisine: it is odious. They cannot even write like everyone else. . . . Everything becomes an excuse for going into a rage.

Then comes the second stage. Nothing and everything sets your nerves on edge: taking off your shoes on entering a house; listening to the talk about marvelous flower arrangements while everywhere in the street one sees frightful wreaths of artificial flowers celebrating the opening of a bakery or a new bride's loss of virginity. The crowd becomes an obsession, in the street, bus, subway, train. The sumptuous furnishings of offices or stores make one smile, when 80 percent of the capital and whole cities are built of wood and look like immense, electrified shantytowns, short on water in the summer and stinking, due to the lack of sewers. The luxury of the Ginza repels you after you have seen the endless streets of the Saniya quarter, where the unemployed are jammed together, nine or ten to a room twenty square yards in size. No city planning and indeed no plan at all, except for some ministerial office with a dozen incompetent functionaries. Political parties raking in graft; an educational system that drives the young to suicide and despair; wives who are slaves to their husbands and who never join them at table; contracts that are not respected, tariff barriers; customs; endless regulations to prevent the foreigner from getting in. Everywhere ambiguity, perhapses, maybes, hesitation, and qualification, the permanent tension of the individual subjected to a rigid social hierarchy, an individual who spends all his time worrying about losing face.

In this period of my life in Japan, my second, irritated phrase was aggravated by three stories I heard. A young European girl working as a secretary in an embassy fell in love with a young Japanese, the son of a family that was neither rich nor poor, merely comfortable. He seemed to be in love with her. A rather inferior student in a private university, he had no clear idea as to his professional future, particularly since his parents had agreed to support him. One day the European girl saw the blind alley she was in and that there was no way out of it, even in marriage, which, in fact, the boy's parents were against. So she decided to break with him. That's when the psychodrama began. The young man, who until then had been a well-bred, courtly, even passionate lover, was transformed into a brutal, foul-mouthed maniac, screaming obscenities in the middle of the street, making scenes in front of their friends, pretending to faint on the sidewalk so that he had to be carried half-comatose to his house. Act Two: The young man began to blackmail the girl by telephone, harass her, demand compensation, though never saying how much. Act Three: The poor girl, frightened to death, came to the office each day with her nerves in shreds, on the verge of clinical depression, and, after the nth telephone call, agreed to a final meeting to decide on the compensation. Act Four: The meeting took place. The young man had completely regained his self-control and calmly threatened her: "Your break with me has made me lose face at the university; you owe me reparation." (The girl passed from tears to stupefaction.) "I demand six thousand yen immediately. My friends are my witnesses. If you do not give me the money within forty-eight hours, I will kill you and then commit suicide." She had the happy idea of confiding in a Japan specialist, who could give her only this advice: "Take the plane for Europe tomorrow." Which she did.

On the intercom my secretary calls me: "It's Professor X. Will you take it?" "Of course!" "Monsieur Courdy, it is very urgent. I must see you. Can I stop by your office tomorrow?" "Agreed. Four o'clock?" "Four o'clock." The next day at the exact time, Professor X, from Y University, stands before me. I wonder what important matter he has to discuss. He has been in my office for almost five minutes and he has not yet opened his mouth. He spends a long time searching for his cigarettes, then his matches, and then he asks if he is bothering me. Finally he begins: "I have a serious problem, and I am looking for an impartial person. So I thought of you." Silence again. He resumes: "For years I have been tormented by a problem of conscience. Three times a week, when I give my course, I do not use the shortest route to reach the amphitheater. I make a long detour, for I know that if I don't, I will meet my old professor. And I can't handle it; I still haven't worked out the right way to greet him." New silence . . . puff on the cigarette. "What do you think?"

I was with a group of ten Japanese journalists, three or four Americans, and two other Frenchmen, all invited by the Korean government. On the second evening, we were asked to give examples of our national talents. I do not know how to sing and I loathe this sort of entertainment, but forced to do something, I improvised a mime of La Fontaine's fable "The Oak Tree and the Reed." I am not Marcel Marceau, but everyone there understood that the oak represented America and the reed Japan, that the oak ended up being uprooted by the storm, and the reed, after bowing its head to the storm, had resisted and triumphed. The Japanese journalists, who belonged to the club of the Ministry of Foreign Affairs, held a meeting afterward to decide on a protest, not being able to bear the idea that Japan had "bowed its head." It was an insult, not because they thought it wasn't the truth, but because a truth disagreeable to them had been put forward in public and, what was more, before their old colonial dependents. As for me, I did not notice until much later the tornado I had provoked. I did not regard the position of the reed as at all humiliating. Summoned to the Ministry of Foreign Affairs, I sincerely begged their pardon, never having had the intention of offending them, but now more aware than ever of what face, or loss of face, could mean.

At stage two, Japan clogged my pores, and I took the plane for Europe without regret, determined never to return. At thirty thousand feet, I began to feel reborn, more relaxed, calmer, trying to answer the question: Who are they? Are the true Japanese those who created this perfumed bath in which I have wallowed for months, or those who transform their environment into a sweatbox in which one loses oneself, undifferentiated, or risks becoming a target when one wants to step forth into the light? My thoughts clung to that monument on Okinawa which commemorates the immolation of the schoolchildren who, in 1945, their teachers leading them, threw themselves from the top of a cliff in front of the American battleships. In that second stage, Japan was for me the bottom of an abyss where the sea breaks with redoubled violence. Another image haunted me: an immense torchlight procession on New Year's Eve. I had joined a crowd at the railroad station in Harajuku and, carried by the current, I climbed slowly, among shadows holding lighted tapers, up to the Meiji temple. Beyond the light of the tapers, I tried to make out what was hidden behind the trees in the park. I wondered who lived there, so vividly did the lights of the procession create the illusion of inhabited depths. The gravel rasped rhythmically underfoot. Hardly anyone spoke, and the murmur that arose made the crowd even more shadowy. How many of us were there, after midnight, in those first minutes of the new year, ascending the Harajuku to the door of the temple? Tomorrow the newspaper would say four million. I had forgotten what we were going to do at the temple, when all of a sudden it appeared in the glade. Men, women, children—with their families or alone—clapped their hands three times as they bowed, cast down their offerings, and then retired, surrounded by the murmur of all those behind them who were coming up. The crowd descended across the park and one by one the tapers were extinquished.

Long after they were extinguished, their flames continued to sway before my eyes. I had certainly not understood anything about Japan. I had not seen anything. My puzzle was composed of pieces which were impossible to assemble. A remark of a French friend, Pierre-Louis Blanc, rang in my ears: "If you leave Japan having a single Japanese friend, a friend whom you want to see again and whom you miss, your stay here will have been a success." Search as I might among all the Japanese I knew, I did not find one who answered to this description. I decided that I must return to Japan to reassemble the pieces of the puzzle I had just destroyed.

1: MEETINGS

TOKYO AFTER A LONG ABSENCE

We had already fastened our seat belts. It was ten o'clock in the morning. At this end-of-October day, the perfectly clear air permitted us to see the ground as it approached. After the desolate expanses of Siberia, I suddenly discovered welcoming green woods which autumn had not yet touched. The sea formed a continuous band that mounted to the assault of the trees, only to lick its feet. This landscape was not familiar to me. I did not perceive, as each time before when I had landed in Japan, the tower of Tokyo, surrounded by the bay, all sunk in the smoke of immense industrial areas, above all Kawasaki, which has rendered Japan notorious for the density of its pollution. It was the first time, a year after its opening, that I had arrived at Narita, the new international airport, situated on the peninsula of Chiba, about 115 miles from the center of the capital. The spacious facade of the installations seemed to stress all the more the emptiness of the large waiting room for arrivals, where almost no one waited for the travelers on our flight. Before Narita was put into operation, the proximity of Haneda, the older international airport, located barely 25 miles from the Ginza, had made it a favorite place for an outing for the Japanese of Tokyo. They had developed the pleasant habit of a kind of escort ceremony for travelers arriving or departing. Narita has killed that custom. My traveling companions and I felt alone and a trifle lost. Customs seemed less fussy than usual. The taxis waited sedately, drawn up in a line outside the exits. The bus to the center of town received the travelers from Europe one by one. Dazzled by the sunlight, I stepped into a bus with air conditioning and pneumatic seats. From the realm of imagination and disorganization, I had once again fallen into a meticulous universe where the least detail has its importance. Nothing had changed. The luggage, carefully ticketed, had been delicately arranged in the baggage compartment. In the pouch in front of each seat there was a plastic box, with a red side, imprinted in Japanese, Chinese, English, German, and French: "If you are sick, show the red side of this box to the driver; he will immediately call an

3

ambulance"; and a blue side: "If you have an urgent need to go to the toilet, show the blue side of this box to the driver." A short time ago, every bus had a hostess, but hostesses had been replaced by a tape recording, which provided travelers with the expected information—that is, how long the ride would take and the approximate time of arrival.

The Chiba highway was jammed, not to the point of immobilizing us, as often happened, but enough to prolong the trip by fifteen or twenty minutes. From the "air terminal" to the station in Tokyo, I observed, after my ten-year absence, the same crowd, the same streets, their severe buildings brightened by new rows of trees, reflecting the efforts and taste of the merchants. Hibiya Park at the foot of the Imperial Palace looked rejuvenated. Here and there were a few new buildings; everywhere, and especially in the Marunouchi quarter, efforts at embellishment by planting clumps of flowers. Tokyo is a city the sun transforms—"a cold city where the sun is hot," to paraphrase the geographer Jules Sion.

In my hotel, I began to telephone in all directions, planning the rather too brief period I would spend in Japan. The familiar sound of the Japanese telephone's dial tone resounded pleasantly; in this country there are no blocked switchboards, no distracting "frying" noises on the wire, even when one calls long distance. The people of Tokyo are fanatical users of the small red telephones installed on the sidewalks, in front of tobacco stores or street stalls. In the center of town, some new public phone booths equipped with touch telephones have made their appearance.

Today's newspaper carried headlines about Deng Xiaoping's arrival. The Chinese deputy prime minister's trip, to initial the Sino-Japanese treaty of peace and friendship signed in Peking on August 12, 1978, gave the treaty a world dimension. On the economic level, there was first of all the enormous potential market that China meant for Japan and the acceleration that Japan's technological capacities would give China's development. It was spoken of as a momentous event, not only because it would become a date in history, but above all because it was the beginning of a return to a historic continuity broken in 1894. The treaty was also a political coup, reinforcing an Asian Asia by eliminating, without naming it, the Soviet Union from the powers in the region. Zhou Enlai's China had pursued this objective since the Bandung conference; Japanese-American security agreements could only reaffirm it.

In my room at the Akasaka Tokyu Hotel, I looked with curiosity at the surprising television images of Madame Deng, visiting a nursery school and weeping at the children's gestures and songs of friendship for a fine lady from the continent where Japanese culture had been born fourteen centuries before. At the Todaiji temple in Nara, the sacred town of Buddhism, the chief priest proudly showed the Buddha, one of the largest bronze statues in the world, lifted into place in the year 752 with the help of Chinese engineers. In 717 the Chinese priest Ganjin arrived on the continent and built the Toshodaiji.

In memory of these ties whose strength has come down through the centuries, Emperor Hirohito, receiving Deng, expressed the desire for a future filled with friendship.

On the other hand, there is a past whose evocation is considered inconvenient. Goro Noguchi is "the best singer of his generation," according to the newspaper *Asahi,* but his singing *"Boku in Totte Seishun Towa"* (What Youth Means to Me) in a recital that November at the Nissei Theater was considered tactless. This long song is simply a reading, against a musical background, of letters written to their mothers by young soldiers who were doomed to die. Recipients of the Order of Culture on November 1 evoked for me an unchanged Japan: the seventy-eight-year-old novelist Kazuo Ozaki, the philosophy professor Ichitaro Tanaka, and the youngest of the group, the fifty-two-year-old Takashi Sugimura, director of the national cancer center. The impending campaign for the presidency of the majority party, the Liberal Democrats, was covered by one of the newspapers, but almost casually, though the new president would become, as is the custom, the new prime minister.

A public that is indifferent to politics is greatly concerned with trivialities. For example, during my stay, a chimpanzee that lives in the Tama zoo in Tokyo took on the aura of a national hero. A television program in mid-October had attracted the public's attention to Joe, and so the program was shown again. The Japanese had been impressed first of all by the courtesy of the chimpanzees, then by Joe's authority and his way of settling differences among his fellow chimps, by his gallantry toward the females, and by his courage in defending the community against all attacks—or what looked to him like attacks—from outside. Mail had poured into the television station, and thanks to the media, a slogan began to circulate: "They are more human than men. Let us be inspired by the chimps." The Japanese Association of Amateur Sports bought the film for the training of athletes, and the municipal government of Tokyo bought it to show aspiring administrators how a community is managed without any checks or controls. Elsewhere in the papers, professors are discontented with their overcrowded classes, building lots are becoming more and more expensive, the value of the yen keeps rising, the defense budget has led to some objections, and economic critics, eager to provide something besides good news, try to pick holes in the seven percent growth rate, the government's goal.

As always in Japan, I was submerged beneath a flood of information and confusedly felt the need to examine my conscience. Basically, what had changed? Had Japan changed? And had the Japanese?

The Paradox of Change: Kazuko

It is eternal Japan that first of all assails me from behind the head-lines of the papers, the eternal Japan that forms men and society and whose immutable character appears the moment one sets foot on the islands. There is an antlike work carried out to impose a few square miles of land on the sea and compensate for the chronic erosion of the coastline, as well as the geographical phenomenon of impercepti-ble stress which century after century thins the waist of the long body which is the island of Honshu. There is the permanent instabil-ity of the crust on which the Japanese live; it is menaced day after day by typhoons, tidal waves, and volcanic eruptions. "Eruption of Mount Usu: A river of volcanic mud has invaded the towns of Toyako and Abuta. . . . Three persons have been carried off. . . . As the result of cloudbursts, the lava of the Usu volcano was trans-formed into a river of mud. The town of Toyako has been cut off and two hundred houses had to be evacuated. At Abuta, mud invaded the pumping station and the city's water supply had been cut off. . . ." I was not surprised by this story. Nature does not change in Japan. The personality it stamps on men can help us understand the pro-found sense of interdependence felt by individuals. Certain sponta-neous gregarious reactions, a need to be rooted all the more strongly since the ground itself is unstable, create a predominantly peasant style of life, even in the cities.

A Western mind poses questions in terms of compatibility or contradiction. I therefore asked myself whether the persistence of a certain type of rural society and rural mentality was compatible with or in contradiction to frantic urbanism. I remember going to the airport of Haneda—today a kind of inland desert—for the inaugu-ration in 1964 of the famous monorail between the station of Hama-matsucho and what was then Tokyo's international airport. The py-lons that supported the single track veered gradually away from the docks and their bases set in the water and crossed an indentation of the bay. In 1978, railway cars with panoramic windows now traveled over rooftops. One got to the airport across warehouses, sports fields, and business areas. Whichever way you turned, the sea was no longer visible. Spaces one or two miles wide have been stolen from the water; the monorail now runs overland, and where the Pacific once existed there are now highways and houses. Urbanization ap-pears everywhere; it is a matter not of "modifying" the territory but of an urban cover of maximum density, sometimes to the limit of what is bearable.

In this fantastic continuous creation which the cities of Japan represent, the family system, which was the foundation of Japanese homogeneity, persists or is being transformed. One finds in Japan all the constraints imposed by modernization, which appeared first of all in the United States and later in Europe. But here the other side of scientific progress—the development of transportation and rise in the standard of living—not only modified or overturned the value system, as it did in the Western industrial countries, it also created the conditions for a complete break with the past, that is, the questioning by children of their parents' whole way of life. At the time I returned to Tokyo, youthful suicides were news, as though they signified rejection of a society which many Japanese regard as unsuited to the present period, but which they instinctively consider indispensable for their survival.

Chance had seated me next to Kazuko on the Paris–Tokyo flight. A marked Japanese type, she wore her hair in long pigtails which attenuated the asymmetry of her face. She appeared nervous, lighting cigarette after cigarette and crushing them out half smoked in the ashtray, which nobody came to empty since we were in the nonsmoking section.

"Are you going to Tokyo?" I asked her in French.

"Yes, and you?"

"I am too."

"So we have a number of hours to pass together. Is this your first trip to Japan?"

"No, I lived there for seven years."

"And is this the first time you're returning?"

"No, I went to Japan in 1963 and left in 1970, but this is my fourth trip back since then. And you?"

"I left Japan three months ago. Since then I've traveled through France and to Brazil. Now I'm going back."

"Where did you learn French?"

"In Paris. I lived in Paris for five years."

"If I may ask, what did you do in Tokyo?"

"Wait, I'll show you."

From a purse repetitiously marked "LV" she took out a card holder, also marked "LV," from which she drew some photographs.

"Do you know Harajuku?"

"Yes."

"This is a women's dress shop in that quarter. I own the shop and have two employees, who run the business in my absence. But in three months . . . I don't know what I'll find now."

"What's your name?"

"Kazuko. Do you think it's a pretty name?"

"Very. I like all Japanese names. My daughter is named Keiko."

"Oh, you gave her a Japanese name? Then you must love Japan. You're married, I suppose."

"Yes."

"So am I. I have a little boy of six and a little girl of three and a half. And you, you have only a daughter?"

"No, I also have a boy of twelve."

"My little girl is not mine. I adopted her. She's my sister-in-law's daughter, or rather the daughter of my husband's brother's wife."

"Your sister-in-law is dead?"

"She left my brother-in-law to run away with her lover. The daughter was taken in by her grandmother, then by a mother-in-law. But it didn't work, she was unhappy, so I took her with me. I don't know whether I did the right thing."

"Do you have regrets?"

"Not at all, but I abandoned everything too—my adopted daughter, my son, my husband. I had decided to go away forever. You know, I have a man's temperament, but like all women I have a weak side and my husband discovered it, and then he took advantage of it."

"Tell me about your husband."

"He is a tall man, thin, very handsome. I think he is an intelligent man. He is an actor and he has sacrificed everything to his profession. Three years ago, he got very sick. A cancer, I think. He had a serious operation. He was in the hospital for two months. Then for six months he was convalescing. I took care of him like a child. He needed me, and he did not understand that I needed him too. I am very selfish, but so is he. I always had to be at his beck and call. He had a very eloquent way of looking at me. Even when I didn't want to, he made me undress, and most often he took his pleasure selfishly. Sometimes it was marvelous for me, but too rarely. I soon got fed up and didn't want him to touch me anymore. He got furious. Each time he felt like making love he would beat me—to put me in the right state, he said. One day he hurt me and I decided to leave.

"Isamu is the president of a small import-export business, he's rich, and he's my husband's best friend. For several months, he was constantly at our house. My husband invited him over almost every day. One might have said that he did it so he could avoid being alone with me. I began quite soon to watch Isamu. The way he looked at me was not simply the look of a friend, and one day I felt he was not indifferent to me. My husband had pushed Isamu into my arms. When we were alone, he boasted to me about his physique, his intelligence.

About three months ago, Isamu called me on the telephone at the shop. He asked me to leave everything. He was on his way to Paris that very day. He begged me to join him at his sister's house on Rue de l'Observatoire. I promised, and I had to keep my promise. I left the next day, entrusting my children to my mother-in-law. I did not hide from my husband that there was no question of my returning. It was silly, don't you think, since I have come back? At Paris, Isamu was waiting for me, with a plane ticket for Rio. I spent three extraordinary months in Brazil. Isamu took very good care of me. Then one day he got a letter from Japan. That very evening we left Rio for Paris, and he left directly for Tokyo. I stayed in Paris, and the next morning he called me on the telephone:

"'Come back to Tokyo. You can go back to your husband and we can continue seeing each other.'

"'That is out of the question. Last night my husband called me.'

"'Come back—I can't live without you. Your father and your mother want you to return. Your children too.'"

Kazuko was speaking to me, but she was really talking to herself: "I'm returning to Tokyo to try and have a new life with my husband, but not because of my children. . . . maybe because of my father and mother."

"What are you going to do when you get to Tokyo?"

"I'm going to telephone my father, and then I shall undoubtedly go to my husband's."

We were approaching Narita airport. Outside the window, the Japanese alps appeared, their slopes covered with cedars.

"I hope that I have not bothered you, telling you about my life."

After going through customs, I saw Kazuko into a taxi. She was waving rather desperately to me, inviting me to take the taxi with her, but I pointed to my suitcase already loaded in the bus. She told the cabby to drive on, and I have never seen her again.

The Paradox of Permanence: The Law of the Group

I was struck by this confession to a stranger. Kazuko's flight itself was banal in Japan. Wives disappear, change their identity, go to live somewhere else, abandoning husbands and children. Attempts to find them are usually unsuccessful. Adults can disappear without a trace. Japanese do not have identification cards but a system of registration at the city hall of their current addresses. Without a record of previous residence, one can live anywhere, cut off from one's past. But modern life is a permanent challenge to those who seek anonymity.

Fourteen of the twenty-three election districts in the capital have adopted computers for the registration of their residents. Here the computer plays an ambiguous role. On one side it depersonalizes, nothing being more anonymous than a perforated card; but at the same time it establishes identity permitting the location of anyone sought. At the end of 1978, 31,691 residents of the Suginami district in Tokyo signed a petition against having their residence registered by computer, insisting that this practice violated their privacy.

As for Kazuko, if she had simply wanted to disappear, she had more chance of doing so if she had stayed in Japan.

How then explain her leaving? Less than Japanese men do women feel the need to be part of the group. They are in fact the pivot of the most homogeneous and steadfast group in Japanese society, the *ié*, or family clan, within which women possess an authority that greatly exceeds any outward manifestation of it. When the structure of the *ié* is undermined, the wife ceases to feel an attachment to anything or anyone. Then why did Kazuko return? Not because of her husband or her children, but because of her father and mother, their welcome and their wish, for they were ready to introduce her again into the family group. For Kazuko, above all else, it was a matter of being reinserted into a group that would restore her to her position as both daughter and mother, her role as wife being confused with that of mother. Kazuko knew deep within herself that by agreeing to return to Tokyo she would be canceling out the habits she had contracted during her recent stay in a society where the concept of the family is essentially based on the relations between the spouses.

I reflected on the biblical example of the prodigal son, which seemed to me to depict a social phenomenon of contemporary Japan: individuals who want to break the chain that binds each Japanese to a group, whether the family clan or the professional, school, or university milieu, and the judgment of "immorality" that attaches to such aspirations.

A Question of Mentality

I had an appointment with Takeo Doi, chief of psychiatric services at St. Luke's Hospital and professor of psychopathology and psychoanalysis at the medical school of the University of Tokyo, the most prestigious university in Japan. A man with a youngish air, he is more than fifty but looks forty, quite pudgy, with an open face and sparkling, mischievous eyes.

"Are the Japanese different? Is there such a thing as a Japanese mentality?"

"Human nature is what it is and the Japanese are human, and I wonder sometimes whether one must insist on Japanese originality being perhaps less important than we think. My colleague Madame Chie Nakane, a professor of sociology in this university, has posited the problem in terms of structures. But I see it in terms of psychology, though there is no contradiction between our conceptions. In fact, what characterizes the Japanese is esprit de corps."

"How, according to you, has this esprit de corps—based, as I understand it, on the cohesion of the rural family—survived urbanization?"

"This was the theme of a congress organized by the Royal Australian and New Zealand College of Psychiatry, which I attended at Singapore. Urbanization is a permanent challenge to the individual's mental equilibrium. Why is the rate of crime, juvenile delinquency, divorce, and all the phenomena of social disintegration palpably less high in Japan than in other industrialized countries? How does

Japanese society maintain its equilibrium despite the precipitous changes which have taken place here in the course of recent years? Attention should be paid to the force of cohesion inherent in our society. Among the Japanese there is a very strong inclination to maintain a balance between the stability of the individual and that of society, which they regard as interconnected. The Japanese do not live as individualists in a unique search for personal equilibrium, nor as "socialists" solely concerned with the progress of society. Japan is certainly not the only country where the achievement of this sort of balance is sought, but it is interesting to note that among us the search is instinctive. I would even go further and say that my compatriots rarely make a distinction between personal equilibrium and social stability. Indeed, the Japanese is not individually an egotist, yet group egotism does exist. He can even be very egotistical when he acts in a group, a phenomenon that has existed at all times. Today this egotism has become more apparent than in the past because there are no more barriers. In feudal Japan, when the egotistical behavior of a group endangered society, an order from on high did away with the conflict: the group that caused the disorder was commanded to commit seppuku. Japan today faces a problem that did not exist yesterday: the problem of a mediated authority.

"Thus nothing has changed, except that, in the absence of authority, group aggressiveness and egotism accentuate rivalries.

Seventy percent of the Japanese live today in an urban community, and their mentality is the same as it was in the past. This is the mentality of the middle class, which adheres to a concept we call *amae,* which means presuming or depending on the love of another. The British psychoanalyst Michael Balint describes this phenomenon very well. When you say 'I love' that means you are in an active process in regard to someone or something. But behind that there also exists a passive process: it is the desire to be loved. In Japanese, one cannot say 'I love you' from the active point of view—there is no such word. Amae is this conception of man's instinctive tendency to create a total harmony with his environment. Thus the sensibility of the Japanese is very acute and it is easy for them to 'put themselves into someone else's shoes.' But this is not due to altruism. It is rather the instinct for the preservation of harmony with one's environment and an innate feeling of dependence vis-à-vis the 'other.'"

"The search for the *amae* is not necessarily the generator of harmony—could it not also become the source of conflicts, for example in sexuality?"

"It is true that each race projects on the 'other' its ghosts and everything taboo—what it can only imagine, but dares not admit to itself."

"How do you explain the fact that pornography from abroad is censored, but not the pornography made in Japan? Is American pornography more pernicious than the Japanese variety?"

"Sex appeal is magnified by exoticism. Just look at the success of Marilyn Monroe or Brigitte Bardot. And look at the advertising posters on our walls—statuesque blondes. In reality, Japan does not differ that much from the West. Sexuality is common to humanity without distinction of race, but Freud is not applicable here. I do not accept the idea of the libido for the Japanese. In Japan, more than any other place, emotion and sex are bound together."

"Is this another manifestation of the group spirit?"

"Yes, but that doesn't mean that I condemn it with the excuse that it sometimes conceals a whole series of individual and egotistic actions. The *amae* is the herd instinct. The egoism of the group often denatures *amae,* which for example makes our relations with foreign countries difficult and in return often leads to our being treated with contempt as Japan Incorporated. But I am still convinced that the Japanese facility for coming together and adhering as a body to certain rules is a factor of stability for both the individual and the society.

"This ability to come together has survived all the traumas of urbanism and modernization and no doubt helps us avoid a rupture in our society. Remember, I am a psychiatrist, a doctor. So I treat sick people. Now, mental illness in France, as in Japan, is a caricature of the culture, whose eccentric side it reflects in some way. In France, the psychiatrist works to permit the individual to rediscover his personality, his individuality. As for me, I work to permit my patients to rediscover the sense of the group, because the individual's inability to be part of a group or to join one is in this country a sign of disequilibrium."

JAPAN FOR THE FIRST TIME

In Yokohama, where I stepped ashore from the *Laos,* one of the three ships of the Far Eastern Shipping Line, I had been at sea, including all the stops, for thirty-two days. The ship had been tied up at the dock for more than an hour; I was not eager to leave my cabin or the salons in which I had been at home for more than a month. I was closing my suitcase when the steward's figure appeared in the doorway: "They've been looking for you everywhere. . . . Some Japanese . . ." I had already greeted the cultural attaché to the embassy, Pierre-Louis Blanc, who had come to meet his sister Josy Anne, and I was preparing to have my last breakfast on board, if they agreed to serve me. I saw behind the steward a small, attractive young woman who stretched out her hand and made introductions in French. I did not catch the names, but she explained to me that she had come with the liaison officer for NHK, the national Japanese television network. They had been looking all over the ship for me for more than an hour; that seemed to amuse her a great deal, because she laughed. Everyone laughed. So I invited all of them to come laugh with me in the dining room and, and at the same time, have some refreshment. The menu was meager; the kitchens were closed. Conversation was reduced to some purely formal questions on my trip and laconic replies to which the liaison man responded with a gurgling sound in his throat, followed by "*Sodeska*," which can, it seems, be translated as "Oh, fine. . . ." The snack was soon ended. Then a Japanese, the chauffeur, took my luggage; and there I was, being driven to my hotel in a sumptuous American limousine sent by the network. The chauffeur had put on his white cap, bearing the NHK insignia. He opened and shut the doors with a ceremonious air. We headed for Tokyo, as I stared in wonder. I couldn't understand what was happening. We kept going down narrow streets through which the car could barely squeeze. There were no sidewalks. A disorderly tangle of electric wires overhead reminded me of an anarchic Buffet. Low wooden houses ran uninterrupted along the road, except for small stores and latticework gates. Not a single modern apartment house was in sight. The car turned to the right, then to the left, and at last a little space, the street was a trifle wider; we passed a railroad station, which I later learned was Shinagawa. After an interminable and fatiguing journey of an hour, I found myself in the middle of a garden opposite a park. I had not yet seen a single large apartment house or building. I had the feeling that I was out in the countryside—a Japanese-style country, populated with hordes of cars. My new home was situated about a hundred yards from the French embassy, a few hundred yards from two or three other embassies, in the very heart of Azabu, a residential quarter in the center of Tokyo. I cursed the embassy's staff, which had put me up so far from everything, and I resolved to change my hotel. The Azabu Prince Hotel is surrounded by pleasant gardens, but the quarter is due for transformation. In front of and behind the hotel, some buildings of three or four stories will replace the green open spaces. I went up Kan-Nana Dori, or Seventh Avenue, which resembles an outer encircling boulevard, totally independent of the network of urban highways. There was an impossible traffic jam, the disorder of urbanization, an inextricable tangle of electric cables, and signs in Japanese.

Whenever I return to Tokyo or Kyoto, to all the cities of Japan I know, I find again the familiar places. Nothing has changed in the Meguro, Setagaya, or even the Shibuya districts. Each day the immense Shibuya station is the scene of the arrival and departure of tens of thousands of people from the suburbs. Every ten minutes the subway trains arrive and depart, without respite, at the first story of a large department store. Before and after the day's work, the consumer is ready to go: From the subway platform, he has only one door to pass through to reach women's lingerie or the toy department. But at night an ever-renewed amazement engulfs the pedestrian in an orgy of neon lights, electrified signs, illuminated newspapers, creating an atmosphere which resembles that of Broadway, if you do not immediately sense its unreal character. On Broadway, a neon light is a neon light. At Shibuya, a neon light looks like a neon light, but you are not sure, so much is the scintillating light the creator of a symphony for the eyes, a symphony which is taken in by the dense crowd that rises and falls around the foreign visitor, as the swell rises and falls around a sailboat in the open sea. The crowd does does not speak loudly; it murmurs and flows, as a wave folds back at the prow of a ship in fine weather.

The quiet, narrow streets, without sidewalks, are bordered by small gardens. Four or five stones permit you to cross a strip of lawn to reach a sliding door with a symbolic bolt, which admits you to a house made of fine, delicate wood. You leave your shoes at the entrance. They are exchanged for zoris, slippers immunized against the outside dust. Along hallways whose flooring creaks, between the shoji, the sliding paper partitions in which a cat, a baby, an adult finds it amusing to prick holes, you head for the room where the host awaits you. There you take off your zoris, push open the shoji, and, kneeling, bow in greeting; then you go into the room, bare feet on the tatami, the floor covering made of rice straw, on which, in the evening, the mistress of the house will spread the futon, the light, pliable mattress used for sleeping.

Nothing has changed in the muffled atmosphere of these streets in a quarter of Tokyo where modernism, together with the auto, has penetrated only discreetly. Nothing has changed in the contrast they offer with the nearby avenues clogged with heavy trucks that make the air unbreathable, air which gives Tokyo its reputation as the most polluted city in the world. The familiar sounds of birds rise up to me. Then the squealing of schoolkids in the neighborhood. There are more and more squealing sounds in the street: "Oaio gozaimasu! Oaio gozaimasu! Oaio gozaimasu!" This morning greeting is articulated increasingly loudly, by a dozen kids who are leaving for school. I get up and suddenly realize that this "good day" is addressed to me. They are all there, boys dressed in black, their caps in their hands, little girls in blue with a sailor collar, their pigtails neatly plaited, stopping by the side of the house. They bow and shout once more, "Oaio!" since they can see me at the window, and then they run off. A little later, I learn that the mothers in the vicinity have spoken about the geijin who lives at Hiroguchi-San's house and have told their children not to forget to greet him when they pass. This is just one more ritual—besides the ritual of the family meal, the ritual of courtesy, the ritual of the bath, the ritual of going to bed, the ritual of relations with one's neighbors. Thus a symbolic universe is created in which the rigidity of certain social relations has as its corollary the imaginative—that is, the anarchic, easygoing, good-natured—side of individual behavior.

Which Japanese is the true one? The Japanese whose delicate courtesy often smacks of the obsequious, or the Japanese who behaves with terrible rudeness toward the anonymous person he meets by chance in the street or a public place? Can the Japanese behave with rigidity and at the same time adapt himself without difficulty to new situations, even the most unexpected? Is he resolutely modern and turned toward the future, or a traditional citizen closed to everything foreign? This meekness bordering on finickiness, is it compatible with the cult of the warrior and the saber, not to mention the innate violence that is given free rein in the martial arts? Is the Japanese loyal or traitorous, generous or scornful, submissive or rebellious, courageous or timid, aggressive or peaceful? How can one disentangle the reality, caught between a tightly structured social setup almost impermeable to outside influences, and institutions in which diversity and imagination bring together all sorts of models at the point of progress? And finally, should one believe in the society's merciless hierarchy or the egalitarianism of its way of life? Japan resembles those glass labyrinths at fun fairs where the mirrors reflect a thousand images of any who venture into their winding passageways. A Japan of innumerable facets appears, a Japan whose institutions reinforce a disconcertingly pluralist image.

Confronted by the violence of the natural environment, the evolution of history has marked off several Japans: The Japans of north and south, separated by the belt of myth which runs from Ise to Sado, passing through Nara, Kyoto, Fukui, and Kanazawa. The Japan of the Pacific facade, and that of the Sea of Japan facade, marked off by the meridians of reality, those of Hokkaido to Kyushu, which follow the fault lines of the earth tremors, from one volcano to another, with special mention for the Tokaido line from Tokyo to Kyoto, where Mount Fuji symbolizes the central meeting point of the meridians of reality and the parallels of myth. At this point, sacred and profane are confused. But the sacred prevails, just as the innate order of the rural mentality prevails over anarchy, whatever might be the force of social disintegration born of urbanization. The reconciliation of all centrifugal forces with the centripetal current, the guarantor of Japan's homogeneity, has led the Japanese, beyond all ecological solutions based on regression, to conceive of a megalopolis, as dream joins reality in a kind of cosmic ambition.

TWO SIDES OF THE COIN

In the course of my first year in Japan, I experienced all the ambiguities and all the misunderstandings. Although he wanted to understand Japan, Arthur Koestler preferred to remain definitively a stranger to an irrational world, where emotionality serves at once as a meeting ground and a language of communication; but he had the ability to show that ambiguities and misunderstandings are not confined to the relations between foreigners and Japanese, but are also the rule among the Japanese. The Japanese language, filled with periphrases and successive approximations to a reality which is never fixed, leaves to each interlocutor the possibility of avoiding the attempt at communication with the "other," thanks to a system of nuanced interpretations of what is said. One can wonder whether this ability to accept or politely reject a message does not become necessary in a society where communication is the iron rule. In Japan one cannot ignore one's neighbor, who sometimes becomes more important than members of one's family who do not live under the same roof. The density of the crowd eliminates any possibility of isolation. So the problem is not how to communicate but rather how *not* to communicate. It was perhaps because he did not understand the individual's profound need of solitude in this country that Lafcadio Hearn, underestimated at the beginning of the century by his fellow Americans, was also isolated by the Japanese, whom he wanted so much to understand that he became a citizen of the Empire of the Rising Sun.

When one wants to know Japan, it is a good idea, like a pilot who wants to land his plane in a fog, not to make a mistake in one's approach, for then one runs the danger of bypassing a world which resembles ours in its external manifestations, while the soul that inhabits it believes in the permanence of its special genius. Thus does this world differ from our skeptical old societies which ceaselessly call their spiritual existence into question.

Coexistence

To discover Nippon, one must look for the keys to the reality of a country, doubtless the only one in the world, which can depend only on its spiritual resources and the genius of its civilization to create the material wealth indispensable to its life in a naked, arid land where legends and myths evoke only misery, servitude, calamity, and death.

In going back to the origins of this civilization and to the elements that have fashioned it, one discovers, at all the high places of pilgrimage where its deepest roots lie, that mind joins matter by identifying with it, now in anthropomorphic forms, now, rustically, in the abstraction of volumes, odors, colors, and sounds. The contemporary Japanese rediscovers music and poetry at the point where life and death are confused and intermingled, where rocks, fire, water, earth, and air offer their testimony.

This faceted reality always involves a judicious synthesis of pragmatism and ideology. The former counts at least as much as the latter, even if it is only a ceremonial costume that camouflages a mercantile anthill. However, it is necessary to ask whether the mercantile anthill is not instead the camouflage chosen by this profound Japan, the object of our quest in these pages. When announcing their father's death to their friends, two sons tried to explain what the Japanese call *akirame*, the resignation which is taken for granted in the face of an inescapable destiny. One son wrote to me: "Death must not lead to sadness. It prolongs life just as life prolongs death. One could not exist without the other." At the ultimate instant, the individual's religious convictions do not play a big part. Shintoism is there only to keep alive the memory of those who have become the ancestors, whose most august line, the emperor's, is traced back to the gods. Since God does not exist in the Western sense, Buddha or Jesus and his prophets are only the insurance taken on an uncertain hereafter. Almost all the Japanese have adopted Pascal's theory of the wager. It does not at all bother them to be at once Shintoists and Buddhists, to belong to a Christian church and assiduously follow the precepts of one of numerous sects that flourish in Japan, bringing together thousands, even millions, of followers in often bizarre practices.

To find the individual Japanese, one must carry out a veritable psychoanalysis. "I like to hide myself behind a mask," the famous writer Yukio Mishima, dead by seppuku in November 1970, told me one day. The reference was to the No. This form of theater, so pure, so perfect, encompasses ancient tragedy, opera, and ballet. Everything is acted in slow motion in a mimetic symbolism that gives the spectacle a great similarity to a religious ceremony, and it is celebrated in accordance with an unchanged millennial ritual. Each actor in the No wears a mask representing a stock character: a jealous wife, a devil, a god, an animal, a miserly old woman. . . .

The success of the No depends less upon the truth or moral of the story than upon the aesthetic effect, brought to a pitch of poetic emotion by the performance of the actors. Behind their masks, the Japanese dissimulate the essential, which they place instinctively in the beauty and perfection of the gesture rather than in the goal sought by the gesture's accomplishment.

The Japanese call all Caucasians *Namban*, "savages from the south," alluding to the Dutch merchants and sailors who were the first to make contact with them, at the beginning of the sixteenth century. That is how my friend Takashi Suzuki, from whom I learned a lot, described me. In our long conversations, the more he talked, trying to explain the Japanese and their mentality, the less I understood. One day, with the serene, detached manner I knew so well, Takashi pronounced these words: "I admire you a great deal and I never tire when listening to you explain and analyze a problem. You are logical and clear, and that's intelligence." I felt the glow of vanity mounting in me; but Suzuki continued, pensive, as though talking to himself: "All this is clear in your words and your mind, but I am not so sure that clarity is the way to attain reality."

Where is reality? This indeed is the question one asks oneself about a country which in less than a century has known feudal society, industrial society, and postindustrial society. They have appeared one after the other, but none can be regarded as a substitute for the previous system. The Japanese admit this coexistence quite frankly, and it is particularly visible in Tokyo. From Marunouchi, the modern business quarter where the large firm of Mitsubishi reigns, to the tangle of alleyways flanked by wooden houses reminiscent of Ueno, clustered around the goddess Kannon's temple in Akasaka, the amusement quarter, where geishas in rickshas coast by the big American hotels and the male and female prostitutes, and finally to Saniya, the district that harbors menials and unemployed, this coexistence is not measured by the contrast between the Toranomon skyscraper and the last wooden house of the ecological "resistance" in Yurakucho. It can be seen in the color of the street, the dress of the passersby, the small handicrafts and trades, the unexpected back alleys, which wind their way between bamboo or wooden mats. Nobody dares cut the umbilical cord which keeps nineteenth-century architecture in the orbit of traditional Japanese space. That is why rebellion and confrontation have, until now, always led Japan to reconciliation. The hardships and shocks have at times been harsh, and civil war has raised its ugly head. So it was in 1960 during the big anti-American demonstrations; in 1968 with the revolt of the students; in 1970 with the "Red Army" terrorists; and from 1973 to 1978, with the demonstrations against Narita airport, symbol of resistance to a rigid, traditional society. Revolt and resignation, confrontation and reconciliation, have been constants throughout Japan's history, and are expressed at the same time in the national structure, *kokutai*, which helps to solidify the feeling of unanimity.

Adaptation to the Stronger Power

Certainly, in the history of the Japanese nation, *kokutai* has been deflected and manipulated, notably by the militarists from the time of the Manchurian incident in 1931 to the end of the Second World War. Modified or transformed, the system of values has never been fundamentally questioned, due to a concept which the Japanese have always fully supported: the concept of *tenko*. A pure product of Japanese culture, *tenko* cannot be found anywhere else in Asia. It signifies conversion, in the sense of the acceptance of a stronger power than one's own. *Tenko* permitted the Meiji restoration to open the doors of the archipelago to the West, but also gave the military the chance to take power and not give it up save under the pressure of the atomic bomb. It is *tenko* that made Japan into an ally of the United States; it also permitted the creation of a modern and economically superdeveloped modern state. Adaptation goes hand in hand with creative dynamism in all spheres, which does not exclude a certain nostalgia, as expressed by the owner of the Toranomon skyscraper in the heart of Tokyo. He decided to give Japan's capital the song of birds, which it had lost, so he created on the roof of his building, thirty-six stories high, a green environment to attract them. And he succeeded.

JAPAN AS IT IS PERCEIVED

Japan is of course enacting the role of a great industrialized country. Nipponese technology competes successfully with the technologies of the most developed Western countries, when it does not surpass them. The average intellectual level of the Japanese people is expressed through eloquent statistics which prove the high quality of a superior educational system and permanently available training, and is confirmed by a student enrollment larger than that of the most advanced countries. The gross national product and per capita income put Japan in the second rank of world capitalist powers. Faced by the world crisis and quite deeply affected by it, more deeply perhaps than such European countries as West Germany and France, Japan is in the process of carrying through an economic redeployment and a civilizing effort which is realistic, spectacular, and dynamic. The advanced capitalist countries, even the United States, look upon this approach to the future as threatening competition, against which they raise protectionist barriers. All this explains in part why the received idea of Japan makes it look different from what it is.

Before presenting the statistics, one should set forth all the human factors that could clarify them. These are astonishing in themselves. A civilization perpetually changing yet always loyal to its roots preserves in its daily life a ritual whose weight gives the society cohesion and homogeneity. At home, in his professional life, and on the street, the Japanese evolves within a regulated and hierarchical environment which gives this country a distinctive efficiency that Western countries too quickly ascribe to contempt for the individual, for imagination, or for the freedom they eagerly defend. So Japan is seen as differing from its outward image as a Western capitalist democracy, economically advanced and politically liberal. This apparent difference is due to a confused idea people have arrived at by lumping it together with its neighbors. In both the United States and Europe, the public is confused about everything Oriental. People glibly attribute to the Japanese virtues or defects that history has taught them, on the basis of European and American encounters with China, Korea, and Vietnam.

The entire Oriental world is yellow, has slanty eyes, and is cunning—and, because of its eyes, cruel. Chinese tortures are legendary, as is the smoke of opium. The women are attractive because of their loose morals. . . . One could continue almost indefinitely this catalog of clichés from the colonial era, kept alive by the reports of various expeditionary forces and priests who were victims of religious persecution.

Then one must add memories of the Second World War, heavily colored by the movies spread throughout the world by the United States Information Service. Thus, propagated by tales and films about war in the Pacific, an image of a particularly cruel people was attached to Japan.

Everybody knows how to answer the easy questions: What is a kamikaze, a geisha, judo, karate, or hara-kiri? The average American or European can even cite a few brand names of Japanese cameras or automobiles. They are convinced that the Japanese imitate us. They know that the emperor is no longer a god and that the Japanese electronics industry has become the undisputed leader in the manufacture of pocket calculators. But if one goes a bit further and asks some questions about Buddhism or Zen, for example, ignorance and confusion appear.

Keiko Kishi, a famous Japanese actress of the sixties, had been commissioned by TBS, one of the most important private television networks in Japan, to film a live show which would be relayed by satellite from the Champs-Élysées to Tokyo. Standing near the George V subway entrance, she stopped passersby and asked: "Do you know Japan?" "No," was the disheartening reply of several Parisians chosen at random. Suddenly an old woman with a glib tongue replied, "Yes," and she added, "It's a shame. These people are very unfortunate: they're dying of hunger and we do nothing to help them." The next day the Japanese papers published the anecdote. To them it was a revelation of the great gulf of misinformation and incomprehension that separates them from a country like France, and the confirmation of what the Japanese have felt since the Meiji restoration: the feeling that they are not well known and not very well liked. How could it be otherwise when writers whose profession it is to influence opinion add to the confusion? Arthur Koestler saw only the robot side of Japan, and Jean-Pierre Chabrol saw an absurd Ubu in every Japanese he met. In 1924, an anonymous person signed the pseudonym Thomas Raucat to a humorous novel, *The Honorable Picnic*, about his stay in Japan. The pseudonym hid a person named Roger Poidatz, a specialist in aerial photography who had been sent to Japan as an instructor after the 1918 armistice. The Japanese first loved his novel, which showed a caricatured Japan, and then hated it, after some charitable soul explained to them that their country had been made to look ridiculous. In fact, the humor of the book hinged not on the described behavior of the Japanese but rather on the encounter between its bizarre characters (a few women and many men dressed as people did dress in traditional Japan) with refined manners, filled with curiosity about everything abroad, and a traveler who acts toward them as if he were a Martian who had just stepped out of a UFO.

JAPAN AS IT WANTS TO APPEAR

The Japanese prefer to appear decked out in the virtues the foreigner appreciates, instead of being burdened with everything that is considered a defect outside the archipelago. So they ally themselves with a system of values that is alien to them. The image they want to present tends to accentuate everything that can merge them into the international community and erase all the originality that might make them a people apart. There is a parallel between this kind of national behavior and the aspirations of the individual Japanese, whose ambition to merge with the mass of his fellow citizens leads him to prefer the grayness of routine over eccentricity. More than anywhere else, in Japan one feels the anonymity of the crowd.

This insistence on behavior that is harmonious with that of other nations and other men has, since 1868, helped to make Japan a country apart and make the Japanese seem like inhabitants of another world—an impression they would very much like to get rid of. Harmony and consensus: these two key words can be traced as much to myth as to reality; they engender the paradox of seeming original in comparison with civilizations like ours, whose progress comes rather from shocks, convulsions, and confrontations.

Since 1965, harmony at all costs, in order to attain the level of the advanced countries of the West, no longer suffices for the Japanese. Their goal is to surpass the West. They are anxious to know whether they have achieved this, and in the Japan of 1970 there was no longer a citizen who was not conscious of his responsibility and didn't feel concern and a burning desire to test the image the Japanese presented to the world.

"Do you like Japan?" The question, in English, is always direct and without frills. It has been asked of me one hundred, one thousand times, by every Japanese I have met. In general, I have always answered with a polite "yes." How could I not like Japan? But when I decided to test a "no," I heard a painful rasping in the throat, quickly followed by another rasp. My questioner, a well-known personality, ended by articulating the traditional "Ah, *sodeska*" and then practically spat in my face: "Come for lunch with me next Tuesday.

We'll talk about it." The tone was almost peevish, and for a few instants I wondered whether I should accept. On Tuesday I went to the prearranged address. M.T. was waiting for me, together with two important associates. This men's lunch involved the usual twittering of the waitresses who knelt around us and dissected the crayfish, as well as the various sake toasts intended to warm up the atmosphere. Toward the end of the meal, my host let fall: "The French are not courteous. I was in Paris recently and I had an appointment with a high official in your government. Forty-five minutes after the appointed time, I left the antechamber of this important personage, after telling his secretary that I was sorry to have to leave, but my short stay in Paris forced me to keep to a strict schedule. That evening when I returned to my hotel, there was a note of excuse written by his secretary and a small package covered with pretty paper, as we do at home. I opened it: it was an ashtray. . . ." (An embarrassed silence on both sides.) "Good; that did not stop me from inviting you to lunch. I would be pleased to repeat my invitation. . . ." The moment had come for me to leave. I bowed, quite determined not to repeat the experience of the "no."

By 1979, the Japanese were so sure they had surpassed the industrialized West that they asked the question "Do you like Japan?" less and less frequently. On the contrary, they were anxious to show that they had no more to learn.

The flawless organization that welcomes guests to the archipelago remains a source of astonishment and sometimes acute annoyance to foreigners. Invited by a Japanese company, the president and chief executive officer of a French company arrived one Monday, with his departure set for Saturday; he was quite relieved, reading the schedule that had been arranged for him, to see that Friday afternoon had evidently been left free. Lunch on Friday was held in a famous restaurant, the Chinsanzo, set in a large park landscaped in the Japanese style with clumps of crooked pines between which flowed brooks straddled by small red bridges. A special pavilion had been reserved. The French executive (whom we shall call Dupont and whom I accompanied) leaned toward me at the end of the meal.

"This tea is horrible," he said in a stage whisper. "I'm going to take a siesta."

Our Japanese host seemed to have guessed what was said.

"Dupont-San," he said, "don't you have anything to do this afternoon?"

"Yes, take a siesta. . . ."

"Ah, sodeska. We have prepared an entertainment."

One of our host's assistants had promptly gotten up and gone to the telephone at the end of the hall.

"Thanks," Dupont protested, "but my wife is waiting for me to go shopping—she wants to buy some pearls. Besides, we have an appointment at three o'clock. . . ."

Our host's second assistant got up just as promptly and took possession of another telephone.

"There, everything is arranged," the first assistant said.

"There, everything is arranged," the second assistant said.

"We are going to let you see Japan's most beautiful horses. The riding school awaits you."

"Your wife has been informed. She will wait for you and expects to leave around five-thirty."

Dupont heaved a sigh which was not one of relief. All that he could do was allow them to go ahead, and so we were taken to the Horse Training Center, which we had been told was a quarter-hour car trip and took us forty-five minutes. Nothing was overlooked, neither the history of the riding school nor each horse's genealogical tree. Finally, there was a demonstration, ten minutes of equestrian maneuvers. The riding instructor never stopped emphasizing the fact that the training of man and horse was the work of a Frenchman. Our return to the center of Tokyo, involving a two-hour traffic jam, gave Dupont plenty of leisure time in which to think. "Why do they force me to waste a whole afternoon in this way to see a horseman, a horse, and a teacher in a riding school?" "Your hosts, Monsieur Director General, have thought to honor you in this way, since the only French gold medal in the Tokyo Olympic Games was won by the horseman Jonquières d'Oriola."

French businessmen find such VIP treatment hard to take; certainly they are less amenable to it than their German or American counterparts. Americans have in general a better knowledge of their hosts' behavior, or know better how to play along with them. A Western businessman who gets off the plane is subjected to a kind of preliminary verbal examination. The Westerner often thinks that he is confronted by his alter ego, when in reality he will find himself trapped in the horizontal structure of the company he is visiting. He will meet three, four, ten interlocutors, and nothing will happen or be advanced because none of them will be qualified to handle his business. By this means the Japanese will test his seriousness, his credibility, the quality of the products he is selling, and his ability to buy those products they want to sell him. Many articles in the West have described the misadventures of businessmen who, exhausted by endless negotiations, have given up the struggle and headed, discouraged, for the airport—only to be amazed on their arrival in the waiting room by their interlocutors bearing gifts and a signed contract. Paradoxically, everything is done to make things appear just as the foreigner wants them. In this way, there is created the impression of an attachment to the values of the visitors; both men and institutions are trained to reflect faith in progress and science, as well as a hankering for universally recognized goals: democracy, peace, economic growth, and freedom.

In wanting to identify themselves with these imported values, the Japanese are not being dupes, but their efforts to efface themselves before their guests are badly repaid and often result in pointing up another image of themselves, which is just as far from the reality as the one they wish to display. Besides, this self-effacement has the effect of making their rituals, behavior, and various customs seem linked with folklore, when in actuality they derive from the deepest sources of Japane,e civilization. So one finds oneself confronted by a Japan with three faces: Japan as it wishes to appear, Japan as it is, and Japan as it is perceived.

THE PROFESSIONAL MILIEU

At the time of my original encounter with Japan, people did not go to Tokyo as they went to London or New York. One had to prepare oneself with great care. Japan did not welcome anyone but specialists. I am speaking not of tourists but of diplomatic representatives, special envoys from large corporations and international companies, and press correspondents. No corporation, government, or newspaper would have thought to send a representative to Tokyo who did not know the Japanese language and civilization, the country's usages and customs, and the psychology of its inhabitants. France was the exception to this rule. That is how I found myself in Tokyo mostly for curiosity's sake, and even more by chance. I spoke English like the average Frenchman, based on what I remembered from lycée, and not a word of Japanese. I had, I think, met a Japanese only once, and I had a curious recollection of it.

In the weeks preceding my departure, I set out in quest of opinions on Japan. The replies of all those who agreed to be interviewed had a common point of departure: "Oh, my goodness! Japan!" The speaker invariably bobbed his head up and down in amazement. He seemed to be taking a deep breath. Something definitive was about to be said. I waited, my pen poised.

"You will be struck by the density of the population. The crowds are oppressive, omnipresent; there is no open country."

"Talking with the Japanese is a dialogue with the deaf. You talk interminably. And you get nowhere. Result: zero."

I transcribe: Japanese, difficult dialogue.

"Never go alone into a bar in the Ginza—they'll strip you clean, leave you only the skin on your rear end. I paid two hundred francs for a whiskey."

I transcribe: Entertainment too expensive for a Western pocketbook.

"The Japanese—who can say? They flirt with you, lead you on, are very cunning, but at the last moment they do a number on you."

"Getting about Tokyo? There are no addresses, no names on

the streets, the taxis drive around like crazy at breakneck speeds and get lost. The first day it's amusing, but when you're working it's something else; it becomes quite wearing on the nerves."

"The food is loathsome."

"The politeness of the Japanese is deceitful—don't trust it. The more they bow and scrape, the more you can expect nasty tricks."

After having met about twenty officials and businessmen who had taken professional trips to Japan, I was completely demoralized. I did not want to leave empty-headed and prejudiced against a country where I was going to live for at least two years. Japan was no doubt a difficult country, the Japanese people were bizarre, that had to be admitted; beneath these truths must be a hidden key. I had to search for it. But where? I finally concluded that only the specialists on Japan could furnish me with the intellectual and moral passport indispensable to finding my way in Tokyo.

In 1963, Orientalists were still pendantically distilling their knowledge, initiating others by slow stages. How could they explain Japan in an hour to a journalist? Their esotericism was genuine, and Japan was a well-guarded hunting preserve that belonged only to a few. After my first interview with one of these eminences, I understood that it would be worth my while to begin at the beginning and work my way up if I wanted to clarify his replies to even such precise questions as: Can it be said that Japanese civilization is a variation of Chinese civilization? How can one explain the collaboration of the Japanese with the Americans despite Hiroshima and Nagasaki?

This was at the beginning of July; I had to sail on August 13. I realized that it would take me ten years dealing with the Far Eastern experts before I would be ready to leave. In the end I turned to books. Thirty-two days on the boat from Marseilles to Yokohama favored long night sessions with a book, and the extended siestas would permit me to reexamine Japan and the Japanese, about whom I finally fabricated a distinctive image.

NHK, that is, Nippon Hoso Kyokai, became my new professional milieu. This was the national radio-television corporation; its setup resembles that of ORTF, the French Radio and Television network, whose permanent representative in the northern Far East I had become. But whereas in France ORTF was a monopoly, NHK, with its two networks, had to deal with the competition of five private networks.

After having settled the problems of my installation in a hotel, I met my first Japanese colleague: Ichiro Matsui, the network's foreign relations director. Bald, with sparkling, almost ribald eyes behind thick lenses, he spoke correct English and "jabbered" a few words in French. His resonant laugh quickly charmed me. His assistant spoke French very fluently. Together with the two special envoys who had welcomed me on my arrival, they represented, I thought, my new human environment, except for our two Japanese secretaries.

The assignment of an office to the ORTF corespondent was the occasion for my first contact with Japanese administration. I had been relegated to a small room on a courtyard, furnished with two old rolltop metal desks. I would have liked a pleasanter decor. Ichiro Matsui had read my calling card attentively, and seeing my disappointment, he remarked with a mischievous smile, "This is temporary. . . ."

It was Mr. Sakamoto who introduced me to my new quarters: "Offices are assigned according to one's hierarchical position. You have a Kokyocho office. The color of the telephones differs in accordance with one's rank. Chairs become more comfortable the higher one rises in the hierarchy."

The same evening I was invited out by the head of the international division, Mr. Hiraoka. At five-thirty, he and Sakamoto led me to a garage in the building, where NHK's black limousine was waiting for us, together with a chauffeur in visored cap and white gloves. My memories of this evening are not unforgettable. The car took us to a bar in the Ginza quarter. The chauffeur ceremoniously opened the door on my side and bowed respectfully, his cap in his hand. We had to go down into a basement. Sakamoto announced at the bar: "NHK" (which he pronounced *enn-ech-ke*). The owner let out a cackling *"Ah, sodeska"* and installed us at a reserved table. Hiraoka ordered beer. Also Sakamoto. So I did the same, while accepting their proposal to taste some sake. At the end of a few minutes, the conversation was threatening to flicker out. Sakamoto began talking volubly in Japanese to Hiraoka, who nodded his head. Sakamoto got up and disappeared. Horaoka did not move a muscle. Then Sakamoto reappeared, smiling radiantly.

"Pardon me, sir. I hope that Courdy-San likes young Japanese girls," with a big, rather lewd laugh. Sakamoto wipes his glasses, but Hiraoka remains imperturbable. I see three young ladies arrive, one of whom is dressed in a kimono, the other two in very low-cut cocktail dresses. Kimono sits on the stool between Sakamoto and Hiraoka, while the other two, who are younger, cluster around me. Seated to my right and left, the girls ask questions about me, first to Sakamoto, now to Hiraoka. Suddenly my neighbor on the right, the girl with the most ample breasts, begins clapping her hands and shouting: "Alain . . . De . . . lon, Alain Delon, Brigitte Bardot, Brigitte Bardot, Yves Montand," etc. The enumeration continues, and I wonder where it will end. Hiraoka smiles; Sakamoto becomes more and more talkative. Kimono, sitting opposite me, surreptitiously makes a proposal under the table, at least I suppose she does, because a leg which is neither Sakamoto's nor Hiraoka's is wrapped around mine. We are now at our third beer. Sakamoto looks at his watch and says something in Japanese. The girls stand up, bow toward us: *"Domo arrigato, sayonara, mata dozo."* Thanks, good-bye, see you soon again. We are already on the sidewalk. The chauffeur is dozing at his wheel, his cap pulled down over his eyes. He wakes up with a start, jumps out to open the door, and we are off. This time I am hungry, and a restaurant welcomes us. It is after eight o'clock, a late hour for Japan. This is a yakitoria. It serves only meat on skewers. The chauffeur is dismissed. I will be taken to my hotel by a taxi. My hosts give the driver elaborate instructions so he will not get lost.

At the hotel a surprise awaited me. My suitcase, left open on my bed was half filled with water from a rainspout. The manager said he was terribly sorry but he could do nothing for me, neither repair the damage nor give me another room. I had to dry the bedsheets and move the bed. The next day it was firmly explained to me that I could not hope to stay for a long time at the Azabu Prince Hotel. In Japan one passed through hotels; one did not stay in them.

So began a long peregrination. My secretary would spend two to three hours a day doing nothing but booking a room for me; at best, I would keep it forty-eight hours. It is true that during this period Tokyo's hotel accommodations were very limited. Some large hotels with a thousand rooms and more were under construction in preparation for the Olympic Games. During this time nothing that happened was to my liking. My office was literally invaded several times a day by young employees of NHK, who came to see me as if I were an exhibition. Generally, the women did not step over the threshold but chatted with my secretary. The men, less timid, would deposit a calling card and then for no apparent reason take possession of my telephone and converse interminably with some mysterious party. When I questioned Tanabe-San, my secretary, she invariably replied: "He had to telephone, and besides, he asked me for permission." Dozens of Japanese wanted to interview me on subjects that did not interest me and had no relation to my job there. But I felt the situation was about to take a turn for the better when Sakamoto, after coming into my office on tiptoe, declared: "This coming Sunday there is a festival near Tokyo. It's the NHK's annual festival. You will see the president. Do you want to come? I shall order a car for you."

It was still hot on this first Sunday in October, and the cloudless sky was perfect for the sort of grand country fair that had been organized for NHK's personnel, who at that time numbered around seventeen thousand. Tents set up in a large field welcomed the guests—in one place with jugglers, in another to enjoy the foods of a Pantagruelian buffet, washed down by floods of beer and sake. In the official tent, the president, Mr. Aben, a dynamic old man apparently enjoying himself, asked me to watch the final procession with him. Each section of NHK had chosen a different theme for fancy dress. I recognized Sakamoto dressed up as a samurai. He had invited me to participate in the parade as a sumo wrestler, but I preferred to present ORTF's prize for the best costume, which was awarded after the president's. Then, a few seconds later, I exchanged calling cards with all those persons whose cooperation I needed in order to organize my work; the director of information and the director of technical services interested me especially, as well as the man responsible for rebroadcasting the Olympic Games. From that moment on, the roadblocks disappeared. The program director, Nagahama-San, gave me proof of his particular friendship, as did Vice-President Maeda, who later became president.

When Nagahama-San was named director of the most important regional television station in Osaka, which practically covered the southern half of Japan, he organized a dinner meeting of program directors and television owners in Southeast Asia. He proposed a toast honoring French television and its representative, and I made a terrible blunder. The atmosphere was completely euphoric. NHK had made a substantial cooperative effort to foster modernization of the young television networks in Southeast Asia. The desire of the new president of NHK was to create conditions favorable to the setting up of an Asian network comparable to Eurovision. In the excitement of the banquet, I raised my glass and in turn proposed a toast: "For Nagahama-San and NHK, *banzai!*" Immediately the Japanese, who filled half the hall, shot up from their seats and raised their arms straight in the air, shouting in response *"Banzai!"* three times. But the delegates and representatives of Southeast Asia, politely turning their spoons in their coffee cups, had not budged.

I later discussed this incident with a very nice Indonesian delegate, who explained to me: "Do you think that Singapore can forget that the Japanese shot thirty thousand of their people, and that after this carnage the Japanese army shouted *banzai!* This word has a resonance of cruelty in all of Southeast Asia." Fortunately, if these words are still charged with bad memories, the reality has changed. The years did their work, creating new political conditions but also a new kind of personal relationship between Japan and the countries of Southeast Asia.

Through the distorting but invaluable prism of television, I began to see Japan in all its aspects. The national Japanese network was for seven years my privileged partner, my recourse in difficulties, and often my support. Each time that I had an impression to the contrary—and that happened quite often during the three first years of my stay there—I had to admit my mistake: I had transgressed, without wishing to, the rules of the Japanese dialectic, overstepped the bounds of the most inviolable usages and customs.

PREPARATIONS FOR THE GAMES

In 1964, Japan was totally concentrated on the Olympic Games. Nothing else had any importance. Tokyo, transformed into a con-

struction site and warehouse, looked like a city that had just been
bombed. Everywhere gigantic construction projects dug down into
the depths of the earth, which had not received such wounds since
the building of the subway. In order to understand really the dimensions of the problem, it is necessary to imagine the largest urban
agglomeration in the world, at that time close to twenty million inhabitants, distributed horizontally around Tokyo, approximately
from Chiba to Yokosuka, over an area seventy miles by forty. Tokyo
proper numbered about eleven million inhabitants, gathered in districts that could be compared to so many villages. The houses were
of wood, with tiny, neatly arranged gardens; they were enclosed by
fences made of planks stained walnut; each district included two or
three streets with stores, a fruit and vegetable stand, a fish store, a
hardware store, and specialized restaurants selling sushi, or o'soba,
or sashimi, etc. The streets and alleys crossed each other, with here
and there a small stream. The pipes and wires transmitting gas and
electricity ran everywhere in a spectacular crisscross entanglement.
Where the street was a little wider, some raised footwalks permitted
the children to cross without danger. There was no sidewalk, and
the streets did not have names. Nowhere was there a sewer. One
could not find a residential section in the usual sense of the term.
Mansions and more modest dwellings stood cheek by jowl, except
perhaps in Azabu, the district of the embassies, and certain parts of
Setagaya. Tokyo did not look like a city, but rather like a juxtaposi-
tion of villages.

However, in 1963, Marunouchi, near the railway station, and
the Ginza, with its large department stores, Shibuya and Shinjuku,
were already urban centers bristling with multistoried structures. At
Akasaka, a few scattered apartment buildings towered over the
wooden houses. A city had been *created* for the games. First of all,
the main avenues of communication: a highway from the Ginza to
the airport at Shibuya and then, subsequently, to Shinjuku, Ueno,
and Meguro; a highway from Tokyo to Yokohama. The work on the
highways completely upset the citizens' lives. When possible, work
was carried on both night and day. To permit life to continue and
especially to make traffic possible on the principal arteries, a system
of beams fashioned of wood or metal permitted workers to close the
excavations during the day and open them at night. Blacksmith
shops rumbled in Tokyo's entrails each night. Entire streets were
demolished to put through the avenues. Other streets were broadened by moving houses on rollers, without knocking them down; the
city highways appeared quite soon, above the roofs. Avenues were
marked out; monuments and stadiums were constructed. At Yogogi
it was a swimming pool in the shape of an overturned boat that
especially caught the eye; at Komazawa the soccer stadium and the
wrestling arena. Elsewhere it was Tokyo Cathedral, to which the
architect Kenzo Tange had given the shape of a stork in flight, the

symbol of happiness and peace. To the Imperial, Okura, and Hilton hotels, completed by 1963, as well as some others, such as the Palace, new Western-style grand hotels were added, including the Tokyo Prince and above all the New Otani, whose sumptuous gardens contain enormous rocks worth several million yen each.

There was no unemployment in Tokyo during 1963 and 1964. Indeed, there was a dearth of manual laborers. An immense movement that had started at the end of the war gained momentum. The rural world was dislodged. Young people, attracted by the opportunity for work, migrated to the city. Victims of an acute housing shortage, they found themselves settled on the periphery in a district called Saniya. Packed five, six, even ten to a space twenty-five square yards in size, they could easily see that Japan was on the move, but they obviously were not the beneficiaries of this progress. Each morning at dawn, in the alleyways, at the street corners, one could witness a kind of "slave" market: recruiters came to choose the laborers they needed on the construction jobs, sometimes giving work to the lowest bidder. There were more volunteers than jobs when the work was reasonably remunerated. When the recruiter left, the people who had been rejected offered themselves at derisory wages for the hardest and most dangerous work.

AUTOMOBILE MADNESS

When I arrived in Tokyo in 1963, traffic was impossible, not because of the number of cars that were circulating but because the streets were narrow and trucks took up all the space. There were no traffic regulations. Everyone drove at breakneck speed; with traffic oriented to the left, how different it was for a Westerner to get about Tokyo at the wheel of his car! Private cars were rare, taxis innumerable, generally tiny Datsuns whose back doors could be closed by a switch next to the driver. You got out of the taxi, turned to close the door, and it swung abruptly beneath your nose, closing with a sharp bang. Some larger cars, of the Prince type, had a television antenna on the roof, miniature Sony or Matsushita sets inside, sometimes in the front. Company cars, with their green license plates, were equipped with white spare-tire covers; rear and sometimes side windows were covered with curtains, often embroidered. At the end of some weeks I understood the reason for this transformation of cars into bedchambers: executives would sleep comfortably during the trip from home to job, or vice versa. Nissan with his Datsun had carved out a conspicuous place in the manufacture of custom-built cars, limousines, and, at the other end of the scale, tiny taxis. I contacted the Nissan offices a few days after my arrival. They sent me, as my secretary made clear after having read my visitor's calling card, the chief salesman.

In Japan you must learn the ceremonial of the calling card. You cannot introduce yourself by sticking out your hand and saying "Courdy" or "Suzuki." Your interlocutor would look at you as though scared out of his wits, take you for a peasant who had just left the countryside, then mumble a shapeless phrase signifying: How do you spell it? You would then get entangled in a relatively complex linguistic process, because when you would say *r* your interlocutor would understand *l*. After a quarter hour spent getting him to comprehend your name, you would do as everyone does: have some calling cards made, in French and Japanese. Introductions can then be made wordlessly, with a simple inclination of the head, to which you add a slight curve of the back if your opposite number is an important person. You proffer your calling card while he hands you his, preferably at the same time. During the exchange you wear a bogus smile, then you avidly peruse the text of the card, which can be long. You should not forget the smile at the conclusion of the ritual; if you are really glad to meet him, you will add, depending on the case, another nod of your head or a second curve of your back. Only then can the conversation begin.

In the case of Nissan's chief salesman, it was not proper for a person of my rank to accept his card directly. It was handed to my secretary, to be transmitted to me. I explained: "I want a small car with a fast pickup to get through the narrow streets, one I can drive myself." Amazement spread across his face, and calmly he explained to my secretary: "These small cars are not suitable for an honorable *geijin*. How could he get around in Tokyo, with its irregular, unnamed streets? The suspension is very stiff, I cannot guarantee the brakes, and it's impossible for these cars to be driven by a chauffeur because the back is too narrow and your knees are cramped. . . . The Prince would be the car best suited to your honorable employer. . . ." He took out of his pocket four pages of fine paper densely covered with cramped Japanese script, and said to my secretary that he hoped she would be so good as to sign them.

"But I would like to read the contract first," I dared to say.

"No," she replied, "it is illegible; even I can't understand any of it."

"Why must you sign the contract and not me?"

"Because you cannot sign with a pen—your signature has no value. I have a personal seal for you which I registered with the district councillor."

She picked up a tiny seal, pressed it on the three pages of what she presumed to be the contract, and presented me with a checkbook. And the deal was concluded. The Nissan Prince, brilliantly brand new, would be delivered to me at Haneda airport on my return from Hong Kong, where I had to go the following day. All that remained to be settled was the matter of a chauffeur. The sales manager proposed that I hire Ono-San, a very cultivated young man who was looking for a job as chauffeur with a foreign company, with the idea of perfecting his English.

Ono was waiting for me at the airport on my return. He was sporting a magnificent white visored cap. He opened the door as if he were the chauffeur of a Rolls. The car was very good-looking, elegantly finished, quite comfortable. It was ten-thirty and I was eager to get home to bed. About a mile from the airport, the motor began to miss, then it stopped. Ono got out, inspected the car, bowed in front of me and said, "*Sumimasen . . .* I must beg your pardon. . . ." He tuned the radio to a fashionable station that broadcasts Western pop music and walked away from the car. He left his cap on the seat. Comfortably seated, I took advantage of the breakdown to read the newspapers.

At the end of an hour, I began to look around me. Traffic had thinned out. All the little wooden houses had their shutters closed. In the half darkness I could make out the electric wires, a gigantic spider's web strung over the roofs, attached on either side of the street. I did not know where I was. My very heavy suitcase was in the trunk. I imagined leaving it there and continuing my trip on foot. I started to keep an eye open for a taxi, but traffic had dried up. Wan electric bulbs lit the street at infrequent intervals.

After two hours of waiting, I saw a shadow appear in the distance. It was Ono, carrying a jerry can. He filled the gas tank without a word, turned the key, and started off without any difficulty. I promised myself to fire him the next day. I slept almost eight hours, and my section of town was already very animated when I was awakened at nine by the *Marseillaise* being whistled merrily outside. It was Ono-San, washing the car. I hadn't the heart to fire a Japanese chauffeur who whistled the *Marseillaise* while working. Afterward we had a great many adventures together, until the day came when he left me to continue his climb up the social ladder.

With the Nissan Prince we traveled together through Tokyo's labyrinths. In the morning he came by to drive me to my office, rarely taking the same streets, and I wound up knowing at least a half-dozen routes for the trip. Nowhere could I find an accurate detailed map of Tokyo. Streets were altered at record speed, and since they did not have names, you had to trust to reference points, but they, too, disappeared. I went regularly to the Marunouchi quarter, near Tokyo's central railroad station, where the Foreign Correspondents Club and the KDD, Koksai Denshin Denwa—International Telegraph and Telephone—were located. I knew that you had to turn the corner of a street where there was a garden. One day, the garden that had served me as a reference point the day before had disappeared; in its place was a construction site surrounded by a fence. The next day the garden was back in place. Once again I got used to it—and overnight it disappeared. But this time it was definitive: a big building started going up.

Ono-San got lost regularly. He would stop at the corner of a street, ask for directions, start up again, drive in a circle, and be right back where he had started from. Each trip outside of those to Marunouchi or the Shibuya center turned into an expedition.

It was a Friday, and I was giving my first party in honor of NHK and a television team that had come from Paris to shoot a Franco-Japanese special report. The French ambassador, Étienne Dennery, would join us. I decided to take precautions. First I sent Ono-San in the afternoon to reconnoiter the route between my office and the Happo-En restaurant. Then I decided to leave an hour in advance. The trip normally took about twenty minutes. At the end of an hour, streets had succeeded avenues, then alleyways had succeeded streets, and we were still not in sight of Happo-En. Ono-San got out to ask for directions from some storekeepers and passersby, and each time there were long consultations. Every so often the person who had been stopped would extend his arms right or left, while Ono-San would also make gestures, as though seeking for approval. (I understood much later that in Tokyo one should never ask directions from a native, for he does not know any more than you do. However, since he cannot lose face, he points out to you what he thinks is the most probable direction. And above all one should never turn to taxi drivers for help. They are habitually recruited in the country, and it is their customer who must show them the way, unless he wants to find himself irremediably moving in the direction opposite to the place he hoped to reach. Finally, one should not, except at one's own risk and peril, ask the policemen stationed on the traffic islands which form a checkerboard across Tokyo. Once, when Ono-San got the bad idea of asking directions at one of these police boxes, they demanded to see his identification, then the car registration, and he then had to answer an interminable series of questions, during which we wasted half an hour.) At seven forty-five we made a remarkable entrance into the sumptuous gardens of the Happo-En. My guests had already been served. They were gracious enough to condone my lateness because I was new to Japan.

Japan's economic growth has zoomed, but the atavism of distrusting the foreigner in any and all situations arises constantly in everyday life, while the number of foreigners living in Tokyo continues to increase. In one year the number of private cars driving around Tokyo multiplied ten times. When I went to Hiroshima at the invitation of Mr. Ueda, one of the directors of the Mazda factories (Mr. Masuda, Jr., owner of Mazda, was president of the Franco-Japanese Association at Hiroshima), I was received at my host's recently built house, located at the end of Hiroshima Bay opposite the temple of Miyajima, a site considered one of the three most beautiful on the archipelago. The house was decorated in a mixture of Japanese style and what in Japan is called the Western style. A monumental staircase led to the first floor, where reception halls and the traditional dining rooms, with low tables and paintings on sliding partitions, were laid out, all in a harmony enhanced by a large window that looked out on the temple. On the floor above, some rooms were prepared for the guests.

Visiting the factory the day after our arrival, and following a minutely detailed program, I was struck not so much by the technology of the assembly lines—they were as perfect as Renault and Ford factories—but by the management organization and the farsightedness of the executives. In Tokyo, in a building near Marunouchi, they had installed an immense studio to make films advertising their products. They intended to add a permanent closed-circuit link between Tokyo and Hiroshima to allow the directors in Tokyo to check on the work in progress in the factory, nearly five hundred miles away.

Precision joined with audacity had greatly impressed me in the shipyards. At the Ishikawajima-Harima yard in Yokohama, they were building the largest oil tanker in the world, *Idemitsu Maru*, weighing 300,000 tons. The precision in construction was such that by consulting the record of expenditures and the work plan, one could deduce with certainty each day's progress in the shipyard. The audacity lay in the decision to launch supertankers when no harbor installation in the world was capable of receiving them, a decision taken on the basis of a national consensus among competing Japanese companies.

NUCLEAR POWER: A PROBLEM OF CONSCIENCE

In the field of electronics, the breakthrough of companies like Sony and Matsushita had taken place by the time I arrived. The Japanese had made their plans with great care, following attentively the efforts of IBM-Japan and the French company BULL before its merger with General Electric. An IBM-Japan engineer, who had come from the United States, commented on the Japanese adaptation to high technology: "Certain components of computers are manufactured by giving the work to subcontractors who have family industries. Even though they do not have ultramodern equipment, these industries are able—one does not know by what miracle—to respect the production standards that are set for them, to such a point that it is impossible to distinguish the Japanese parts from those manufactured in the United States." Photography, now a national industry, has imposed itself on the world market. The Canon company has proved to be particularly aggressive, even though its optics do not surpass German or American optics. The French manufacturer Robert Angénieux has confided that he is not upset by this competition, but perhaps he forgets the increasingly incisive and effective commercial methods the Japanese have perfected. Foreign visitors to the archipelago regard these "made in Japan" products as imitations, and the professionals were surprised some years ago when the International Patents Congress, held in Tokyo, put on the agenda the problem of the imitators of Japanese patents. Japan had reason enough to declare, "Do not copy us," when the legend of the Japanese as champion plagiarists was still being circulated.

In 1968, a Japanese newspaper ran a lead article saying, "A computer can now speak Japanese, but space research still encounters difficulties." It is true that technological innovation has caught Japan unprepared for establishing research facilities on a scale as gigantic as that required for building an atomic reactor or launching a spacecraft. The repeated failures of the Lambda and Mu rockets have given a distinctively bad image to research too dispersed among a multiplicity of uncoordinated units and having at its disposal only meager and scattered funds.

However, the Institute of Space and Aeronautical Sciences at the University of Tokyo attracted the attention of the scientific world by perfecting the four-stage Lambda 4S rocket, running on solid motor fuel. I went to see it launched at Uchinoura, the site of the Japanese space center. Located to the south of Kyushu island, it is hard to reach. A narrow winding road twists past the imposing Sakura-jima volcano and over hills and rice fields to arrive, at the foot of an immense cliff, in a village entirely devoted to rockets and space flight, just as the village of Tokai-Mura north of Tokyo is devoted to the atom. Street lamps are shaped like rockets, and for the peasants, too, space has become an integral part of the folklore. About eight in the morning we appeared, a group of observers, armed with our passes, at the entrance to the base on top of a cliff overlooking the sea. After visiting the operational center, we went down to the bottom of the cliff, where the launching ramp is located. A few hundred yards behind it, a hangar contained the meteorological satellite, which had not yet been attached to the rocket's fourth stage. Technicians dressed in white were bustling around the satellite, but watching them, one got the impression of an amiable improvisation. They screwed something on, only to unscrew it a few seconds later. When one questioned the technicians: "Well, will it go?" they replied: "Maybe. . . ." Finally, everything was ready. The solemn moment had come. The countdown began; the blast-off was achieved correctly, and the rocket rose into the sky. The first stage fell away on schedule, then the second stage. . . . Suddenly, immense stupefaction: a barely visible white dot descended to the horizon. The rocket had fallen into the sea before sending the satellite into orbit.

A professor in our group explained what he called the "drama of conscience" at the University of Tokyo: "We do not accept the fact that our researches can serve military purposes. That is why we have always refused to equip our rockets with a system of radio guidance. This might be one of the basic causes of today's failure."

Unfortunately, the white smoke emitted by the Lambda is thickened by the black smoke of corruption. The man a French colleague nicknamed "Professor Nimbus" was discharged, and the government promised "reorganization" of the research. But the chaos continued. This was why the antagonism between the University of Tokyo Space Institute and the Ministry of Technology came into the open, while the ministries of transport and telecommunications announced competing space programs.

In May 1968, the Japanese government replaced the National Committee for Space Activities with a Commission of Space Activities, to which it entrusted the setting up of a new program of coordinated space development oriented toward perfecting new rockets and satellites. The National Agency for Space Development, formed in 1969, completed the organization, under the aegis of the University of Tokyo. Now the coordination of programs is assured, and effective international cooperation permits the Japanese to make real progress in the fields of telecommunications, meteorology, and geodetics, and to participate in projects as important as is NASA's space capsule. As for satellites, Japan no longer lags far behind Europe, while it has leaped forward in rocketry with the Nu rocket launcher. In 1978, Japanese efforts were basically concentrated on the perfecting of scientific satellites for the observation of particles and solar explosions, of X-rays and gamma rays. Additional money was allocated for the study of satellites for telecommunications and meteorology.

In the sphere of atomic research, the Japanese imported their first breeder reactor from the United States. Afterward, agreements with Great Britain and France as well as certain exchanges of technology permitted them to develop their nuclear resources rapidly until they found themselves confronted by a combination of ecological and antimilitarist sentiments and protest movements of all sorts. In 1968, in particular, two occasions of discord slowed up the development of the "nuclear" research projects: the chance to construct an accelerator for sophisticated particles, and the acceptance by Japan's Society of Physics of funds from the American army to cover the expenses of an international congress on the technology of semiconductors. Although the subvention was rather small, about $10,000, it precipitated an inquiry which revealed that fifty-four researchers from nineteen universities had accepted subsidies from the same source, totaling in the ten previous years a minimum of $2 million. The Society of Physics gathered its wits and declared that from then on, no subvention from the American army would be accepted. The Institute of Research in the atomic industry finally completed at Tokai-Mura the first Japanese reactor; water-cooled and using enriched uranium, it could supply 50,000 kilowatts of power.

Today Japan's energy choice is definitively concentrated on the development of nuclear power. The electricity supplied by nuclear power stations rose at the end of 1978 to almost 10 million kilowatts, representing a little more than 7 percent of the electricity supplied by all the power stations. The present program, revised downward, foresees a supply of 33 million kilowatts in 1985 and 60 million in 1990. To make sure of its success, the Japanese are perfecting a new technique for light-water reactors. They have chosen their new generation of energy sources, those of a super-regenerator for fast neutrons; parallel to this they are studying a method based on the introduction of heavy-water reactors. Japan's objective is to ensure about a third of its supply of natural uranium through importing minerals developed by companies in which Japanese capital is invested. When it comes to enriched uranium, they are now developing the technique of ultra-centrifugal separation, with the aim of building a pilot factory in 1985.

The removal of radioactive waste is considered a key stage in the cycle. Here again, a pilot plant is planned for 1985. The technology of thermonuclear fusion will also be mastered somewhere around 1985. Research is being conducted within the International Agency for Atomic Energy, with the cooperation of the United States. The Japanese are further studying the commercial possibilities of atomic-powered ships before proceeding with their program. Politically, their concern is not to be left behind in this field, conscious as they are of the country's maritime vocation.

THE OTHER SIDE OF ECONOMIC GROWTH

Until 1970, economic growth went hand in hand with opposition movements (though they were not very coherent) which the left seemed proud to benefit from. When leftists lost their two chief "causes" with the return of Okinawa to Japanese sovereignty and the end of the Vietnam War, only a grand national plan could mobilize the forces of opposition and protest. It was thought that Minamata and the mercury pollution of the products of the sea would help to crystallize resistance, and the student-peasant movement against the opening of Narita airport appeared to mark a beginning. Perhaps the price to be paid for dizzying economic growth would be higher than the price of the World War II defeat. The ecological rebellion might destroy what the outcome of the war had not been able to break: national consensus. Increased individual income and general prosperity were accompanied by a growing awareness of the serfdom imposed by urbanization and modernization.

"Supervised Demos"

This new serfdom is symbolized by Kawasaki and its metal industries at the gates of Tokyo, wedged into an urban zone between the capital and the port of Yokohama. In the elementary school in the factory district, the teachers have to distribute gas masks when a contrary wind and dense smog push the smoke and fumes toward them. In one of the back streets of Kan-Nana Dori, the traffic police have to return to their posts every half hour to get a whiff of oxygen. Growth bears within itself the promise of being called into question. In Japan, the street demonstration has always been considered a form of political expression, and also of emotional release, though it is organized and completely controlled even in its "spontaneous" outbursts.

At the beginning of my sojourn, the first protest march I happened to witness amazed me. Men and women marched in serried ranks down the street, preceded by people carrying signs. It was a Saturday afternoon. There were not many people in this demonstration compared to those I have seen since, but it did bring together a number of people walking twelve abreast for more than half a mile. The end of the procession was made up of young girls who, one behind the other, advanced in a snake dance, zigzagging to the rhythmic shouts of *"Wan-Chai . . . Wan-Chai . . ."* Slogans shouted through a loudspeaker mounted on a car at the head of the demonstration echoed all along the ranks and the crowd repeated them. Another car with a loudspeaker, a police car, drove along next to the parade, and the front ranks were stopped by about fifty helmeted policemen. I asked for an explanation: The police are told of a demonstration in advance. They are asked for a permit, and the route is the result of negotiations. The degree of intensity and ardor have also been foreseen, and police are assigned proportionately. When you see policemen wearing only caps, then the demonstration is not going to be nasty. It is more serious if helmets and truncheons are in evidence. That Saturday it was a demonstration of streetcar employees who, anticipating the elimination of urban streetcars and agreeing with the move, were demanding guarantees that they would be reassigned.

Anti-American Waves

After the emperor declared the Olympic Games open, protest movements became more and more numerous. The Japanese demonstrated against the Americans and their presence in Japan: military bases for ground, aerial, and naval forces; the anchoring in Japanese ports of units of the Seventh Fleet; the occupation of Okinawa by an American administration. When, on November 12, 1967, Prime Minister Sato was going to Washington on an official visit, two thousand students waited for him at Haneda airport. They were wearing helmets and armed with clubs, and had a reserve of homemade Molotov cocktails. The police attached to their helmets transparent plastic visors which could be lowered over their faces. They were equipped with shields and long hardwood poles. The students, first to attack, assaulted a police truck. A young demonstrator climbed behind the wheel and, incautiously backing up, crushed one of his comrades. The police answered this assault lackadaisically. Final outcome: one student killed, two hundred students and six hundred policemen wounded. The prime minister took the plane for Washington, expressing his regret for the student's death. Zengakuren, the National Federation of Japanese Students, has organized 690,000 students in 426 associations. At the beginning of 1968, the hottest year, three factions competed for the students' support.

On January 15, 1968, it was announced that the *Enterprise*, the atomic airplane carrier of the U.S. Seventh Fleet, was coming with its escort on a visit to Sasebo, on Kynshu, arriving January 18. Students assembled at the private University of Hoesi, where they spent the night. At dawn on the sixteenth, they headed for the Tokyo station to take the train for Sasebo and the Japanese-American naval base, near Nagasaki. The confrontation took place, but this time the police had received orders not to give any quarter. One hundred and thirty students were arrested; three hundred succeeded in boarding the train. They were joined en route at Osaka by Kansai students, then at Fukuoka, a university town, by Kyushu students. So despite the police, three thousand students reached Sasebo. However, 5,700 special shock troops had been deployed around the American base. Akiyama, a student leader, decided to mount an attack against them. But the police response was devastating: young boys and girls were seriously beaten, even struck down. Tons of water mixed with a blinding, nauseating liquid was poured. Because of rough seas, the *Enterprise* arrived the next morning at nine-thirty. The night before, the opposition political parties rallied more than fifty thousand people, who came from all corners of the archipelago: Socialists, Communists, and members of the Komeito, a centrist party that rose out of the powerful religious organization Sokkagakai. In its calmness their demonstration was a contrast to the students' action. On the morning of the nineteenth, when the *Enterprise* was already at the dock with its two escort destroyers, Akiyama was still waging war, but this was just a last-ditch, gallant gesture, for he had hardly a dozen able-bodied men left. At midday, Akiyama boarded the train under the noses of the police, who did not make a move to stop him, and he shouted at the forces of order: "I'll be back in three days."

At that moment the Japanese writer Makoto Oda, president of the Committee of Intellectuals Against the Vietnam War (Bheiren), rowed with some friends in a frail skiff right beneath the gigantic airplane carrier. Through a loudspeaker he harangued the American sailors, who mocked him from the ship's high decks. "Desert," he shouted to them. He showed them a small green paper pass for those who chose not to return to the ship. At one thirty, the *Enterprise's* sailors and pilots came ashore. At the street corners, charming girl students distributed the green paper that Makoto Oda had shown them. In Japanese on one side and English on the other, one could read: "Against the Vietnam War: If you want to desert, call the telephone number below. You will get an answer. If you do not know how to telephone, present this paper to any Japanese and he will do it for you." GIs and sailors read the paper carefully and automatically put it in their pocket, saying, "Thank you." Some banners appeared, on the initiative of the majority Liberal Democratic party: WELCOME U.S. ENTERPRISE. Merchants had festooned their shops with American flags and banners. The "rest and recreation tour" began. The bars filled up; girls began their striptease numbers in the cabarets; the souvenir shops cranked up their iron shutters or pulled back their blinds, displaying their merchandise; the restaurants were packed.

After January 1969, the situation got much worse. Akiyama's students erected barricades inside the universities. Professors were taken hostage. The students stored up paving stones, manufactured Molotov cocktails, held political meetings. From time to time, they sallied forth into the city to confront the police. The movement gradually won over all the universities in Japan. The return of Okinawa to Japan was the rallying cry of the day.

One winter evening about six-thirty, the avenue that leads from the Ginza to the Shimbasi station in the center of Tokyo was blocked at its two extremes. On the Ginza side, students wearing blue or red helmets, with black kerchiefs tied around their necks, advanced, armed with poles or lances, in compact ranks, while from the other side the police advanced. We were caught between the opposing camps with our television crew when the confrontation began. We were perfectly distinguishable, Westerners without helmets. Nobody touched us. Some students avoided us and even begged our pardon. A diluvial rain began falling, and everyone started to run away. The police had had the time to fire some tear-gas bombs, and the crowd rushed, weeping, into the adjacent streets. The forces of order have a very special piece of equipment: A kind of portcullis or iron gate which seals off a street is pushed straight against the demonstrators; cord nets are then stretched out and cast over those who advance doing a snake dance.

The biggest battle occurred in mid-January, at the University of

Tokyo, where 8,500 men were mobilized to clear the library, an immense structure in the center of the campus, held by Akiyama and three hundred students. Demonstrators and police gave each other the once-over. Carrying identifying signs, we requested permission to go and see the students. Once across no-man's-land, we were greeted by an effigy of General de Gaulle, large as life and nailed to plywood, on his kepi the letters "ORTF," on his sleeves "RTL," and on his belly "Europe No. 1," with a television screen encircled by barbed wire. We learned that Akiyama and his men had been visited some weeks before by May 1968 combatants from the Sorbonne. Akiyama sang the praises of the French students and of their international and proletarian revolutionary spirit. A few hours after we left, police attacked the building. It took them twenty-four hours to overcome the small group of students; helicopters even dropped tear-gas bombs on the balconies. One consequence of this encounter was that the Japanese army constructed a life-size model of the university library for its antisubversion exercises.

After Okinawa's return to Japan and the renewal of the security treaty, order again reigned on the campuses. The disenchantment that followed these intense moments created favorable conditions for an extremist fringe, the Red Army, which, as it increased its violence, encouraged a return to normality in the majority of Japanese society.

The Red Army has given the Japanese a negative image of a "revolution" that runs counter to their deepest feelings. Its violence shocks their conscience, since it acts outside the ancestral rules of national honor. Today the Red Army shows itself only rarely, but its "desperado" and marginal aspects have a typically Nipponese character; it represents the other side of the coin. And certain parallels can set one musing. Some days before his suicide, Yukio Mishima instructed his *tatenokai* (private army) in his doctrine of action. "One must," he said, "carry out to the very end any action one has begun, carry it to its logical conclusion." When I visited Akiyama one day in a clandestine printing plant in Tokyo, he used pretty much the same terms when assuring me of his determination.

PASSENGERS

The Japanese bus passenger takes his seat noiselessly, paying no attention to the people bustling around him. After the first mile, he dozes off. The hostess lulls him with an uninterrupted tide of words, everything to be learned about the region you are traveling through, from the fields growing corn, barley, and rice to the number of male children in the primary schools of the village you're just passing. At times the hostess stops, out of breath. The Japanese, dozing in their seats, may open an eye. If the hostess is a neophyte, she blushes, stammers, and picks up the thread. The more experienced intone a traditional song. Who cares! Everything is back to normal, the passengers can doze off, the humming voice recommences, but suddenly a phrase is repeated. The hostess announces: "Ladies and gentlemen, here is the sea. . . ." The passengers deign to lift their heads to admire it. Some take out their pocket cameras and press the button once or twice; others glare at their watches and go back to sleep. The entire bus is awakened by a bump. The hostess had in fact announced: "Ladies and gentlemen, you will feel a jolt, since we are going across a grade crossing. . . . We are crossing it. . . . We have crossed it. . . . Thank you for being so kind as to accept this slight inconvenience, for which the company begs you to forgive it. . . ."

All hostesses do not behave this way, but the old tradition of bus travel survives in the provinces. At Nagoya, a company has launched a study of the influence of the lunar cycle on its drivers' moods and ability to drive, and has found variations. There are some days when it is better not to take the wheel. A schedule of leaves has been established on the basis of this study, and the company has shown that in ten years the rate of accidents attributable to drivers has diminished by thirty percent.

Traveling on the train is faster and more comfortable. It is also the least expensive means of transportation, if one excepts the *Shinkansen* superexpress runs on the Tokkaido line. But train travel is no longer what it was. With modernization has come depersonalization. In the past, on the local lines, you felt truly at home and did not hesitate to take off your shoes and even your pants, play cards, have a conversation with your friends. The train took the place of a family living room. Certain people, extremely thorough, took the precaution of bringing along a hanger to keep the crease in their pants. Women were satisfied to remove their shoes. But in 1963 the railroads made an effort to eliminate customs that did not coincide with Western good manners. What would the foreigners, the *geijin*, think of undershorts? Exhortations were therefore carried by loudspeakers through the compartments: "Do not take your pants off in the train." By the time of the Olympic Games, the new discipline was in effect, even on country trains.

The Japanese railroad system has been able to perpetuate traditions of courtesy among its employees, as well as an entire ritual. The departure of a train like the *Shinkansen* from the central Tokyo station is initiated by a stationmaster employing certain very precise gestures, accompanied by a salute. This salute is returned by the train's personnel, including those in the restaurant car, where the employees are lined up next to the windows to bow as the train passes the stationmaster. This salute is the signal for service to begin. The *Shinkansen* travels at an average speed of 135 miles an hour and is equipped with a telephone. The painter Miró, traveling with Aimé Maegt, was surprised to receive by telephone, between Tokyo and Kyoto, the news of the death of André Breton. The French delegation at the World Congress of Interpol in 1966 was interviewed by the French radio network over the same wire.

Today, airplane travel has been fully integrated in normal life. All the towns on the archipelago are regularly served by the state-owned Japan Air Lines and by two private companies. Japanese airlines are for the most part customers of the American aeronautical industry, but glance sidelong at Europe's Airbus. They usually offer a high standard of service and food which is palpably superior to that of Europe or the United States. Personnel, trained to conform to Japanese standards of politeness, remain considerate and attentive under the most trying conditions.

Traditionally, the Japanese go from place to place en masse, and often communally. A school, a company, a department in a company, take a cultural trip at an appropriate season; one also comes across a club, or a group of neighborhood families. The travel agencies take care of everything—bus or train, hotels, hostesses, guides. One can see these groups in the temples of Kyoto, on railroad platforms, in the mountains, or at the seaside, clustered behind a banner waved by their guide as a signal to assemble. These gregarious migrations through the archipelago, so characteristic of the modern country, contrast to the traditional homebody tendencies of the women. Only a few years ago, one quite often heard Tokyo mothers say that they did not know the capital's center at all or knew it poorly. But everything evolves—even as the great Japanese migration inside the archipelago has become a worldwide migration.

Europe and the United States have accustomed themselves to this ubiquitous Japanese tourism and made a good profit from it. It is not unusual to see groups of Japanese arriving in winter to ski on the slopes of the Austrian or French Alps.

SHOPPING

To immerse oneself in a Japanese crowd, one must go to Tokyo, Osaka, or almost any big city. The spectacle of Tokyo's Shibuya station when offices let out is especially hallucinatory in the summer, when a wave of white shirts with open collars comes swirling across the square, under the gaze of a statue of a dog, symbol of faithfulness.

When it gets hot and humid outdoors, it is pleasant to take shelter in a big department store—a phenomenon the Japanese believe that they invented. The atmosphere that they have been able to create—an artificial universe where all desires, all proclivities, can be immediately gratified—certainly represents an undeniable incitation to buy; it also pleases the stroller. At the foot of each escalator, a charming young Japanese woman dressed in an iridescent kimono bows in welcome and begs you to watch where you step, while a hostess with white gloves furtively wipes away with a cloth the dust that might cover the railing on which you are going to rest your hand. Throughout the day, elevator operators murmur muffled set phrases of thanks and apology at each floor. Everything you would want is here: a roof garden with a bar, a nursery where mothers can leave their babies without fear, and of course restaurants and automatic machines serving sodas, ice cream, pastries. Whole floors display silks and kimonos in all price ranges. If you wish, you can buy your wedding kimono, have a sumptuous obi wound around your waist, even get a headdress like a Kyoto geisha after having bought the right wig, and then be ready for your marriage. The big store can even lend you its special chapel in which to hold the ceremony, and put a priest at your disposal.

It is perhaps preferable to stroll in the streets and visit the small stores where prices are lower. In Tokyo, the Akihabara quarter is famous for stores selling electronic equipment at noncompetitive prices, as well as kimonos, cultured pearls, and cameras.

The crowd is everywhere. You cannot deepen your knowledge of Japan except in contact with it. It is interesting to meet the crowd in the morning in two places which, for different reasons, are typically Japanese in character: the fish market at Tsukiji and the stock exchange at Nihonbashi. The Japanese are no doubt right when they say that the Tsukiji market is the largest fish market in the world. Each day, more than two thousand tons of fish—fresh mackerel, tuna, smoked salmon, shellfish, clams, whale, shark, seaweed, etc.—are sold there, as well as more than eight hundred tons of vegetables.

One should go to Tsukiji in the first hours after dawn to see the activity at its height. More than thirty thousand people move through it every morning. Three-thousand-ton trawlers come up directly to the dock, ready for the auction. Neatly aligned sharks are no longer frightening, and the blood-tinged tuna are cut up then and there, to reappear as sashimi on the plates of restaurant customers in the Ginza.

The saddest spectacle is that of the whales. Recumbent monsters that will never rise again, they touch the spectator's heart not so much because they are an endangered species as because the myth of Jonah recalls the friendship and solidarity of this animal and man. Tsukiji also recalls, more prosaically, the importance of fish in the Japanese diet and the problem of its fishing fleet, which brings Japan into competition not only with its immediate neighbors, such as Korea and the U.S.S.R., but even with French, English, and American fishers. An ultramodern fleet, equipped to process the fish immediately and transport the catch over long distances, has given the Japanese fishing industry worldwide importance and the reputation of roving the seven seas—which, according to some people, will be literally emptied by Japanese fishers. Out of remorse for the immense slaughter, religious ceremonies of expiation used to be held by the fishermen's organizations, the merchants who sold products of the sea, even the Ministry of Fishing. One such ceremony took place on March 22, 1932. At Tsurumi, in the great temple of Sojiji belonging to the Buddhist sect of Soto, and at another temple, near Odawarea, Buddhist services were held for the consolation of the spirits of the fish caught to nourish the Japanese nation. The next day, the priest of Tsurumi held a ceremony at sea for fish who had died a natural death.

The building of the Tsukiji market goes back to the end of the seventeenth century, when the shogun Teyasu was installed at Edo, ancient Tokyo. At this time, the sea reached as far inland as the Ginza, and the shogun gave the order to fill it in so as to permit the building of the market. During the Edo period, the arrival of bonita in the market symbolized the return of summer.

Tsukiji, a daily meeting place, the central market of the largest urban concentration in the world, a belly filled by the sea, today combines within its precincts town and countryside, fruits, vegetables, and meats as well as fish, but the dominant "catch" here is the excitement of everyday life.

Another daily meeting place in Tokyo is the stock exchange, located at the Nihonbashi bridge, the center of Edo. The stock market was for many years hermetically closed to the outside. It required a world of crisis and the strong rise of the yen to internationalize Tokyo's stock exchange. Today its operations are attentively followed by the entire world. On balconies connecting to form a promenade, troops of tourists cluster behind hostesses brandishing banners for national groups. For years, when the dollar caught a cold the other currencies sneezed. Today, though the yen is not, like the dollar or the pound, an accredited currency in international trade agreements, it communicates its moods to Western currencies, thus attesting to Japan's position among capitalist countries.

Tokyo's stock exchange functions within the framework of a different organization from those in other industrialized countries. Although inspired by the American model, its regulations include original clauses, especially as regards the professional groups allowed to carry on their activities in the exchange. Mr. Sato, a stock market employee of Nomura Securities, explained it to me: "There are no individual members of the stock exchange in Tokyo. Only firms can be admitted. They number eighty-three engaged in buying and selling. They are the regular members. The companies authorized to serve as intermediaries, called *saitori*, are limited to twelve."

We walked through the large hall from one section to another. Here negotiations are carried on for stocks in fishing companies, mines, or construction; over there, stocks in textiles; elsewhere, stocks in foodstuffs, electronic equipment, and vehicles. A dozen booths, each consisting of a counter shaped like a horseshoe, faced each other in pairs, and harbored a double desk. Several booths were set on a dais, each responsible for buying and selling eight stocks chosen from among the most quoted.

The Tokyo stock exchange has been in existence since May 1878. At the beginning of the Second World War, the military government replaced the private organization with a semipublic one. At the end of the war, the liquidation of huge industrial and financial concentrations, called *zaibatsu*, led to the organization's dissolution. It did not resume its activities, in their present form, until May 1949. There are a dozen stock exchanges in Japan, but 95 percent of the volume of business is handled by the Tokyo and Osaka exchanges. However, their role is not fundamental in corporate financing: companies turn to the financial market for less than 10 percent of their needs.

JAPAN BY DAY, JAPAN BY NIGHT

Capitalist Japan has opted for efficiency. Whether in a professional milieu such as television, in the world of large corporations, or in the collective behavior of the Japanese people, one is struck by the precision of the system. But the jolts and jerks that upset men and gear wheels have become more and more perceptible, reawakening old challenges or creating new ones. The big corporation becomes subdivided, the large rural family splits apart, destroying the traditional village, the educational system crumbles, the major religions give way to sects, new feudal systems appear while paternalism is gradually vanishing. However, in reaction, there is a return to fundamentals, preserving much that is essential. One might ask, contemplating the classic dichotomy between Japan by day and Japan by night, whether the Japanese invented nighttime Japan as a refuge for their traditions and their freedom of cultural choice, and then invented daytime Japan as a convenient way to enjoy the benefits of progress without being depersonalized.

Night begins in Japan when workers leave their offices, around six-thirty, sometimes earlier. The men do not go home immediately. Their wives, the managers of the households, have given them a small amount of pocket money before they left for work in the morning.

Satoshi Watanabe is a modest functionary of the Plan Agency. He collates statistics about education. His work is arid, but his way of approaching it allows him some escape. He can make long telephone calls without being noticed. And he doesn't deny himself. At six o'clock his workday ends. He opens his wallet; this morning his wife put a thousand-yen note in it, and he sees that it is still there. Usually he buys a pack of Peace cigarettes each day, but today he smoked only the three cigarettes remaining in the pack he bought the day before. Astonished at having smoked so little, he considers the possibility of trying to stop smoking completely. He goes to get his jacket from his locker and leaves the ministry murmuring, "Sayonara, neither first nor last. . . ." His boss, at the other end of the room, pretends to be absorbed in a document.

Outside, Watanabe lets the crowd carry him along. He moves through a labyrinth of streets, whose illuminated signs betoken gaiety, to a small bar, like thousands that exist in Tokyo. He goes down into a basement by a narrow staircase and emerges in a *sakura*—actually a small *sakura*—a bar. The best places are occupied. Watanabe wedges into a small space in a corner. The counter accommodates twelve people; a few more may squeeze in. Watanabe is a regular customer. The woman who owns the place serves him, without being asked, a double Suntory with ice. Hiroko, Watanabe's favorite waitress, is busy serving another customer. When she has finished, she goes over to Watanabe.

"Did your day go well?"

"As usual. I had a lot of work."

"Satoshi-San is a very important functionary," Hiroko says, speaking to her boss, the owner. "He will soon move up in rank—isn't that so, Satoshi-San!" Watanabe nods in agreement. Hiroko lets out a sonorous laugh as she goes to serve a customer. Returning, she says:

"You're wearing a new tie, aren't you?"

"It's a gift from my wife."

"She has good taste, but she made a mistake, because now you can go and seduce the young girls."

"If you agree to be seduced, that would suit me fine."

"Why not? But remember I like thin men, so you have to lose a few pounds. Do you go in for sports?"

"A little soccer on Sunday morning. I go to the bank of the Tamagawa River with some pals to kick the ball around."

"Would you take me with you some Sunday?"

"Why not?"

This sort of dialogue, repeated each day, is made up of jokes, verbal provocations, allusions to a possible meeting outside the bar—but during the two years that Satoshi Watanabe has been going to the *sakura* in the Shinjuku, he has not yet made a date with

Hiroko. Watanabe looks at his watch: "Already seven o'clock. . . ." He climbs up the stairs to the sidewalk and proceeds to the subway to return home.

Life by night continues. People go to restaurants in Japan from six-thirty to seven o'clock. So the evening starts early, the nightclubs welcoming their first customers at eight. The music halls begin their last shows at eight-thirty. The Nichigeki, an enormous round building at the center of the Ginza quarter, contains movie houses and a stage for ballets and music hall spectacles on the seventh floor. In the sixties, the music hall presented satirical shows that evoked sickly smiles on the faces of Westerners. The sketches dealt with the sexual life of priests or the queen of England. Christians or Buddhists were raked over the coals, as well as feminists and homosexuals. The Nichigeki was sure it would provoke a real diplomatic storm. When the English ambassador heard the report from his first secretary, he could not believe his ears.

"Do you mean to say that Prince Philip and Queen Elizabeth make love in their bedroom in Buckingham Palace, which has been reconstructed in detail on the Nichigeki stage?"

"Yes, sir."

So his excellency the British ambassador went to see with his own eyes the outrage against his queen. The next day he wrote a note of protest to the minister of foreign affairs. He got a prompt response; the minister had informed his colleague in the Ministry of the Interior of the deep concern of the British ambassador and the British colony in Tokyo. Unfortunately, the law did not permit any intervention, but there was every reason to believe that the producers of the show would be grieved to learn that they had shocked their British friends and customers. The sketch was withdrawn from the show a few days later, in exchange, according to well-informed sources—as the journalistic cliché has it—for a lot of cash.

Bar Crawling in Tokyo

The Japanese love the spectacular Lido-type show, which can be seen at its best less than five minutes by car from the Ginza, in the Akasaka quarter on the perimeter of the flashy Japan shown to foreigners. The New Latin Quarter or the Copacabana can serve dinner to up to a thousand persons, providing male patrons with a pleasing and sometimes risqué female companion to help them enjoy the night show.

In the grandiose, futurist genre, one cannot do better than the Queen Bee, where you can choose a sketch of the sort of woman you prefer, incarnating the physical and intellectual qualities of your ideal woman. Your choice is immediately submitted to a computer, which in turn picks out from among the thousand hostesses of the club the woman who corresponds to your expressed (and sometimes unavowed) desires. You wait at the table you have reserved until a phone call comes from the electronically chosen one. A few seconds later, she appears—and you may well learn that a computer's aesthetic choices do not inevitably jibe with yours, the machine having an annoying tendency to underestimate physical qualities in favor of intelligence and propriety.

In the side streets, numerous geisha houses, behind their paper partitions, cater to a refined social group. If you get there at the right time, you can see a ricksha, pulled by a man as in the old days, come to a stop before the house. In the half darkness of twilight, the geisha—shimmering in her embroidered kimono, her tall headdress bearing a half circle of combs, her chignon raised to display above the kimono collar a tapering powdered neck—steps out of her cage with precaution and enters a small garden, skipping from stone to stone. The sliding door splits open to admit her.

In the same street, a trifle farther down, discotheques—the Byblos, the Mugen, or, higher up on Roppongi, Chez Castel—offer a delicious atmosphere compounded of a mix of the globe's races, sexes, and nations. You enjoy the ambiguity of thinking you are in Paris or New York, but reality, when you come back out on the street, reminds you that you are in Tokyo. At the corner of Roppongi, you suddenly come upon a small itinerant stall, lit by a carbide lamp, where you can eat noodle soup, and near the Ginza, you bump into some small trestle tables similarly lit. There, men, women, young girls, old people, stop, hand over a few coins, and receive their horoscopes in exchange, sometimes consulting with the male or female seer. Fortunetellers are numerous at Akasaka along a street flanked by stores, at the end of which the stroller will discover the temple consecrated to the goddess Kannon. There is no shortage of visitors who go there to purify themselves with the smoke from the incense sticks thrust into a hanging cauldron. The temple is surrounded by establishments selling sex—striptease joints, porno movie houses, special Turkish baths—while the streets are crowded with groups of young people on motorcycles, with tourists, with Japanese in quest of adventure or simply curious. Behind this picturesque ambience is a whole community of craftsmen, storekeepers, and practitioners of bizarre or unfamiliar trades.

Shinjuku: Day and Night

Situated at the other end of Tokyo, Shinjuku shares the picturesque aspect of these sections of town when night has fallen and the lanterns appear. Shinjuku perfectly embodies the split between day and night. One part, constructed in the last ten years, represents daytime Japan, while its old alleyways on the other side of the railroad tracks acquire a personality only at night. The daylight side, an immense square shaped like a ship, flanked by buildings that contain large department stores, is a succcessful example of modern architecture. The buildings are not more than ten stories above ground, but they extend underground, where another city swarms, with its streets, garages, stores, and docks for ships, which are continually being loaded and unloaded. The nautical illusion is completed by two chimney stacks set in the center of the square, contributing to its harmony and ventilating the underground city. The Japanese come and go, squeezed together, emerging from the subway, swallowed up by the anonymous masses that oppose the day side, to the night side, each emptying into the other, according to the hour—the traditional and the modern, leisure and work, idleness and efficiency.

It is at Shinjuku that certain avant-garde spectacles have been created, spectacles that made authors like Terayama famous; it is there also that well-known writers, such as Yukio Mishima, presented their most daring theatrical works, like *Madame de Sade,* which was later put on in Paris. In the small theaters under the ground, everything is permitted.

It was the Shinjuku movie houses that showed the first films of Nagisa Oshima, such as *Journal of a Thief,* which included in its Japanese version in 1968 sequences offensive to Western sensibility because of their violence and their vulgarity. For instance, the camera panned between a woman's thighs, showing her in the act of urinating. Already in the sixties, in Shinjuku as well as Shibuya, the porn movie houses attracted an increasingly large audience.

Across the way, at Katchoutcha, in a rustic decor of old intertwined poles and multilevel platforms resembling farm granaries or storerooms, teenagers gather. For the modest sum of a few dozen yen they get an orange juice. The can rent a booklet of the music and words of folk songs from all over the world translated into Japanese, or sometimes printed in the original language. An orchestra gives the signal, and the audience of pimply youths and blushing girls is transformed into a diligent and studious chorus. You can hear them on the street, although they do not manage to drown out the crystalline clash of billiard balls in the ubiquitous pachinko parlor. Pachinko is a slot machine in which balls run over a circuit on a vertical grille, dropping with a characteristic noise into holes of differing value. From time to time the jackpot pours out. The player can exchange any winnings for chocolate bars or small trinkets. Pachinko is not expensive, but numerous impenitent players are capable of spending several hours a day at them and losing a good part of their modest salaries.

An Encounter in Kagoshima

At night the Japanese, in a kind of controlled way, throw off repression and inhibition. We arrived, two French colleagues, in a small town of south Kyushu, Kagoshima. A taxi took us to the center, to a district of bars and restaurants.

We ate at a classic steak house, typical of many such places in Japan since the Japanese began eating meat. After we sat at the counter, the cook cut up a raw steak to broil on the grate together with some bean sprouts. A young Japanese woman came over and in faltering English asked us: "Where are you from?"

"France."

She introduced herself as Yukiko and immediately called over one of her friends, and we were quite soon prettily hemmed in.

"What are you doing next?" Yukiko asked, not at all timidly. Having eaten, we had no choice but to follow them. They hailed a taxi. Nothing is more exciting than to let oneself be led through a strange city at the other end of the world to a mysterious destination by two flirtatious young women. All the more since these young women seemed quite bold. Speaking Japanese, they made some rather equivocal judgments on our respective anatomies, laughing uproariously and without any modesty, and then the cab stopped in front of a cabaret whose sign was composed of three ideograms that were incomprehensible to us.

"My brother is the leader of the jazz orchestra in this cabaret," Yukiko said. "I'll introduce you to him."

We were taken in through the wings onto the stage. The customers were sitting at the bar or at tables; some couples were dancing on a dance floor so small as to encourage intimacies. The orchestra leader also played the saxophone. Yukiko motioned to him. He stopped playing. She briefly explained something to him. In less than three minutes, a table next to the dance floor had been evacuated and a place was made for us. So we danced until late into the night; the cabaret had a special license that enabled it to stay open until two in the morning. Yukiko and my Parisian friend seemed to be hitting it off beautifully. He offered to take her home. The cab ride lasted forty-five minutes, and upon arrival, Yukiko, who had become a bit mussed in the course of the trip, rearranged her clothes and her hairdo, calmly got out, addressed some words to the driver, and took the hand of her "dear little Frenchman." He thought that his hour of Japanese happiness had arrived. Yukiko gave two raps on the door of a garage and, after passionately kissing her eager companion, disappeared mysteriously, the garage door closing behind her before my colleague had time to react.

A little after four o'clock just before we were to leave, the next afternoon, we were surprised to see Yukiko arrive. Her brother the saxophonist and her girl friend accompanied her. They had come to say good-bye and give us their addresses.

FORWARD FLIGHT

On the first Sunday of October 1964, the 80,000 seats of Tokyo's Olympic stadium were almost completely filled. If some seats remained empty here and there, it was because a great many foreigners had been expected and supplementary seats put aside. If the audience squeezed together a bit, 100,000 spectators perhaps might have been accommodated. At the official grandstand, Emperor Hirohito, the empress, and the prince and heir apparent had made their entrance. A pulsating melody announced Yoshinori Sakai, bearer of the torch, who came running into the stadium. The young woman made a complete circuit and then sped lightly up the stairs that led to the urn holding the sacred flame. Sakai was born in Hiroshima in August 1945, and the Japanese chose her as the symbol of the new Japan. The television sets spewed out their images to an indifferent world, which was waiting for the sports competitions. But when the delegation of Japanese athletes entered the stadium and the applause of the crowd was followed by delirium, one understood that something was indeed taking place. Had the new Japan chosen this as the starting point for industrial competition, taking vengeful pride in an international manifestation, transmitted to all the countries of the world by radio, television, and newspapers? For many Japanese, this day no doubt marked the end of humiliation. As for the foreigners present in Tokyo on that day, they became aware of the existence of a national determination whose goal nobody could define with certainty.

Some weeks later even more people assembled in the same stadium under the aegis of Sokkagakai, one of Japan's new and most important religions. The youth, enthusiasm, discipline, and cohesion of this gathering could not help but recall a certain Japanese state of mind which, in the past, had been responsible for the most terrible catastrophes. Was Japan once again going to abandon itself to its demons?

Like most foreign observers in Tokyo, I asked myself this question and I collided with a strange paradox which reveals the West's a priori attitudes. Any refusal by Japan to go along with the process of growth accepted by the industrialized West was interpreted as a return to the militaristic isolationism of the bad old days. And now Japan's enthusiastic adherence to this very process seemed to threaten the system of values that guaranteed Japan's loyalty to its western partners.

Indeed, Japan cut quite a good figure six years later, when the emperor proclaimed the opening of Osaka's Universal Exposition at the beginning of April 1970. Not a spat button was out of place. Some foreign pavilions had the signal honor of being visited by His

Majesty. He started with the United States pavilion (how could he have done otherwise?), which exhibited the famous LEM, just returned from the moon, and an exhibition of photographs in which the official U.S. information services presented, in contrast to the LEM, an average America with its poor whites and its forsaken blacks, its ordinary houses and its population delivered up to work, unemployment, and the serious problems of all industrialized nations. His Majesty visited the U.S.S.R. pavilion, or rather GUM, the big department store in the center of Moscow, pleasant-seeming with its bric-a-brac clustered around a Soviet space capsule, its salesgirls with generous breasts, and its blond representatives with deeply sunken eyes, supplied or not supplied with KGB credentials. His Majesty paused in the German Federal Republic, whose stand was transformed into an auditorium sheltering Stockhausen, playing Stockhausen, and displaying Stockhausen. The technique was perfect, and His Majesty deigned to listen courteously, although, it is said, he is not very receptive to this kind of music. His Majesty still had about a quarter of an hour to make a detour to the French pavilion, an inflated balloon, the pride of France's architects, which had to be equipped with a rigid framework so as to withstand the Osaka winds. It had been realized that the dimly lit escalator, which led upward to the marvels of French technology, could become a problem for the imperial couple, and the escalator had been gone over with a magnifying glass, its mechanism minutely examined. Nothing had been left to chance, but a corner of the carpet at the top of the escalator did not completely adhere to the flooring planks and this detail had escaped even the imperial security guards. But, thank God, His Majesty lifted his foot at the right moment, while the empress stepped off at the other side. The victim—and that was only just—was the grand chamberlain.

Mr. Watanabe and Technology

The Japanese went through the Universal Exposition in mounting wonder and amazement at the world of tomorrow. A big Japanese bank proposed to revolutionize its daily operations by doing away with the formalities of checkbooks and signatures, and simplifying the procedure of deposits and withdrawals. From now on, no more clerks.

Mr. Takahashi Watanabe presents himself before what still looks like a teller's window, but there is no one behind the bulletproof glass. Mr. Watanabe feels quite alone. He looks around him. In front of the other windows stand other Watanabes who have come to withdraw money from their accounts. Behind him still other Watanabes await their turn. Ordinarily Mr. Takahashi Watanabe presents his signed check. He is never asked for identification; either he pays with a credit card or he withdraws money from the small branch office in the part of town where he is well known. Besides, the Japanese do not have identity cards, except for their auto licenses or their passports. At the exposition Mr. Watanabe follows the instructions, announcing his full name in a "loud, intelligible voice"; announcing the number of his account; announcing the sum required. He now has only to wait. In three minutes, a packet of banknotes is put within his reach. The computer has in record time identified Mr. Watanabe's voice and the number of his account and verified his solvency. The computer cannot be tricked; I tried to imitate Mr. Watanabe's voice, reeling off the number of his account and the same amount of money as he did, but nothing came out.

But Mr. Watanabe has not reached the end of the surprises. He discovers in the Matsushita pavilion a machine that delivers his daily newspaper to his home through instantaneous television transmission. On an air-conditioned sidewalk rolling over plastic bubbles, Mr. Watanabe travels from one pavilion to another to see the world that will be his tomorrow. Modernism does not frighten him; his only concern is whether he will earn enough money to buy everything.

In 1970, before the crisis, Japan seemed to be condemned to a forward flight aboard a rocket and in a seat turned backward which did not allow one to see what one had just left but forced one to look into a far-off past at what appeared to be an anachronism. Mr. Takahashi Watanabe started asking himself questions about time and dreaming about one of those black holes beyond our universe. Projected into the most distant planets of another solar system, Mr. Watanabe clearly discerned this Japan of the past to which all his senses bind him and where everything seemed to harmonize so much better.

Bike Ecology

Sometimes Mr. Watanabe reacts. Little by little, he has seen his purchasing power attain the level of that of the citizens of the West German Republic. He will soon exhaust all the joys of his super-equipped kitchen; he has been able to buy a car, which his wife drives with ease in Tokyo when she does her shopping and visits her friends. For ten years he has been living like the citizen of a rich country; he is proud of it.

But Mr. Watanabe has some moments of nostalgia. One day, on behalf of his own health and his wife's, he decided to attempt the ecological life. He opted for a biking weekend, as have thousands of his compatriots lately. Thus he contributed to healthy competition, with the goal of being "Better than the Dutch." In fact, many Japanese believe that by straddling two wheels they are exorcizing the demons of pollution that issue from auto exhaust. But instead of riding in the street, they have taken over the sidewalk, sometimes bumping into pedestrians. As a result, the pedestrians have paid the price for this ecological movement.

Concerned about public order and the chance to exploit this new fashion, some astute minds have created the Center of Bicycle Sport. About eighty-five miles from Tokyo, among the undulating hills of the Izu peninsula, in an incomparable site that enjoys a view of the Pacific, a series of tracks through fields and forests has become the exclusive realm of the bike. Groups of bike tourists arrive there each Sunday in bands of ten to fifteen, their *o'bento* in their knapsacks. The majority arrive by train after a trip of an hour and a half. At the station, you get your permit and go to the bike-rental agent. You can choose among three sizes and three models. The rental fee includes a helmet and shoes. The first time, it is best to start off on the beginners' track and take a lesson, or at least get some advice. The control tower, as in an airport, dominates the situation, seeing and hearing everything. You should not be astonished if, suddenly, you hear a peremptory injunction, as peremptory as the polite Japanese language permits: "Watch out, keep to the left!" The tower has a video recorder that can keep watch all around, for a radius of three miles.

You go to the bicycle center in a family group, with friends, or on an excursion organized by your business or factory. You go to please your wife, to lose weight, to get plenty of oxygen. In the framework of this unique sports setup can be found a bicycle university, equally unique, aimed at turning out professional bicyclists. Lined up in an immense gymnasium whose plate-glass windows open on greenery, two hundred stationary bikes are ridden by two hundred students who, each day for three years, work at achieving speed and endurance. When the whistle blows, the students begin pedaling at top speed. After their three years of study, the graduates will be hired by the professional clubs in the cities. Four thousand professional bicyclists give exhibitions in fifty municipal velodromes.

Ah, how edifying to participate in Japan's new ecological fad!

II: DUALITIES

1: Myths and Reality

Japan's crucial historical periods are always found at the meeting point between the image of themselves that the Japanese present and the reality of which they are conscious. Japan did not agree to enter into contact with the outside world until 1868, if one excepts the period that runs from 1549, date of the arrival in Kyushu of St. Francis Xavier, to 1638, date of the expulsion of all missionaries and white merchants.

After remaining open to the world for scarcely one hundred years, the Japanese, under assaults from outside, and thanks to the rapidity of change, saw their cultural identity and the future of their model of society seriously threatened. They began to ask themselves questions, although the Japanese show only a limited interest in history as a rigorous record of events, because in their case it has so often been confused with legend by the historians themselves.

The separation of myth and reality was not achieved until the sixth century. Until then one finds a mythical Japan, which, at the moment of its birth, seven centuries before our era, was plunged into darkness as a result of the anger of Amaterasu, the sun goddess. To escape her brother's sarcasms and jibes, Amaterasu withdrew into a cave. Thanks to a plot of the gods, the goddess was finally lured out of the sacred cave by an object which glistened with a divinity superior to her own: a mirror. Having emerged, she could no longer return to her cave because of a rice cord which had been surreptitiously tied behind her. Since that day, the light of the sun shines on the islands of the Rising Sun.

Two collections of annals, the Kojiki annals, which can be traced back to 712 B.C., and the Nihonshoki annals (720 B.C.), are regarded by the Japanese as the first documents in their history although, in reality, the oldest copy of the Kojiki, preserved in the province of Saitama in the temple of Shin Fukuji, dates from 1371 A.D. This fudging of dates has made it possible to maintain the idea of an emperor-god and divinely established imperial institutions. But do the Japanese really believe all this? Have they ever believed it?

Again, the ambiguity that is evident throughout this book. For example, how can one reconcile the fact that the Japanese have been able, until recently (the 1945 defeat), to regard and revere the emperor as a god, when one sees that the word "god" exists in Japanese only in the term *kami*, which signifies divinity and applies both to the gods of mythology and to animal guardian spirits like the fox or to mineral guardians? The Kojiki, composed of forty-eight volumes divided into three parts, deals with the first period of Japan, or the dynasty of the gods, which the Japanese call the mythological epoch and which ends in 660 B.C. with the advent of the emperor Jimmu, the first whom Japanese historians can place in a historical, non-mythological epoch.

But the complexity of the Japanese calendar, based on epochs which correspond to the emperors' reigns, does not allow us to fix any precise dates. The Japanese trace the imperial lineage back to Jimmu, but Jimmu is a posthumous name. The first emperor was actually called Kamu-Yamato-Iware-Hiko. He lived on the southern island, Kyushu, and having heard about a rebellion in central Japan, he and his brother raised an army, crossed the inland sea, and arrived at Osaka, at that time called Naniwa. Then he headed for the province of Yamato, where in the end he overcame the resistance of the local potentate. Prince Iware-Hiko then established himself at Kashiwara, where he organized a government and was proclaimed emperor. It was said that he attacked his enemies by taking them from behind, claiming: "I am the descendant of the sun, so I do not have to fight facing him. I fight with the sun at my side."

Emperor Jimmu, founder of the empire, died at the hour of the dragon (eight o'clock) on the eleventh day of the horse, at the age of 127. When the solar calendar was adopted in Japan in 1873, this day was considered to be the third of April of the year 585 B.C. Since then, the calendar has opened a new chapter with the advent of each emperor. Hirohito, the present sovereign, ascended the throne in 1926 and decided to call his reign that of the *Showa*, or "radiant peace." Therefore, 1983 represents the fifty-eighth year of the Showa era. Yet everything is not so simple, because the Japanese continue to utilize the lunar calendar (especially in the countryside) and the Chinese calendar side by side. Each year within the framework of a twelve-year cycle bears the name of an animal. The same symbols are used for the hours and serve as reference points on the navigation compass. Thus one finds in order: rat, steer or bull, tiger, rabbit or hare, dragon, snake, horse, ram or ewe, monkey, cock, dog, and wild boar, even though the official calendar utilized today is of course the Gregorian.

It was in 1549 that Japan encountered the West for the first time. This first contact was long overlooked, as much by the Japanese as by Europeans and Americans. Only very recently, in the post-war period, has it been popularized. In the United States and Europe in 1976–77, the novel *Shōgun*, by James Clavell, dealt with the rivalry between Dutch Protestant missionaries and Portuguese Jesuits in feudal Japan, racked by internecine struggles among the various clans. In 1972, the official movie presented by Japan at the Cannes Film Festival was entitled *The Silence*. It told the story of the Jesuit priests who landed clandestinely in Japan after 1638, the date of the expulsion of all foreign missionaries.

The period from 1549 to 1638 was marked by the martyrdom of Japanese Christians burned at the stake or crucified by the thou-sands, at first on the order of Shogun Hideyoshi, founder of the Toyotomi dynasty, and later at the instigation of the founder of the Tokugawa dynasty, Shogun Iyeyasu. And although Christianity was to leave only faint traces, the Jesuits made a minor but deep cultural imprint symbolized in our day by the University of Sophia in Tokyo, whose graduates generally occupy important positions in public ser-vice, political life, teaching, and journalism.

Japan's second encounter with the West has never been over-looked. It was on June 9, 1853, that Commodore Matthew Perry appeared with his fleet in the waters of Kurihama Bay near Yoko-suka. The Tokugawa dynasty was coming to an end. The acceptance by Shogun Yoshinobu of Commodore Perry's "message of peace," while the warship *Plymouth* pointed its cannon at Japanese soil, in the end hastened the return of the emperor to real power. The emperor took control and moved into the Edo Palace, the present Imperial Palace in Tokyo. He sent the imperial Iwakura mission all over the world to create ties that Japan would soon make explicit demonstrat-ing its humility before the West's great achievements and its skill in making them its own, and thus entering upon an irreversible process of modernization.

During the nineteenth century, Japan had remained a feudal, backward empire. Under the pressure of the *Namban*, the "savages from the south," the shogunate had been obliged to accept invidious treaties, similar to those between the "big powers" and China. The shame of these treaties divided Japan into two camps—the shogun party, which approved them as inevitable, and the conservatives, at-tached to the tradition of Nippon. In 1868, a true, Japanese-style revolution took place, and the emperor, who called his period Meiji, "enlightened government," so hastened the "Westernization" of Ja-pan that in less than a generation he obtained a formal revision of all the unfavorable treaties. Feudal Japan gave way: from the south would come the English, Dutch, and French; from the north the Russians; and from the east the Americans. The intellectuals had been divided between nationalists, the *kokugakusha*, and intellectuals of the so-called Dutch school or persuasion, the *kangakusha*. The former defended the concept of the imperial state closed to the foreigner, the latter that of Western modernization and support of the shogunate. The Meiji revolution abruptly ended the debate.

On the occasion of the 2,549th anniversary of the foundation of legendary Japan—that is, on February 11, 1889—Meiji promulgated a constitution. It made some limited concessions to modernism by creating a national parliament, but it maintained the office of foreign affairs as a domain apart. In fact, the new constitution established a system in which a whole series of councils became influential organs of decision. The ministries formed one council, while the military leaders formed another. There was still the privy council. In this setup, the role of the prime minister was not clearly established, and the role of the Diet was limited to parliamentary interpellations, resolutions, addresses to the throne, and representations to the government. From this moment on, the ministers of the army and the marines could be chosen only from among the generals and the admirals respectively, those who kept their distance from the government and were directly attached to the imperial household.

The idea of the emperor's infallibility and inviolability gave birth to the doctrine of *junsoju-no-Kan*, which set the stage for pinning the blame for disastrous decisions on the bad advisers who surrounded the emperor.

After the First World War, Japan emerged as a state dominated by an absolute power. To Marxists the imperial regime was dominated by big landowners and the bourgeoisie, and reflected the total negation of the people. In the thirties, according to the Marxists, Japan could only act in terms of the class struggle. The military caste responded harshly to this challenge. It provoked the Manchurian incident in 1931 in order to have a pretext for hardening its position and reinforcing its military occupation in northeastern China. It forced the imperial government to reject four successive offers of a treaty of nonaggression made by the U.S.S.R. in 1930, 1932, and 1933. The axiom in foreign policy was to create one's own sphere of influence. Of course the United States also had its sphere. In 1938 the axiom would become the concept of a sphere of co-prosperity which would lead the Japanese from conquest to conquest all the way to the borders of Southeast Asia.

For Japan, the enemies were the Russians and the Americans. The Japanese withdrew from the League of Nations, and the defeat of an uprising by extremist officers in 1936 did not stop the military plots whose culmination would be Pearl Harbor. Japan waged a cruel war and then was subjected to one. The 1945 fire bombings of Tokyo resulted in 200,000 victims. On August 6, 1945, there was Hiroshima, and then, on August 8, Nagasaki. The emperor finally decided to break the silence in which he had lived, shut up at the bottom of his bunker in the Imperial Palace, where he presided over the council. Wanting to handle tactfully the emotions of shame which he knew would be bound to overwhelm his subjects, Hirohito did not say: "We have lost a battle" or "a war," but instead stoically declared: "The fate of arms has not been favorable to us."

The American occupation forces became allies. Those who refused to accept the inevitable committed suicide in accordance with the seppuku ritual. Thus the country returned to the same ambiguity as in 1868, and modern Japan, allied with the United States, has achieved its present status thanks to those who fought most furiously against the Americans.

MYTH

The "gateway" one uses to enter Japan takes on great importance. I had the luck to come ashore at Kobe, my first Japanese port of call. But Kobe and its harbor landscape would not have left any particular memory if, after barely ten minutes on the train, I had not been transported into the strangest universe that can be conceived—the ancient capital of Kyoto. One must not go to Japan without seeing Kyoto, just as one cannot stay in Japan without returning to Kyoto again and again, with the aim of rediscovering a kind of lost paradise and escaping the racketing hustle and bustle of everyday social life, the demands and obligations of Tokyo.

I can no longer count the number of my pilgrimages during the seven years of my stay. Each was associated with a meeting, a vision of Kyoto, a Japan ceaselessly renewed, as inseparable from my itinerary as Buddha is from the piece of wood in which he is carved. The first time I went was with an organized tour, and Japanese tourism is without doubt the most organized, the most minutely regulated, and the most learnedly pedantic and boring of all those I have encountered. So I have kept but few memories of this first contact, save for images imprinted on my retina through the windows of an air-conditioned superbus.

Black tiles shining from rain, a willow tree, the shore where silk was washed, but above all pine trees, always pine trees standing erect or reflected upside down in the lake, pine trees which let their cones fall on the crags above the gold of the Golden Pavilion. Kyoto is indissoluble from the Golden Pavilion, Kinkakuji. I love it in the winter when the gold has disappeared and everything is folded away beneath the snow. Each footprint on the paths along the lake leaves the trace of an intrusion around the solitary building. The departed tourists have been replaced by those who dream of an inviolate, untouched Japan, where one could not be admitted except by privilege. I have photographed the pavilion in the summer, scintillating in the morning heat, surrounded by the birds' chatter; I have been ready to enter and to enjoy the profundity of space thanks to the mirrorlike effect of the lake's surface and, beyond, the mystery that makes the horizon of undergrowth soar. I have tunneled under the blossoming trees in the springtime, hemmed in by groups of students, boys in black and girls in navy blue, whose shouts alarmed the barely opened young buds. The Golden Pavilion cannot dominate the springtime symphony in Kyoto; but in the fall it gains the upper hand, restored to its rightful place by the carpet of yellow leaves that lie so softly underfoot.

In July 1950, an arsonist's fire destroyed the Golden Pavilion. Thirteen years later, I could not get out of my mind the thought that I was admiring a copy.

Yukio Mishima made the fate of the Golden Pavilion his concern. Mishima's novel *The Temple of the Golden Pavilion* encompasses several levels: the motivation for the crime; the perturbation of a young woman traumatized by Hiroshima, who cannot rediscover her faith; the myth of beauty destroyed by fire, and the obsession with fire which can be found everywhere in Japan—fire the destroyer but also the purifier and generator of renewal. Young Mizoguchi, the novel's hero, is a lonely man because he stutters and is obsessed by his own ugliness. Welcomed into the monastery of Rokuonji after the intercession of a prior, he is reconciled for a time with a milieu of which he seems gradually to become a part. But owing to the influence and actions of a friend and a few blinders of his own, his hard-bought equilibrium is endangered, and Mizoguchi finds himself alone again. His hatred for those who reject him and his ardent desire to impose his existence on them causes him to attack the symbol of beauty the Golden Pavilion, whose destruction by fire will avenge his ugliness and purify it.

It is this analysis of Mizoguchi which interested Yukio Mishima, that expert in the motivations of the Japanese soul. As seen by Mishima, Mizoguchi is quintessentially Japanese. He subsumes in himself all the phantasms that agitate the Japanese soul: a complex about physical appearance, a complex about not being loved, an adoration of beauty, violence, and resolve, the extremism of the individual stripped of his social context.

The character of Mizoguchi and that of his author, Mishima, deserve to be examined. Thirteen years after the death of this fabulous novelist, the Japanese identify with the myth of the author and his hero. A hero makes a clean sweep by fire and emerges from his solitude, the solitary author, unable to sweep away a civilization which has lost all meaning, is driven to die by his own hand, in the hope that his "extremism" will create a future that cannot be connected with an already dead past. Mishima himself explained Mizoguchi to me: "On the one hand, a simulacrum of eternity emanates from the human form which is so easily destroyed; on the other, from the indestructible beauty of the Golden Pavilion emanates a possibility of annihilation. . . . Setting fire to the Golden Pavilion, a national treasure since 1890, would be to commit an act of pure abolition, of definitive annihilation which would reduce the sum of beauty created by the hand of man. . . ."

The Obsession with Fire

At Kyoto, seeing all those alleyways bordered by wooden houses, one is reminded of the Japanese fear of and fascination with fire. Japan's history is full of disastrous fires, the most recent being Tokyo's veritable destruction during five consecutive nights of incendiary bombing, at the beginning of August 1945. "Everything turned red," a witness told me. "Women and children rushed through the streets, most of them transformed into living torches, and those who had been able to escape by a miracle ran through the flames and acrid smoke all the way to the shore, where they leaped in, only to be boiled to death." Final count: 200,000 dead.

Each town, each village, on the archipelago has constructed a fire alarm system. It is not rare to see small metal towers projecting above the roofs; at the top, reached by a ladder, is a platform from which one can detect the source of the fire and ring an alarm bell that brings fire engines on the run. The institution of professional firemen goes back to 1602, the year when Edo (as Tokyo was then called) was totally destroyed by fire. In 1657, 100,000 people perished in another gigantic conflagration, the "great fire of Meireki." In 1772, 223 city streets succumbed to flames. In 1923, the great earthquake was followed by a terrible fire which destroyed 366,000 houses and caused the deaths of 60,000 people.

From these historic catastrophes was born a certain philosophy about fire, which popular tradition calls "the blossoms of Edo." Not a day passes in Tokyo when firemen are not summoned to put out a blaze. So it is hardly astonishing to find fire at the center of the "public theater" art of Rakugo. In a theater in Shinjuku, the backdrop depicts a fire in a section of Tokyo at night. A bell summons firemen, who come at full speed. The entire neighboring quarter gathers in the street. "Where is it?" asks the fishmonger, her head wrapped in a blue kerchief, the symbol of savage determination, and her hand wielding a knife (in Japan, one speaks of the fishmonger's knife, not the butcher's). "Behind the station," answers the peddler of o'soba, pointing his finger at the flames, while the fortuneteller has left his stand, lit by the swaying light of a carbide lamp. The wife of Minoru, the manager of the public bath, invites them all to come up on her terrace to get a better view. Then cries of joy: "That's it!" The big store has caught fire. Now it is the turn of the vegetable market . . . and look, the houses of the real estate agents. Bravo! The crowd applauds. Finally, justice is done and over there . . . Sakuragi-Cho's public bath. "Hurrah," cries Minoru's wife, "our competition is ruined!" But on the Minoru balcony and the streets all around, it can be seen that the fire has gained ground and . . . everything is burning, since justice must be done.

The joy in fire is expressed by fire festivals. The most spectacular one takes place in Nara at the end of June, when an entire hill is set on fire. The fire starts slowly at the base of the hill; it lights up all the surrounding area, and spreads toward the summit, while the crackling sound of the mounting flames increases. Music for the eyes, colors filled with sounds. I was in search of the sacred and suddenly discovered it: fire spraying up on the mountaintops like water, for there is no separation between the two elements. One night on the outskirts of Kyoto, I saw the initiation of young boys at a festival. It was the middle of winter. Under the fire sign and by the light of torches, hundreds of naked boys, gathered in the temple courtyard, were being drenched with ice-cold water while dancing to the beat of drums and gongs.

At Nanao on the Noto peninsula, the fire festival at the end of July is connected with purification in the sea after everything has been burned, outside and inside. To travel from Kyoto to Noto, one must leave the Pacific coast behind, and follow the alpine depression filled by Lake Biwa, then cross Fukui, classical site of Zen Buddhism, and Kanazawa, old city of the samurai. The peninsula of Noto is covered, on a gentle slope, by well-cultivated rice fields that stretch all the way to the Sea of Japan. The population is less dense here, and for the first time since my arrival, I had the impression of living in the country and breathing deeply. A Shinto temple dominates the village of Nanao, which contains about fifty houses with thatched roofs, and with sliding doors that grate as they close on mysterious hallways. All the temple's light comes from an interior courtyard, which has a broad opening onto the fields. On this July Friday, everything was calm on our arrival: nobody in the fields, not a soul at the temple, except for the Shinto priest, to whom we made offerings in exchange for authorization to film the Matsuri. Night fell quickly, as usual, and by the light of a row of bulbs stretched across the front of the temple, we saw the arrival of clusters of children, timid adolescents, then young people, women, and, finally, men. The men were shouting, carrying one of their number in a kind of flowered palanquin adorned with an immense cask of sake. Having reached the temple, each person performed his devotions, prostrating himself and meditating briefly. Some clapped their hands three times, and then, having bowed, went to place an offering: a few yen in the alms box. Surrounded by lighted candles, the priest in his ceremonial kimono chanted an invocation. Suddenly, shouts resounded in crescendo, while from the motionless palanquin the man in charge of the sake served it in square wooden cups. He swigged at the rate of one cup per dozen servings. The consumption of alcohol gradually abated and the palanquin, swaying dangerously, was borne, yard by yard, all the way to the place of the ceremony, at the foot of an immense pile of logs surrounding a central pole about sixty feet high. Wooden sticks on the circumference were lit; the fire spread toward the center and then upward, while sake warmed the entire village. For a long time after everything was extinguished and the bulbs on the temple's facade had become dim, we stood there in the cool of the night listening to the fading noises of the festival, our ears still throbbing with the sound of the drums and the beat of the gong.

But the importance of fire cannot be comprehended unless one has experienced the night of O'Bon, the Feast of the Dead. In a prolongation of Tokyo Bay, the Pacific rolls majestically to the foot of Mount Fuji, which is generally wrapped in its disdainful cloak of mist. Kurua, a very small cape on this rocky coast, is dominated by hills covered with underbrush, cut through by cultivated fields and small pine woods. Along the bus route from Zushi to Miura, one first passes the emperor's summer residence, then the teahouse of the crown prince, with the door ajar for the maid who comes to do the weekly cleaning. Perched on a promontory, sheltered by a pine tree, its elegant tiled roof was the landmark at which I asked the bus driver to stop. A little farther on was the beach house I had rented during my first summer in Japan, and there some friends and I tried in vain to get to sleep that early morning of July 15. The penetrating drum resounded in our ears, but I recall how much we were intrigued by a very peculiar sound, a sort of dry clatter that punctuated each drumbeat.

We got up, and a few seconds later, on the beach, we clustered around the platform on which, keeping time by clapping their hands, dancers turned tirelessly in a circle. They were wearing the traditional dress, with the band signifying resolution tied around their heads, and their feet were shod with wooden clogs. These were producing that strange, oppressive sound we had heard from a distance. Under the pines, in the light of the lanterns, one could make out some dangling white papers, odes to the dead, ready to be burned on the following day. The flames are supposed to attract the souls of the dead, which are sent back into the darkness when the fire is extinguished the next day. Paper prayers, paper happiness, dear death implored, begged to come and mingle with the living . . . life sent back among the dead, since one cannot exist without the other.

On July 16, while I was strolling on the hills, I ran across a small temple surrounded by statues carved in stone, some rather crude, others artful. Some of the sculptures wore small red neck pendants. I examined these guardian angels without finding a single one that resembled another. When I questioned the priest, who was very long-winded, I learned that Jizo is the guardian angel of dead children. According to the revelations of the Buddha, the children's souls go to the Sai-No-Kawara, which is, as it were, the Styx of Greek myth. There, the innocent are gathered together by a female demon, Shozuka-No-Baba. Taking off their clothes, she sets the children to work piling up stones to facilitate their arrival in paradise. Yet she undoes the work as fast as they complete it. Then Jizo comes, full of love and pity, and chases away the demon; comforting the children, he covers them with large leaves. The red pendants represent the covering devised by Jizo to dress the children stripped bare by the female demon.

Taking advantage of the priest's agreeable disposition, I switched the conversation to the subject of the O'Bon. "For three days," he told me, "the living and the dead are reunited. On the thirteenth, each family burns incense on the graves and in each house at the altar of the ancestors. When night has fallen, lighted lanterns are hung over the graves, and white papers at the doors. Then the spirits of the dead are asked to return to their homes; lanterns are provided against holes near the highway and the path. The spirits arrive and one speaks to them as if they were alive. . . . On the fourteenth, one spreads on a low table some symbolic portions of dishes the deceased loved, together with sweet potatoes, sesame seeds, soybeans, and water. . . . On the fifteenth, bowls of rice are cooked as a farewell, celebrating the souls' departure for the Meido, the celestial world of darkness. Farewell fires are lit in front of the houses." The O'Bon, which we had witnessed the day before, celebrates the liberation of souls from purgatory, the opening of the gates of heaven.

The Legend of Fuji

It was now the sixteenth of July, and strange to say, the air at dawn was completely free of humidity. From my bedroom, I could see Fuji's cone, which generally can be seen only in winter. Almost perfect, it rises 12,388 feet above the five lakes that reflect and surround it, like so many mythical sites from which one can contemplate the sacred mountain. Fuji-San is to Japan what Mecca is to Islam. There is not a single Japanese who does not want to climb Fuji at least once during his lifetime. Every mountain represents a holy personage connected with shamanism, and on each mountain, ascetic practices bearing the name *shugendo* are performed. By meditation and rigorous physical training, certain men succeed in perpetuating the bond between the living and the dead, earth and heaven. *Shugendo* is connected with a kind of magical ritual enacted during the annual festivals and celebrations designed to maintain or reestablish man's harmony with nature. Fuji participates in this communion, if only because of the incalculable number of pilgrims who climb it in July and August (more than 100,000 each year), the two months when Fuji loses its white cap. A feverish animation reigns on the slopes of the volcano and in the surrounding villages, especially at Gohra, the start of the tramway that takes the traveler across the mountain all the way to the summit of Sounzan, and then to the banks of Lake Ashi, more commonly known as Lake Hakone. One can reach Fuji by six different roads, each provided with ten resting places or stations, which permit those who have decided to ascend on foot to take a breather. In general, people ascend to the fifth station by car. One can get past the next two on horseback. But then comes the fateful part: the pilgrim, alone, must make an individual effort to climb up one of the peaks from which he will be able to see the sunrise.

In the past, Fuji was an active volcano. Though it has been dormant since 1707, nobody thinks that it is really extinct. A local proverb says: "He who climbs Fuji once is a wise man, but he who climbs it twice is a fool." People climb one of the eight peaks which encircle the crater, but nobody, so far as is known, has gone down inside the volcano to explore it. This inviolate cave of the gods has a bad reputation. Some years ago, a BOAC plane transgressed the recommendations of the control tower at Haneda and flew straight over the crater to permit its passengers to take photographs. Suddenly, the plane was cut in two. It took several days to recover all the bodies strewn over the mountain slopes.

In November 1977, a veteran German mountain climber, disregarding the official prohibition, undertook the climb up Fuji, accompanied by a friend who was also an expert mountaineer. They reached the summit in ideal weather: not a cloud, and a high temperature for the season. They began to go down into the crater. What happened afterward has been reconstructed. In a few seconds, the weather deteriorated. Strong gusts of wind flung the two men on the ground and along the ice of the lake, playing with them as if they were boys' tops. Three days later, their bodies were found nearly a mile apart, the faces swollen and disfigured.

Fuji's religious character arises directly from the celestial *kami* who came to take possession of the earth and whose wife, the granddaughter of Izanagi and Izanami, direct ancestors of the imperial line, became Fuji's goddess. Although she did not take part in the initial creation, Mount Fuji is today worshiped by several sects, the most famous of which is known by the name Kakugyo (also called Fujiko). According to the teachings of one sect, love of the *kami* of Fuji purges men of their faults. These prayers are addressed indirectly, to the sun, and here can be found in its original form the beginning of the myth of purification by fire, which the sun symbolizes. Thus we are right at the heart of the Empire of the Rising Sun. . . .

The Legend of Ise

To get from Fuji to the holy sanctuaries of Ise Jingu, one descends the mountain toward the sea, traveling down that vital artery of Japan which is the Tokaido, a dorsal spine that connects Tokyo with Osaka and along which almost half the country's population is concentrated. Along this spine one passes from prehistory to history without knowing very well where the former ends and the latter begins. Today the temples of Ise Jingu are the center of Shintoism, since this state religion has lost its official character without losing its sacred character. At Ise it is Amaterasu, the sun goddess—or, more exactly, the divine ancestors of the imperial family—whom people come to invoke. The structures date, it is thought, from the fifth or sixth century. A temple called the *geku* encloses the *naigu*, the principal sanctuary. Periodically the two sanctuaries are dismantled and rebuilt on a nearby emplacement, then reassembled on their original sites. This transplanting of sacred buildings is explained by the myth of the holy cycle, according to which life and death are interdependent.

Shintoism describes itself as an aid to the reconciliation of man and his environment; its purpose is to merge spirit and matter inseparably. From the legendary myth of Fuji the Japanese are led naturally to the prehistoric myth of ancestral divinities and then to those—in historic times—that revolve around Buddhism. The myth on a human scale becomes the religious myth linked with the evolution of the entire society.

Myth and Reality

From the moment one lands in Japan, preferably at Kyoto, one is saturated in these myths, unless one remains under the influence of that tenacious image the Japanese do so much to foster—the Japan of steel and concrete, champion in all categories of industrial growth. The vast enterprise dubbed by the Americans "Japan Incorporated" certainly flaunts before us its elevated highways, its skyscrapers, its monstrous traffic jams, its factory smokestacks, and its pollution, but at the edge of the urban areas an iron curtain drops which turns Tokyo and Japan's large cities into artificial islands where foreigners are marooned in their hotels, their cabarets, and their restaurants, not to mention the business offices that wait to receive them. In the eyes of the pragmatic Westerner, reality surrounds him; myth exists on the other side.

Everything that is typically Japanese has between carefully placed in the category of folklore. Why shouldn't one discover Japan in the Akasaka quarter, near the Hilton Hotel? One will find a Japanese garden there, a Japanese house, Japanese rooms, a Japanese kitchen, geishas, hostesses, souvenir stores. One could attend a Japanese wedding, a concert of Japanese music, or exhibitions of Japanese prints and *ikebana*. During the first weeks of my stay in Japan, caught up in the life of the grand hotel, I thought this factitious Japan was the only one that existed. Then I received a call from the secretary of the Association of Newspaper Editors, Nihon Shimbun Kyokai, who asked in excellent English: "Would you like to attend our annual meeting? It is being held this year at Kanazawa. The association will make all arrangements for you. After the meeting, we have planned a visit to the region. . . ."

Crossing the archipelago from the Pacific coast to the inland Sea of Japan is an experience that I have renewed many times. As in Kyoto, I found myself in another Japan. Kanazawa is known as one of the centers of classical culture in the so-called Kamakura epoch. The Buddhist monastery there boasts a famous Chinese library formed in 1266. In a town of warriors, the annual procession of samurai in August produces an orgy of costumes and chariots that carries one right back to the most lavish period of the Middle Ages.

This excursion with the newspaper editors turned into an initiation. Our special bus rolled along the sea in the direction of Kyoto. At the end of an hour, the road branched off toward the interior. About the middle of the morning we entered an immense park of cedars, in the depths of which stood various temple buildings, connected by arcades. Here, at the very heart of Zen, the only purely Japanese expression of Buddhism, we had walked straight into the midst of myth and history.

Zen Buddhism

Autumn had left its mark with a carpet of yellowing leaves on the ground beneath the trees. At the end of the covered walk I saw a monk much larger than the others, who was tirelessly sweeping up the dead leaves. Eddying, they kept covering the places he had just swept clean. I recognized a fellow Westerner and questioned him in English. "Is that Zen, always beginning the same task over again?" He nodded, no doubt wishing to add: You would do better to keep quiet—you will never understand anything about all this.

For a long time, Zen will remain linked for me with the cedar forest that surrounds the Eihei-Ji temples. One is a little shocked to encounter a vast modern functional building there, but by walking along the corridors that open to the forest, one reaches the room of meditation. It is there that the tall priest urges us to attempt a Zen meditation. He knows who we are and what we represent. The directors of Japan's newspapers, the editors in chief, the editorial writers, the representatives of the international press, are all there on their knees, sitting back on their heels. At the end of a quarter of an hour, I have cramps in both legs. I do not understand a single word of the sermon. Getting up to film the ceremony, I find myself again, in the second that follows, in my place, completely stunned. I have not seen the blow fall. One of the young monks threw me down and yet I felt nothing. Did he lift me in order to set me down kneeling on the tatami amid my Japanese colleagues? Did he fling me over their heads? Nobody else has budged. My colleagues repeat the sutras after the monk. . . . My God! Where is my camera? I must have lost it in the scramble. A monk passes behind me, leans over my shoulder, and deposits it at my feet.

The ceremony completed, we are led into another tatami room. Having removed our shoes, we are invited to sit down on a cushion. A lacquer tray in front of each of us contains small saucers filled with foods impossible for a Westerner to identify, except for the white rice, which is served cold, badly cooked, gluey. I taste a tepid soup with a sharp, bitter taste, then slowly strip away the envelope from the chopsticks, taking note of the order in which the dishes are being eaten. There appears to be no rule. The foods are vegetarian, and impossible to bolt down. A monk reads to us; I understand nothing. It appears that we are literally hemmed in, as though to be conditioned psychologically. I later learn the importance of this conditioning. It tends to create a harmony which increases one's receptivity to meditation. On coming out of the temple, a colleague explains to me the severity of the rules governing Zen Buddhist monasteries. In certain respects it recalls the rules of the Trappists or Benedictines. The young monks rise at three o'clock in the morning; fasting in the cold, they walk down the corridors to the room of meditation. In a posture which Westerners find difficult to tolerate, they begin to create an empty space inside themselves, meditating so as not to meditate; they read the sutras aloud until they are exhausted. When sleep overwhelms them, the book slips slowly from their fingers, their heads incline to the side, and some snore, attracting the attention of the priest in charge of discipline. He walks down the rows armed with a club, the *kyosaku*, with which he strikes them on the shoulder, causing the guilty head to straighten up, the hardened brain to force itself alert. The regimen of reciting the sutras continues, its aim the mastery of life.

Our buses left the park one by one, going along the edge of Eihei-Ji's cedar forest. We finally reached Kyoto, via the road beside Lake Biwa, the largest Japanese lake, whose beauty has earned it the cognomen "eight marvels of Omi." According to Japanese poets, the eight marvels of the lake are: the last lights at Seta; the return of the boats to Yabase; the snow at sunset on Mount Hira; the nocturnal rain at Karasaki; the flight of wild ducks at Katata; the sound of the Mi temple bell in the dusk; the autumn moon at Ishiyama; the sun and breeze at Awazu.

Esoteric Buddhism

The legendary myths regarding the origin of Shintoism are almost all Japanese. The historic myths, on the other hand, come from Chinese and Korean sources. Indeed, Zen as a doctrine restores a harmony of concepts inherent in the Indian, Chinese, and Japanese cultures, especially, after Hindu Buddhism, the Confucian and Taoist teachings. The islands of the Rising Sun have adapted and modernized the old beliefs of continental China.

I discovered and made contact with one sect, the Shingon, which practices "esoteric Buddhism," long after my arrival. The temples of Muro-Ji, near Nara, were built to shelter nuns of the Shingon sect.

Esoteric Buddhism essentially affirms a Buddhism of nature, the true temple of man. It was raining on Muro-Ji one Monday in October, and you might have thought you were alone on the paths and lanes, but you are never alone in Japan, even to meditate beneath an umbrella. At eleven o'clock in the morning, the grove was suddenly invaded by shouts, laughter, and a forest of umbrellas. Young girls and boys, hundreds of students, were performing one of those innumerable rites that punctuate their lives, making it their duty to go back, whenever they can, to the sources of their civilization. Before the central temple, each student will bow and clap thrice before going away to other temples, other forests, other myths. When I left Muro-Ji that Monday afternoon, it was still raining. I headed for Kobe, where a car ferry would take me somewhat south of this belt of myth that encircles of "waist" of Japan.

The Japanese go to the island of Shikoku, the fourth island of importance in the archipelago, chiefly to visit Kotohira, where one of the most frequented sanctuaries in Japan can be found. To reach the top of Kompira-San, you must climb a hundred steps flanked by souvenir stands selling banal picture postcards as well as objects unavailable in Europe and America except in sex stores. The myths of sun, fire, and water have joined with Buddhist thought to create a specific idea of man and his spiritual nature. But the Japanese have never been able to accommodate the immaterial and inexplicable except by relating them to the senses, discovering well before Father Teilhard de Chardin the intimate bond between spirit and matter and the impossibility of one's existing without the other.

Phallic Cults and Fertility

A good Japanese friend insisted that I visit a temple in a small village near Nagoya, outside the usual tourist circuit. From the end of May to the beginning of June, Tagata Jinja welcomes thousands of Japanese who come to pay homage to the phallus (a few miles away in another temple on the side of a wooded hill, woman's sexual organ is celebrated). Wooden phalluses float in a small holy lake; sterile women seek fertility by bathing in it. At the temple door priests were selling amulets representing the female sexual organ, together with prayers to be recited later on at home.

At the Tagata Jinja festival, the entire municipal council parades in ceremonial costume, preceded by an orchestra of traditional instruments. Shinto priests dressed in their holy robes surround the "object," which has been sculpted from the trunk of a very large tree, and is pushed along on a cart. Behind this giant phallus comes the choir of village virgins; they carry a dais bearing a plaster statue symbolic of virginity. Then come widows in black and white ceremonial kimonos, each holding in her arms, like a baby, a life-size phallus. At the end of the procession, in traditional costume, come the young men in two rival groups. The first group carries an uprooted tree, still covered with leaves; the other group tries to gain possession of it, and as the procession continues, this game gets violent at times. It is said that any youth who succeeds in outwitting the vigilance of the group guarding the tree and manages to seize one of the branches, no matter how small, will be assured of virility for the coming year. The procession continues through a rice field and reaches the temple of Tagata, where the phallus is solemnly brought inside. In the courtyard, priests and monks sell commemorative objects, while from the top of a platform, rice patties fall on the crowd and are caught by the most daring.

It should not be thought that this is an isolated festival or a purely local phenomenon. We visited the island of Sado with a Parisian television crew, hoping to witness the holy dances called Kagura, which persist in their original form in many villages. Around the bend of a rice field, a country temple appeared; it was filled with phalluses that had been carefully carved by the entire population. A little farther on, we were surprised to see a permanent stage in the village square. A puppet show was presented for us. Some of the puppets had been handed down for more than two hundred years. We watched the movements of these extravagant figures without understanding a word of the dialogue. Our cameraman shot the puppets in close-up and from all possible angles. Suddenly the male puppet lifted his kimono, exposing a huge shapely penis, and began peeing on the cameraman.

Women and Spirits of the Sea

South of Sado, at the farthest point of the Noto peninsula, the small port of Wajima on the Sea of Japan serves as a rear base for the island of Hekura. It is inhabited only in the summer, by a population whose essential activity is gathering shellfish. On the Pacific shore, the women have become popular with tourists, thanks to the king of pearls, Mr. Mikimoto. On the island of Toba, in the open sea across from the holy sanctuaries of Ise, he dresses the women in white and has them dive and bring up for the tourists' pleasure pearl-bearing oysters, which are then opened in front of the visitors. Traditionally, the women have the difficult job of gathering shellfish sold for food, particularly conch with three holes, called *awabi*. Each year the divers of Wajima migrate with their families, traveling four hours by sea to the desolate island of Hekura, which is simply a heap of volcanic rocks. When I landed at Hekura with my camera crew in the middle of July, I did not know what awaited us. I thought we might be flung back into the sea. It was almost worse; we were greeted by complete indifference, and found it impossible to secure a place to stay or to make a single serious contact. The people avoided us—on the run. Even the Japanese who accompanied us did not manage to exchange two words with the natives. The local grocer finally agreed to rent us a room we shared with fifteen boys and girls, separated by the veils of our respective mosquito nettings. It took several days to convince the women to dive before the eyes of our cameras. There are no white clothes here. Wearing a narrow loincloth and a belt holding a knife, the young divers hunt *awabi* in the coves, at depths of ten to fifty feet, with only a flimsy apparatus to maintain the correct pressure in their eardrums. Living under a pseudomatriarchal regime, they dive like this every day, while their husbands take care of the children and do the cooking and cleaning. They gradually got accustomed to working half-naked in front of us, above all when I showed them the book of photographs the Italian writer Fosco Maraini had published ten years before, *Hekurajima*. No European had visited the place since he had taken those photographs. They recognized their older sisters, their mothers and cousins, and the book was a big success in the village.

One must travel about fifteen miles southwest from Hiroshima to reach Miyajima, also called Itsuku Shima. From the shore one catches sight of the large floating sanctuary, famous as one of the three most beautiful sights in Japan. The cluster of Shintoist shrines connected to each other by covered walks on pilings is devoted to the worship of the three daughters of Susano-o, the brother of the goddess Amaterasu. At high tide, the principal towers and the temple's entrance portal are under water, and the sea reaches the level of the covered walks, giving the impression that the temples are floating. These shrines were already in existence about the year 800, as documents attest, but they have been rebuilt several times in the course of the centuries. They contain the oldest No theater in Japan. In mid-July, the festivals of the O'Bon are celebrated with particular brilliance by a nocturnal procession of boats and the lights of innumerable hanging lanterns.

REALITY

In Japan, reality is first of all physical, and the violence of the natural surroundings leaps to the eye. My first visit to Hokkaido occurred some months after my arrival. It was not quite spring. I arrived by plane at Sapporo, the capital of the northern island, where the Winter Olympic Games of 1972 were held. A hard northern city, Sapporo is inhabited by a particularly hospitable population, but the city's sights did not occupy more than a day, so I left next morning by train for Asahikawa, a city at the center of the island, where a very large, very cold plain extends to the foot of the Daisetsuzan mountain range. The station at Asahikawa, open to the Siberian winds, made me hope that the wait for my connection would be brief. But one's hopes are not always granted, and it was only after several hours of walking up and down and stamping our feet that we were en route to Biei.

Land of Fire

In forty-five minutes we were at the foot of Mount Tokachi, an active volcano whose smoke holes could be discerned above the forest, well before we arrived at the hot springs of Shirogane-Onsen. The only hotel, which had not harbored a Western visitor for eleven years, received us with courtesy and deference.

For three days, skis on our backs, we clambered up the sides of Mount Tokachi, all the way to the shelter, where each afternoon at four o'clock an old man dressed in white rang a bell, the signal to go down. Descending the slope, we felt under our feet rumbling explosions that reminded us Tokachi was still very much alive. The proprietor of the hotel is familiar with the capricious volcano, which at times threatens as if in a sudden attack of rage, waking up the inhabitants in the middle of the night with grumblings or explosions, and at other times is quite sober and content, not even tingeing the sky with white smoke.

Coming down from Tokachi, one observes a break in the northern end of Honshu, the central island in the peninsula of Shimokita. There rises Osore, the mountain of the witches, which represents Japan's most demonic landscape. Osore's active volcano is a good example of the constant interpenetration of myth and reality. The scene: a crater lake four miles in circumference; lava has always flowed all the way to its banks. The higher one ascends toward the summit of the crater, the more crevices appear in the volcanic rock, releasing smoke from the volcano's center, while here and there beneath one's feet, boiling water surges. Then the lava comes to an end and the forest encircles it, like a royal crown, all around the upper edge of the crater and halfway down the slope. In autumn, the wooded crown turns all colors, the red of maples and the green of spruce, the white of beech and the yellow of chestnut. Along the borders of the lake are some Buddhist temples; beyond, some piles of stones. They have been placed one on top of the other in the shape of lanterns—*ishi doro*, symbolizing the souls of the dead. Jizo, guardian angel of dead children and of souls in distress, rises up here and there, stiff and fantastic, now in the full light, now veiled as though shadowed by the smoke of the volcano. Pilgrims walk about among the stones and stop sometimes, accompanied by a medium, to invoke the souls of their dead and enter into communion with them. Every year, toward the end of June, hundreds of mediums, usually blind women, travel here from all over the archipelago, together with a considerable number of pilgrims who have come to experience a privileged communion with the hereafter. When I got to this strange place, a storm was raging, the wind blowing in strong gusts. The roof of a temple was carried away before my eyes. Violence and desolation contrasted on this November day with the stoicism of the Japanese pilgrims, whose behavior was equaled only by the impassivity of our cameramen, confronted as they were by the furious elements.

The island of Oshima, near Tokyo Bay and opposite the Izu peninsula, is dominated by another active volcano. One can climb on foot or donkey back all the way to the crater's rim. Strings of barbed wire mark the danger zone, where eruptions are not infrequent; at all times of the year one is likely to hear explosions and rumblings and to see lava being flung up in the sky. The most violent and no doubt the most majestic volcano is situated at the southern extreme of Kyushu, and there are in all about twenty volcanoes that, on one occasion or another, have erupted violently. This danger seems to us to impose a challenge, but the inhabitants of the archipelago have apparently not as yet decided to accept it. This is perhaps the only perpetually renewed challenge against which the Japanese have not mobilized their technology or their imaginations to escape the logic of absurdity: building while knowing that their work will be destroyed, living under the shadow of death and opposing it by life, thus feeding an endless cycle.

An earthquake surprised me one day in my fifth-floor office in Akasaka. Before I had time to realize what had happened, I was flung to the other side of the room, without being harmed. The Japanese have learned to live with such events—they have become part of their civilization. There is a proverb: "Earthquakes, lightning, floods, fire, and his father—here are the five things that fill a Japanese with fear and trembling."

The first earthquake recorded in the archipelago's history is the one that gave birth, in 286 B.C., to Mount Fuji and, consequently, to the depression in which Lake Biwa lies. Since that date, the earthquakes that have become cataclysms cannot even be counted.

On September 1, 1923, at 11:58 A.M., the great earthquake of Kanto killed more than 60,000 persons and destroyed 366,262 houses in the capital.

Legend says that an enormous catfish lives under the earth and provokes a quake each time it moves. It is held in the bowels of the archipelago by a rock located in the enclosure of the temple of Kashima in the province of Hitachi, 230 miles north of Tokyo on the Pacific side. With the idea of touching the fish's head, a gentleman of the Mito clan tried to pull up the rock, but he could not succeed—it was embedded too deeply in the ground. The memory of the 1923 earthquake is preserved in the temple, which contains the bones of thirty thousand victims deposited in barrels. Two statues of Buddha made out of calcified bones are displayed in the memorial enclosure, and each year they attract a numerous, pensive crowd on September 1.

Flooded Lands

The violence of the natural environment is revealed in another relatively frequent calamity: typhoons. Given the poetic names of women, they are detected by the weather bureau, which broadcasts news of their progress and intensity. Winds, frequently accompanied by rains, are channeled in often broad concentric spirals. Thus, on the periphery of a typhoon, one can feel only the equivalent of a wind of force three or four, together with a few drops of rain. In Tokyo, when the radio sounds the alarm, employers dismiss their workers. The streets empty, traffic stops, the wind begins blowing in strong gusts, while a noise mounts in the city. Muffled bangs resound everywhere as merchants in traditional Tokyo nail down their wooden shutters. The piercing noise increases; the sky darkens. The physical damage is often quite considerable; human lives lost to typhoons average more than a thousand a year.

Tidal waves, which are rarer and generally accompany earthquakes, act as reminders of the profound inhospitality of nature here and the price paid for the sweet mildness of the ephemeral intermediate seasons, the time of the cherry blossoms—they often last only one day—or the blossoming of the maple trees that redden the mountains in the autumn.

2: The Puzzle

Solving puzzles is a favorite pastime of every inhabitant of the archipelago, whether foreigner or native. You gather the pieces one by one—pieces that happen to come to hand, those you make yourself, or those you borrow—and assemble them in a thousand and one ways. Of course, we are not talking about an actual puzzle, but an attempt to reconstitute a country from all its component parts, parts that characterize Japan's daily life, its institutions, its civilization, and its history. Nothing is more natural for a foreigner than to try to solve the puzzle of the country which has welcomed or has interested him.

One's observation of one's neighbor or oneself has no value unless it is lucid, critical, and suffused with humor. The observations of Takashi Suzuki have all these qualities, especially since they aim at one goal only, intellectual stimulation, and try to attain it by a kind of incessant provocation.

During the riotous events of May 1968 in France, Takashi Suzuki was in Paris on a business trip. On his return, he was deluged with invitations to dinner by the French diplomatic colony, each of whom hoped to benefit from an eyewitness version of the uprising. In the course of one of these evenings, in mid-July, a well-intentioned lady asked the question that was on everyone's mind: "Now tell us, Mr. Suzuki—this revolution, what was it like?"

"I do not know, madame. I am Japanese and it is very difficult for me to evaluate a typically French event. Yet I can say that I found the paving stones in the French capital much too heavy. . . ."

I can't recall who introduced me to Takashi Suzuki. It was at the beginning of my stay; the writer Maurice Mourier, then the young cultural attaché, and his wife, Pascaline, had invited us both to their small Japanese house at Gotemba. Tall, thin, dressed in Chardin clothes, Suzuki looked little more than fifty. Ten years later, he had barely changed; he was said to be seventy. Alert, Voltairean, he had a multiplicity of calling cards which permitted him to gain access—with equal competence and great distinction—to the most diverse milieux. Because he belonged to the exclusive alumni club of the

79

University of Keio, he had innumerable connections. Through him one could get into contact with the minister of justice or the chief of police just as easily as with the most hippie of intellectuals or the most extremist of students in the city. Officially he was a talented painter whose works were already selling for high prices in Japan. And just as officially he presided over Royal KK, an importer and exporter of films for theatrical and television distribution. A promoter of the Committee of French Elegance, he taught aesthetics in a Kyoto university and amused himself during his insomniac nights by solving very complicated mathematical problems. As a member of the Committee of Intellectuals Against the Vietnam War, he participated in protest parades every Saturday alongside the writer Makoto Oda and the sculptor and philosopher Taro Okamoto. Takashi Suzuki belonged to the liberal branch of Japanese thought, which has always represented one of the deepest currents in the archipelago while constantly favoring and giving strong support to a conservative policy.

The Meiji Restoration

Takashi Suzuki helped me to understand how Japan has lived with a great national contradiction, doomed to appear the victim of all its ambiguities and to undergo the fate of the "unloved." This contradiction, seen from within and through some great moments in Japan's history in modern times, first appeared with the Meiji restoration in 1868.

The Meiji restoration was accomplished by the samurai, those guardians of tradition and honor. In the name of those values, they drove out the shogun and restored the emperor to power. The shogunate had betrayed the people by accepting, after the bombardments of Kagoshima in 1863 and Shimonoseki in 1864, the iniquitous treaties imposed by the Western powers. The samurai launched the slogan *"Sonno joi"*—a directive to drive out the barbarians and revere the emperor—but at the same time their leaders were f∙ced with the problems involved in transforming an archaic feudal state into a modern nation, and their decision to modernize Japan by agreeing to enter into commercial relations with the Western powers—the United States, Great Britain, the Low Countries, and France—filled them with shame.

Traditional methods were ill-suited to confronting the demands of the new situation. The samurai's swords and its code of honor—Bushido—were insufficient to stem the invasion of the foreigners. This profoundly troubled all those who had overturned the shogun, and split them into irreconcilable factions which clashed over the projected annexation of Korea. The opposing sides were called the "party of war" and the "party of peace," the "imperial faction" and the "national faction," the "feudal group" and the "capitalist group."

These different appellations give an idea of Japanese divergences, provided one does not forget that both groups were originally samurai and that both had supported the restoration of the emperor. The struggle between them began to take on the aspect of a civil war, which was then translated into the revolt of the Satsuma clan, among whom the famous Takamori Saigo had retired. Saigo has remained in history as the prototype of the intransigent samurai. Having agreed to support the revolt of those samurai who had been unable to adapt to the modernization of Japan, Saigo lost the fight in 1877. And after, measuring the consequences of a revolution that he had helped to instigate but whose fruits he did not recognize and whose reality he disavowed, he committed seppuku. The denouement of the conflict came in 1910 with the definitive annexation of Korea.

For Takashi Suzuki, liberal reformer, the structure of modern Japanese society differs very little from the one established during the years that followed the Meiji revolution in 1868.

"When you observe Japanese society," Suzuki tells me, "you lose sight of the essential question: Why has Japan with its energy handicap passed through the crisis without too much trouble? How did it overcome it? By what miracle has it emerged as the second strongest economic power in the world after the United States? Of course, one can find fault with its policy of lifetime employment, the fragility of its trade union structures, its workers' mentality, but these are just details. What counts is the strength produced by the coming together of the Japanese inside the institution: family, business, and nation. The Japanese draws his imagination and his capacity for innovation from the group. That has not changed since 1868. It is the way his mind works.

"If I divide a whole into four parts by drawing one vertical line and one horizontal, your logic leads you immediately to see each of the sections as an entity. This is clear and sharp, while for me the division of a whole into four parts is an expedient, a method of approach which does not change the whole. Besides, does the division correspond to the reality? The reality is ambiguous. It is obvious that, say, the French Revolution had nothing in common with our 1868 affair."

This evaluation of Japanese society by a friend, a reformer in the Japanese samurai tradition, recalls a statement on the opposite side, made by a traditional conservative, a direct heir of the spirit of Takamori Saigo: Yukio Mishima.

"The revolution must always be made within the tradition." Thus did Mishima pass judgment on the Meiji revolution. Carried through by the samurai, it sacrificed its promoters to the country's modernization. "In Japan there are three classes—the merchants, the peasants, and the samurai. I work as a peasant, but I preserve the spirit of the samurai." This quotation from Mishima shows us simultaneously the ambiguity and the identity crisis of the Japanese.

Some of the samurai of 1868 successfully converted, and entered the despised caste of merchants. Others, returning to their lands, were often forced to hire themselves out to the peasants and gradually became the poorest class, and as society's transformation continued, they were disdained and forgotten. The values of honor, chivalry, and loyalty lost some of their significance in a society committed to complete modernization, a society in which infrastructures of production and consumption were gradually being set up in imitation of the West. Edwin O. Reischauer, the American expert on Japan, has spoken of the "revolution against tradition." It is true that the Meiji revolution was made in the name of the military, warlike tradition, and this tradition did not immediately profit from the reform of the structures of a feudal state (which had in fact ceased to be feudal because of the abolition of samurai privileges). But the revenge of "tradition" was not long in coming, since some years after Saigo's suicide, Japan entered on the path of imperialist expansion and the domination of the military. Later on, thanks to a "compromise" with the liberal reformers, the traditionalists put the finishing touches to their victory by the annexation of Korea.

Militarism: 1931–1945

Even in the minds of the reformers, the modernization of Japan had to begin with that of the army, an idea shared by all social classes and summed up in a popular slogan of the period: *Fukoku Kyohei* (A rich country and a powerful army).

The first part of this program would be greatly compromised during the international economic depression of the thirties, which affected Japan severely. The most aggressive military men, the people who had settled accounts with Korea in 1910 and wanted to finish off China, took advantage of the situation to cast discredit on the politicians and even on the army's general staff. Secret societies organized commando groups to carry out assassinations and tried to bring pressure to bear on public opinion, and the Japanese army in Manchuria created an irreversible situation by deliberately provoking the incident of September 18, 1931, when some Japanese officers sabotaged a trunk line of the Manchurian railroad, accused the Chinese of responsibility, and used this as a pretext for conquering Manchuria. This led to the creation of the puppet state of Manchukuo, of which Pu-Yi, a creature of the Japanese, became emperor. When the League of Nations condemned the Japanese invasion, Japan quit the League.

All this did not suffice for the extremists, for whom recourse to direct action became the rule. Yukio Mishima later succeeded in awakening a certain "samurai" nostalgia with a film evoking the atmosphere of excitement, which led to the army's resumption of control after the conspiracy of February 26, 1936. On that day, a group of young officers led a revolt in Tokyo's first division and in a few hours murdered the minister of finance, the guardians of the great seal, two former prime ministers, and one of the three ranking generals on the army's general staff. But the officers failed to overcome the imperial guard, and were brutally punished. One lieutenant went home after the failure of the putsch and informed his wife, who immediately knew the consequences. The man and woman unrolled a sheet of parchment and slowly drew on it the ideograms of their last will and testament. Then with great solemnity they undressed and made love for the last time. The wife carefully prepared the instruments of seppuku and got ready to give the coup de grace with the traditional dagger, which she always carried. The ceremony unfolded in accordance with the ritual. The officer drove the sword into his belly as deeply as required. Then, slowly, he carved out his entrails. When he had completed his act and reached the peak of suffering, his wife cut off his head and drove the dagger into his heart. In Mishima's movie, *Yukoku*, or *Patriotism*, we are not spared a single detail. Mishima played the part of the officer. At the 1966 festival of short subjects in Tours, neither the jury nor the audience could take this assault on their sensibilities. The majority left the theater before the end of the film.

Later, Mishima would repeat in reality the very acts he had simulated before the camera, not without grandeur yet leaving a generally derisory impression. Mishima's seppuku offered unmistakable proof of his attachment to the patriotic values he espoused, yet his tragic suicide caused, even among his friends—save for the small private army that surround him—more stupefaction and compassion than support.

August 6, 1945

The repercussions of the last traumatic event in the history of modern Japan echoed far beyond the borders of the archipelago. We decided to cover the ceremonies marking the twentieth anniversary of the dropping of the bomb on Hiroshima with a special fifteen-minute television report. We had no idea what we were going to put in the film when we found ourselves at the epicenter of the bomb's explosion, the dome of the Chamber of Commerce, whose ruins are preserved to bear witness to the event. Around the building's calcined skeleton the memorial Park of Peace has replaced the center of old Hiroshima, which was completely razed. On August 6, 1965, there was a very large crowd of people in the park. Delegations had come from all over the world. Japanese national television had the idea of reconstituting, with models and drawings and the help of witnesses, the urban center of Hiroshima as it had been at the moment of the explosion. The sole survivor from that area told this story:

> "I was head of the office of industrial promotion, and we would usually begin work at eight o'clock. My secretary would go to the basement and get the files I had to use during the day. Every afternoon, as regulations prescribed, all dossiers were put back in the basement. On this particular August 6, 1945, it seemed to me that nothing was normal. It was ten after eight and my secretary, usually so punctual, had not yet come in. She arrived at fourteen minutes after eight, and did not even offer an excuse. When I began to ask her for an explanation, telling her to go down and get the files, she told me to go down myself. That was really unheard of. Besides, everybody seemed nervous. So I went down into the basement, extremely worried about my co-worker's attitude.
>
> The files were kept in the second basement. While I was preparing to look for the documents, I heard in the distance the rumbling sound of a plane, then the siren began moaning, sounding the alert. Hiroshima had never been bombed yet. After this, I don't remember anything. I woke up later. All the documents were scattered about. I was surrounded by chunks of plaster and the debris from the building. It was black. I climbed up to the surface, groping my way hesitantly. Everything was razed to the ground, stripped bare, the trees and the people who wandered about were like ghosts, whom I divined rather than actually saw. I walked all the way down to the shore. As far as I could see, all was ruins. Then I picked up some stones and threw them into the water.
>
> The city around me was strangely silent.

On August 6, 1965, as night fell on the Park of Peace, boy and girl students were playing a game in the dark. Farther on, in the city hospital's small modern private rooms, thirty-odd "atomized" patients had died during the past year, twenty years after the event. But near the cenotaph on which are inscribed the names of the victims—a list which grows longer each year—one must, if one wishes to remain objective, remember the afterword in the published diary of Dr. Michihiko Hachiya, in 1945 the director of the hospital of the Ministry of Communications:

> Dr. Lodge was a young medical officer. He came each day for a month to examine the patients. Although we did not speak the same language, we understood each other. He was a gentleman and my entire staff and all my patients were anxious to regard him with friendship. There are no frontiers where there is sympathy and understanding. . . .
>
> Colonel John R. Half, Jr., also came to see me quite frequently. His general headquarters were in Kure. I think that he was the chief surgeon; he was tall, certainly the tallest of all the Westerners I had met. . . . These two doctors drove the fear and hostility out of our hearts and left us full of hope. . . .

This generous and realistic attitude is one bequest of history; the attitude of the kamikaze pilots who purposely crashed their planes on the decks of American battleships is another.

MYTHS AND REALITY

The traumas of history in the archipelago help in understanding the "Japanese puzzle." The "Mishima puzzle" helps us understand the Japan of the samurai, as it exists in the depths of every Japanese citizen's heart, but the samurai of the 1980s, who have the courage to live the ideal they profess, are today a derided and deluded minority. The "Suzuki puzzle" begins with the same set of postulates. The Meiji's reformers finally made treaties with the West only because they were forced to by circumstances, and are hence responsible for Japan's modernization. Japan began going to school with the West for practical reasons and in order to become efficient. Little does it matter, therefore, that the Japanese have borrowed certain things, so long as the compromise does not affect the essentials. When a place is made for the foreigner, it must not interfere with the inner life of the Japanese.

Each individual in this country participates inwardly in the conflict of the currents represented by Mishima and Suzuki. He tries as well as he can to get them to coexist. The myth offers a kind of intellectual and moral shelter. It is idealism and art, ethics and aesthetics; it is the Japan that looks forward to the night, free of all restraints, and the Japan at home, sheltered behind the shojis; the Japan we see in the movies and on the stage, and also the rural Japan, independent of civilization.

On the other side is reality, practicality, efficiency, economy, production, enterprise: the daytime Japan, carefully structured and scheduled, of work, of ultrarapid transportation, of achievements visible to everyone; it is also the Japan of political parties and trade unions, of demonstrations and protests.

But as in all coexistence, there is interpenetration. The myth sometimes enters reality, just as reality gets mixed up with the myth. The supreme art of the Japanese is the ability to balance these distinctions.

MYTH AND REALITY IN LITERATURE

Professor Yoshio Abe tried some years ago in the magazine *Esprit* to set forth an approach to Japanese cultural identity. Undertaking extensive historical analysis, he presented his compatriots as confined within the rationalistic Western concept of universality, in contrast

to the irrational particularism of Japanese civilization, whose importance was being neglected. And what if this vaunted Western universality was only a particularism which had benefited from universal
diffusion? "The concepts Western/universal/advanced and Japan-
ese/particular/backward lie behind every cultural choice that tends
to replace something native with something Western. This emotion
and this concept have been the source of an inferiority complex in
regard to the model imitated. . . ." One should also remember the
irritation which the success of the Japanese "pupil" can arouse in
certain American and European circles.

Yukio Mishima

Should the Western/rational/universal concept be revised and become Japanese/rational/universal? For Yukio Mishima, as quoted
by the critic Tadeo Takemoto, ". . . there are quite a few movements in Japan which want to establish ties between what is local and
what is foreign. But isn't this the business of the souvenir salesmen?"
Mishima protests on the other hand against a certain pseudo leftist
interpretation of Japanese history, according to which the Shinto
myths which present the Japanese emperors as gods who came down
out of the sky, and the people they vanquished as local, outcast gods,
would in fact simply be a picturesque way of describing invaders who
conquered sedentary agricultural populations because they happened to be better organized. This does not mesh with the official
thesis to which the Japanese turn every time they feel the need to
comfort themselves about their original cultural identity. In this
sense, Mishima's fight to preserve the myths led him to express the
need for an imperial cultural system.

"I am a very serious Japanese writer," he told me during a long
discussion in his Spanish-style house in the Omori quarter. "I do not
love literature. It is a little like a Don Juan who does not love women."

On another occasion I saw him perform one of those "rituals"
to which he had decided to submit himself. During the summer of
1969, he had come to dinner at my house with his wife, Yoko. Some
Tahitian men and women friends of mine began to dance. He became interested and asked them to teach him this dance, through
which he could express both his violence and a certain sexual ambiguity. That night he told me confidentially that he was about to
crown his work by a literary monument which would sum up his life
and thought, everything to which he had dedicated himself. The
work would be entitled: "The Sea of Fertility." At the same period,
Mishima wrote to various friends: "I have divided my life into four
rivers: the river of books, the river of the theater, the river of the
body, and the river of action, and these four rivers will all empty into
the sea of fertility."

My first meeting with him, at the end of 1965, had taken place under the sign of "the river of the body." The Korakuen center for sports and leisure activities, located near the Ochanomizu and Ichigaya railroad stations, is very well known in Tokyo. In the basement, at street level, there is an immense, rather somber gymnasium. Lacking embellishments, but excellently equipped, it is frequented by men of all ages and professions, but most come from a rather lower-class milieu. I became a member of the gym, knowing that I would see Mishima there twice a week.

Aware of his taste for physical culture, I worked conscientiously with the dumbbells. For two weeks he did not come; no doubt he was traveling. The third week I was seriously toning up the muscles in my abdomen by repeated push-ups, when a professor from the Franco-Japanese Institute came over and interrupted me. Mishima was there, right behind me, wearing shorts, his torso naked, just as I had seen him in many newspaper photographs. All that was lacking was the band of resolution tied around his head. With extremely bright eyes and a very flat face, this small, rather ugly man radiated intelligence and assurance. His handshake was hard and energetic. Our conversation was brief, but we agreed to meet at the Foreign Correspondents Club, that gathering place where the news of the entire Far East is concocted. Journalists are automatically members by right, but all the embassies are represented by one or several of their members, especially those in the information services. So the Foreign Correspondents Club is a meeting place for journalists, diplomats, and secret agents from all over the world, as well as many Japanese officials who find it a useful medium for the diffusion of their information/propaganda throughout the world.

It was in this setting that I met Yukio Mishima once again, after he had come with Takashi Suzuki to dine at my house in Shimouna. That meeting of my two "mentors" had not been very cordial. Takashi Suzuki regarded Mishima as a fascist, despite the apparent contradiction between that opinion and Suzuki's acceptance of the mythical version of Japanese history. A similar contradiction appeared in Mishima's actions in favor of an "imperial culture" despite his relative support of Western progress and a certain American-style consumer society.

In April 1966, at the press club, Mishima agreed to answer a few questions put by my colleagues. He spoke on ritual suicide by seppuku, saying, in substance: "The sincerity of Westerners is hard to believe in because one does not see it. In the feudal period, it was thought that the seat of sincerity was located at the level of the intestines. Therefore, to show our sincerity, we must open our abdomen and put its contents clearly on display. It was a symbol of the will of the samurai, who knew that it was the most painful way to die. It proved his courage. This method of suicide is a Japanese invention, which foreigners could not copy."

Some days later, Mishima declared to me: "There are two forms of suicide, that of the strong and that of the weak. I admire the first and hate the second."

Mishima's work is typically Japanese and representative of the country's mixture of myth and reality at the confluence of the sacred and the profane. The river of action which formed part of his life plan ended for him with his seppuku on November 25, 1970. I was in New York, where it was about four o'clock in the morning. In Paris it was ten o'clock. My colleague there, Philippe Labro, who had read the dispatches announcing Mishima's suicide, telephoned and woke me up. I felt that I was living in a waking nightmare. Labro asked me some questions about the meaning of the suicide. I answered mechanically. At seven o'clock, my wife, Anne-Marie, woke me again; she had just learned about it from television. CBS and NBC broadcast some pictures that had been filmed by Japanese television. One saw Mishima's head roll on the carpet, after the slashing blow from the saber of Morita, his friend and the first member of his private army, who killed himself immediately afterward. These horrible images are still in our memories, and I shall never forget the day that followed, as I dragged myself about, haunted and obsessed by this suicide. I preferred to remember Mishima's river of writing, which bore on its current his fascinating characters, Japanese men and women in a living Japan in which there coexisted, as among living men, the realities of the present and the ghosts of the past, the dreams of today and the speculations of tomorrow.

The drama surrounding a compromise with tradition was described by Mishima in one of the novels which has most contributed toward making him known outside Japan: *Confessions of a Mask.* On this occasion he was compared to André Gide and Mishima felt flattered, though at the same time he said that the comparison did not seem to him to have any real basis. He preferred to compare himself to Raymond Radiguet, to whom he owed his vocation as a writer. "I had the revelation of my vocation when reading 'Count d'Orgel's Ball.'" At first Mishima wrote short stories. He was very concerned about the impact of his work, so his disappointment was great at the glacial reception accorded one of his novels, *Kyoko's House*, which was perhaps a little too long, and from which he had expected much. Nothing could make up for this failure, he felt, even the success of *After the Banquet* and *The Temple of the Golden Pavilion.* For two years there was some talk of his getting the Nobel Prize, but in 1967 Miguel Angel Asturias beat him out, and in 1968 the Swedish jury finally chose Kawabata, because he was older. At this time Mishima became a clearly "committed" writer. He published *Runaway Horses* and *Spring Snow,* and then announced the tetralogy which would crown his work: *The Sea of Fertility,* the image of a desertlike region on the moon.

On July 20, 1969, at 10:56 P.M. Eastern Standard Time, Armstrong had just set foot on the moon; Aldrin followed him soon after. I and my television crew were in front of the Sony building at the entrance to the Ginza, trying to gather the reactions of Japanese passersby who were watching the event on the screen set up there. At one moment the moon's surface was reflected in the water of the aquarium and Mishima could have imagined, as he knew so well how to do, a sea of tranquillity different from the one Armstrong and Aldrin were in the process of discovering. I ran to the telephone. He seemed to me the only person who had the breadth of mind to comment on this event. I telephoned him a number of times, but never got through to him. I did get hold of him some hours later. He poured out his thoughts, fascinated by the event.

"When a virgin has been forced, she has lost her virgin nature and as a consequence has changed in her nature. I have the impression that we have murdered something, like a dream which we kill by waking up. The dream is dead now. I would weep over men if I had the time, but above all I weep over the moon for having been raped."

When I left Mishima and Japan in July 1970, our relations had become rather cool because I had publicly cast doubt, in a symposium he organized for a magazine, on his sincerity in regard to the formation of the *tatenokai,* his private army. He had outfitted his soldiers in sumptuous uniforms—they were ridiculous and worthy of a third-rate operetta. I claimed that this was not an expression of patriotism but an exacerbated narcissism, and I added that it could be a matter of an aging man who wanted to see himself reflected in the bodies of young and virile athletes. Some days before my departure, I was astonished to receive a telephone call from him, in the course of which he said to me: "I've just heard that you're leaving Japan, and I want you to know that I am very grateful to you for having given me the chance to learn the Tahitian dance. . . ."

Four months later, almost to the day, he killed himself. I was sorry I had not fully appreciated the extent of his commitment. I should not have been misled. Perhaps he was right when he said there was no sincerity in the West. But to complete the puzzle one must go further. Expressing an important preoccupation of the Japanese, critic Tadeo Takemoto made himself the echo of Mishima's anguish: "I feel in myself the profound appeal of the sacred, which stipulates the existence of some supreme attribute. It would be rather limiting to think that there is in this quest only the desire for a return to imperial authority even if of divine descent. The absence of the metaphysical is cruelly felt in a civilization of strictly determined behaviorism. Mishima, more receptive to these problems than most of his fellow Japanese, expressed above all a quest for God, everywhere present but so profoundly absent in our hearts. This void is the cause of the people's anxiety."

From Akutagawa to Kawabata

Akutagawa, the samurai-peasant of Japanese literature, was not the first writer to commit suicide. Ten writers have put an end to their lives during this century, the last one being no less than the Nobel Prize winner Yasunari Kawabata. Among those whose names have traveled to the West, the name of Ryunosuke Akutagawa has a particular resonance. He committed suicide by swallowing cyanide on July 24, 1927, explaining that he had an "indefinable anxiety." He wrote numerous stories, some of which are very well known in Europe and the United States. In "Rashomon," Akutagawa conferred on the traditional Japanese tale, a subtler truth than could be expressed in realistic works. What is the truth regarding Takehiro's death? The truth of the bandit Tajomaru, who declares that he was responsible after raping the victim's wife? The truth of the wife, who says that she killed her husband and then tried to kill herself so as not to survive the shame of having been raped? Or the truth of the witch, who "spat on the soul of the deceased," announcing that he had committed suicide because his young wife had not only survived the rape but had taken pleasure in it? Akutagawa expresses in his writing and the choice of his subjects a certain skepticism as well as an aesthetic perfection characteristic of the Japanese mentality at its most profound. One can wonder whether the "vague disquietude" which led him to suicide did not arise from his search for the undiscoverable truth.

Yasunari Kawabata committed suicide two years after Mishima. More than anyone else, he derived his sensibility from that Japan whose nature and people he communicated as a poet. I knew Kawabata only through the articles the Japanese press published about him from time to time. When he was awarded the Nobel Prize, Mishima wanted to be the first to congratulate him, particularly since Mishima himself had secretly hoped to win that honor. Kawabata was president of the Japanese Pen Club, which had shocked Arthur Koestler by its refusal to take a stand in the Pasternak affair, when the Russian author was forbidden by his government to go to Stockholm to receive his Nobel Prize. They whispered in Tokyo that Mishima would have had the Nobel if the Pen Club had not lobbied to get the prize for their president, without his knowledge. Other rumors claimed that Mishima had lobbied on behalf of Kawabata, who had encouraged Mishima at the start of his career, and could in fact be considered his master.

Rereading Kawabata, one can discern the bridge which allowed Japanese literature to pass from its traditional to a "new" culture. It was a process of integrating foreign elements, domesticated one by one but not allowed to implant themselves like introductions by a colonial power. Mishima's ambiguity derives from his feeling himself a colonial in cultural matters, reinforced by the guilt which was also felt by Kawabata in the school of young writers that came into existence under the shadow of defeat. It should also be pointed out that after the Meiji period, cultural integration was painful, and the intellectual world had more difficulty than the business world in accepting the new state of affairs.

Tanizaki

The writer Junichiro Tanizaki seems to have really succeeded in crossing over to modernism during the first half of the twentieth century. He died in 1965, a key year in the modernization, after the inauguration of the new Japan by the emperor in October 1964, when he solemnly opened the Olympic Games in Tokyo. Tanizaki is typically linked with the aesthetic tradition of traditional Japan. He even went so far as to make it a profession of faith. He was able to communicate to his readers the Japanese art of living, which did not prevent him from including in his work some typically Western elements. The precision of his descriptions recalls Mishima's minute detail. This is a quality characteristic of authentic Japanese writers, whose writing is concerned with veracity of detail while yielding to the poetic vision evoked by the words themselves.

The hero of Tanizaki's *Diary of a Mad Old Man* goes to the Shinjuku Kabuki in a Hillman driven by a chauffeur; he gives his daughter-in-law Satsuko a silk Cardin scarf; the breakfast menu is Western. . . . Tanizaki thus distills Western elements of comfort, but the West remains purely external. Without making any claims for Japanese universality, at no point does he let you suppose that he believes in Western universality. The relationships he establishes among his characters in *The Key* would make no sense in Western society.

MYTH AND REALITY IN THE THEATER

Myth set aside, tradition forgotten, the sacred neglected—and lo! the appearance of a "modern" Japanese theater, rather dim and faded, which is called *shingeki*. The realistic plays of the Western theater at the beginning of the century have replaced the traditional Japanese theater, condemning its aesthetic. The Kabuki is especially regarded as a form of reactionary theater and, since 1945, even as fascist theater. But the young generation of avant-garde authors and stage directors has, paradoxically, refurbished the repertory of the Kabuki so that its myths and the movements of its actors are tied in with some purely contemporary preoccupations—the idea being to show the spectator what every Japanese bears in his deepest being. The Japanese universities call this mythology the "collective imagination" or the "collective unconscious," and Moriaki Watanabe, professor of literature at the University of Tokyo and a specialist in Paul Claudel, has written that this new theatrical language "permits us to detect the archives of the Japanese psychic infrastructure."

Kabuki and Its Heritage

Kabuki interests us insofar as it is a mythological translation of a Japanese reality. In Tokyo today, two theaters present Kabuki spectacles. One is the old Kabuki-za, whose traditional facade resembles that of a temple near the Ginza; despite less sophisticated stage equipment than the national theater's, it provides a more authentically Japanese atmosphere. The modern national theater is situated on the other side of Hibiya Park, facing the eastern moats of the Imperial Palace; it permits much more ambitious staging. The Kabuki's classic spectacle is presented as a play that alternates dialogue, dance, song, and music in an entirely original creation, the immutable repertory being literally renewed and transformed by the actors. All are male, including those who act the female roles.

A typical play, *Sukeroku,* is one of the most popular Kabuki theater pieces in Japan. In it, Ikyu, the samurai, representing the power of oppression, is mortally ridiculed by Sukeroku, the man of the people, at Yoshiwara, the old, very famous brothel district in Tokyo, where everyone, rich or poor, aristocrat or commoner, is treated as an equal. But the popularity of this play is not due only to its subject. The scenic utilization of what is called the "path of flowers," *hanamiti,* ravishes the audience. To enter the stage, the actors must use this passage, on the left side of the set. It is sometimes mirrored by a narrower passage on the opposite side, *kari-hanamiti.* Kabuki stages have a great range of unique stage machinery. The revolving stage, which permits an instantaneous change of set, was invented in Japan and has been used by the Kabuki theater since the eighteenth century. Wooden clappers punctuate dialogue or important declarations. Musicians and singers, dressed in the traditional medieval costumes but not made up, always occupy a corner of the set, while next to them stands the narrator behind a small lectern. He reads his text in a declamatory style. Sometimes the musicians play behind a bamboo curtain at one side of the stage. Opposite it is a kind of music box, which the Japanese call the *geza.* Though it often goes unnoticed, this instrument is played by very specialized musicians. The music box gives the signal for the actors' entrances and exists and punctuates all musical effects. It can also resonate, imitating the sounds of water, rain, and bells. When the play requires it, an orchestra is used, especially when the action involves a dance. The samisen, a stringed instrument that looks like a small guitar, acts as a kind of orchestra conductor. As for the dramatic performances, one should note the use of the *mie*, a method the actor employs to dramatize and accentuate his action by freezing his posture. It is the theatrical equivalent of the freeze frame in film.

Among other important elements of Kabuki, one should not forget the prompter, or *kurogo*, who is dressed in black, his face concealed by a mask. The *koken*, near the prompter, moves the furniture, which is usually just a chair. His face is visible.

According to Moriaki Watanabe, modern Kabuki is characterized by "two contradictory requirements, one stemming from a re-reading of the repertory in the light of modern psychology, and the other from the reincarnation of the Edo Kabuki's aesthetic tradition." But the Kabuki's dynamism is literally paralyzed by the monopoly of a single company. The style of certain actors, like Juro Kara, reflects Kabuki's mythic origins; that of others, like Tadashi Suzuki, the Kabuki of the eighteenth century, when it was at its aesthetic peak.

Juro Kara, born in 1941, has had the idea of adopting the formula of a strolling company of players, as it existed in the past in Europe and Japan, carrying about a red tent to remind people of the "original matrix" which gave birth to the theater of cruelty. But Kara is a poet, and his theater is filled with symbolic objects: "The eyes of gigantic, silvery dragonflies gathered by a beautiful small beggar girl; a handcart which flies over Tokyo on fire . . ."

Tadashi Suzuki, director of the small Waseda theater, was born in 1939 and began his career in the university theater in the 1960s, which was deeply marked by the struggle against the Japanese-American Security Treaty. He mixed his dramatic scenes with extracts from one of the most famous Kabuki authors, Tsuruya Namboku (1755–1829), whose specialty was everyday life in the Edo epoch. Typically Japanese, filled with such characteristic objects as the "poisoned knife" which cuts like a razor, Suzuki's decor is purposely sordid. This permits him to revive an "aestheticism of murder," which is the basis of Namboku's dramaturgy.

Shuji Terayama, famous for almost twenty years (he was born in 1934), initially created plays inspired by folklore, following the lead of other comtemporary authors, such as Kinoshita or Chikao Tanaka. And under the strictly political heading one should place such names as Kunio Shimizu (born in 1936), Makoto Sato (born in 1943), and Yoshiyuki Fukuda (born in 1931). These authors make use of romanticism to illustrate the problems that confront Japan because of modernization, eroticism, and violence. These, indeed, were Yukio Mishima's three preoccupations when he acted the stage role of the martyred St. Sebastian, or that of the officer of the coup d'état who committed suicide by seppuku. "I draw," he said, "my inspiration from my Eros, or more precisely from our tradition, which is at the heart of my Eros as a snake is hidden at the bottom of a spring. . . . I like to be called not a man of the extreme right but a traditionalist. . . . Tradition is dying in Japan. I have decided to create an army to save tradition. . . . We have no force capable of protecting an independent idea. . . . That is why I have created an army. It is composed of one hundred students. . . . They are men who did not want to become involved with the left and who felt alone. As for myself, I love solitude and I detest it. My writing is solitary and I have neither the intention nor the desire to influence anyone. I am not responsible for whatever consequences my writings may have. When Goethe wrote *Werther*, many young men committed suicide, following Werther's example. Did that make Goethe responsible for these suicides?"

The No

It was out of a love of tradition that Mishima composed his famous modern No plays, declaring that they were linked to the fifteenth-century tradition. The No is a much more rooted theatrical form than the Kabuki. It is a theater of masks: emotion must not transpire through the mobility of the face, but through gesture, mien, and the language of the body. A mystical theater tied to Buddhism, it has a repertory of about three hundred plays. The masks carved in wood are fashioned to represent very precise characters: an old woman, an old man, a man and a wife of mature age, a young man, a young woman, a blind man, a good divinity, a powerful divinity, a terrifying divinity, a monster, a wild animal. . . .

The plays are divided into six groups:

Plays of gods, or *kami-mono*, pay homage to courage and to a divinity. These No plays are also called plays of the "second actor," because at the start of the play it is the supporting actor who first enters the scene, dressed as a Shinto priest.

Plays about warriors, or *shura-mono*, present stories of battles as recounted by an aristocrat or a samurai who has assumed the appearance of a commoner and reveals his identity in the last scene.

Plays about women, called *kazura-mono*, have the female roles taken by men. The story introduces a young woman who dances, sometimes also an old woman or the spirit of a plant.

Plays about madmen are based in general on the madness of the principal character, most often a woman. Thus *Sakura-Gawa* is the story of a mother who goes mad after losing her infant.

Universal plays are primarily dramatic, though some belong to the epic or lyric genre.

The final category consists of plays that create on stage a whole supernatural world, filled with devils, lions, orangutans.

In a No spectacle, a series of short plays, in which the performance is valued for its deliberate pace and its perfection, is interspersed with *kyogen* (mad words), comic sketches that relax the spectator's tension, performing the same function as the satiric interludes in ancient Greek tragedy.

For a time, the No plays lost a good part of their audience. Cries of alarm were raised: No was dying. Then the apathy, which had lasted for thirty years, ended and the No plays found an audience again. It is a pity that they no longer have the social cachet they once possessed. To be seen at a No play was felt to be a sign of taste, but today's No plays have fans who experience them as though they were a ceremony.

Bunraku and Takarazuka, Gagaku and Kagura

Traditional Japanese theater also includes Bunraku, most notably the puppet theater in Osaka, which, at the end of the seventeenth century, presented plays by a celebrated author, Monzaemon Chikamatsu. The text is declaimed by a narrator, while the puppets are handled by manipulators who wear black and are visible to the audience. The plays performed today are dramas of social customs or historical events. They recount typical conflicts of aristocratic Edo society, most often conflicts caused by passionate love.

In reaction to the classic theater, Takarazuka attracts the crowds; in it all the parts are played by women. Founded in 1919, the Takarazuka music hall is associated with a name for a village about eighteen miles from Osaka, a resort well known for its hot springs. An amusement park with merry-go-rounds and the usual traveling booths surround the music hall buildings. One sees few men there, and usually they are teachers of dance, singing, or music. Invited by one of them, I was taken by car through streets bordered by wooden houses in which are lodged the "young ladies," who indeed are recruited very young. Each house harbors residents of a particular age; they are model dormitories, and strict regulations bar men from troubling the "vulnerable" girls—that is, the adolescents. As in the Kabuki, where male homosexuality is inherent in certain roles, in the Takarazuka there are lesbian associations; hence the players' fame is as much the result of scandal as of talent.

Gagaku is music for the eyes, which must be seen as it is played in the Imperial Palace at Tokyo. Twice a year, at nine o'clock in the morning, the palace opens its doors to a thousand privileged guests. The concert hall is glacial, thoroughly uncomfortable, but when the orchestra members are seated right and left on their platforms, eyes and ears are transfixed. Excitement grips the spectator. The wind instruments—a round oboe, a mouth organ, and a transverse, German flute—alternate or harmonize with stringed instruments such as a pear-shaped lute and a table zither, or with percussion instruments such as a drum in the shape of a sandbox and a small or a large gong. This visual music accompanies Shinto marriage rites or Buddhist ceremonies, presenting a sonorous obbligato to the chanting of sutras.

Ennen is more directly tied to Shinto rituals. The actors belong to a religious community, and the plays are performed once a year on a fixed date, at varying sites. Such ceremonies have been presented since the twelfth century; they experienced a decline in the fifteenth, as the influence of the big temples diminished.

Kagura, a kind of popular No play also connected with Shinto ritual, is performed inside temples or in certain traditional villages, where the troupe is composed of the villagers. It is a kind of profane communion that lends itself to a whole range of amusements once a year. Similar rituals could be found in Europe during the Middle Ages, and vestiges persist in Europe's annual village festivals, some of which have not completely lost their sacred character.

MYTH AND REALITY IN THE CINEMA

The Japanese cinema tends to jolt the novice. This should not astonish us, when we know the Japanese feeling for the importance of beauty. The young generation of Japanese filmmakers possess brilliant qualities and sometimes show a promising inspiration. Yet, untrammeled and undisciplined, they sacrifice the rigorousness necessary to produce a masterpiece, pushing their theories to extremes. More than any other art, the cinema expresses the conflicts of Eros, "hidden at the bottom of the self like a snake at the bottom of a spring," the conflict of tradition with modernism, and of myth with reality.

In the 1960s, the big companies that had been responsible for the high noon of the great directors closed their doors one by one. In 1966, one-third fewer spectators watched films than ten years before. For the first time in a long while, no Japanese film was shown at the foreign film festivals. Three incidents illustrate the crisis of Japanese cinema in this period. The organizers of the Berlin festival in 1965 had accepted a Japanese film. But the Japanese authorities, not at all concerned with the filmmakers involved, denounced the film as erotic, whereupon the filmmakers, in protest, refused to send it to Berlin. Three Japanese films submitted that year to the Venice jury were disqualified. At Cannes the organizers were just as severe, stating: "This year the entries do not possess the qualities which have so moved us in Japanese films shown in previous years."

Akira Kurosawa, the most famous filmmaker in Japan, then played double or nothing by accepting offers from foreign producers. He involved his own production company in these co-productions, but it did not have the scope of the Toho company, with which he had earlier made five films. *Red Beard,* shot in three years, had to wait another ten years before being recognized and acclaimed abroad.

The five big Japanese film companies saw their studios deserted by the younger generation of directors, who had become independents. Among them was Nagisa Oshima, who made a sensation at Cannes in 1977 with *In the Realm of the Senses* and conquered the 1978 audience with *Phantom Love;* and Hiroshi Teshighara, the son of Sofu, famous throughout the world for his *ikebana* schools. In 1965, as the author-director of *The Face of Another,* Teshighara presented a cinematic psychoanalysis through the story of a man who usurps another man's identity by taking on his physical appearance thanks to plastic surgery and a mask.

In 1963, Teshighara had triumphed with *Woman in the Dunes,* a philosophical story that caught the attention of Europe and the United States—the same audience that had already saluted *The Island* as a masterpiece, establishing the reputation of Kaneto Shindo abroad.

In order to survive, the filmmakers did not hesitate to go into pornography. The big companies also counted on films about the *yakuza,* bandits who roamed Japan in the sixteenth and seventeenth centuries, pillaging and exacting ransom while sometimes protecting the weak and oppressed against the nobles' abuses. Some young independent directors—such as Sinsuke Ogawa and Yoichi Higashi—gained favor with a certain public by politically committed films that supported the new left.

Nagisa Oshima epitomizes cinematic genius. My first contact with Oshima's work dates from the release of *Diary of a Shinjuku Burglar* in 1966. I was chiefly struck by the discovery of an unexpected Japan. This discovery was deepened and enlarged by some of his other films: *The Ceremony, In the Realm of the Senses,* and *Phantom Love.*

In the Realm of the Senses, according to Oshima himself, is the story of a man and woman who confuse their real existence with their deepest sexual impulses, creating out of whole cloth a world of pleasure which unites them until they elect to die.

Phantom Love is also a story of love and death. An aging ricksha driver is married to a beautiful, still-young woman who responds to the advances of a young man. The lover kills the husband and with the help of the wife throws his body in an abandoned well. But the crime haunts the lovers, and the ghost of the victim appears before the wife and the people of the village. The lovers cannot escape human justice.

During the Cannes festival in 1978, Oshima pointed out what was Japanese in this film. "The lovers might appear to you cast into hell by their sexual impulses, but in my view it is the rumbling of the earth, the murmur of the wind, the soughing of the trees, the song of the birds and insects, in short it is all of nature which guides the couple in its descent into hell. . . . Traditional Japanese art often makes use of ghosts. The ghost in my film is quite different. He is born from folklore which the Japanese have been able to preserve and perpetuate from generation to generation. It is an authentic ghost, of a sort rarely seen on the stage or screen. For Seki and Toyoji, as for the people of the village, it is not a question of the imaginary: they have really seen it and walk straight into the supernatural world. However, today's spectators, I am well aware, will not see a ghost except by making an effort of the imagination."

Two great men have revealed the true Japanese cinema: Kurosawa and Mizoguchi. (One should add, to be fair, Kinoshita, Ozu, Kinugasa, and Uchida.) It was in 1951 that Kurosawa received the Gold Lion at Venice for *Rashomon*. He was not all that happy about it, for *Rashomon* did not seem to him a major work. The scenario had been imposed on him by the producer. Besides, Kurosawa's filmography is sufficiently abundant so that one can believe him when he states that this film is representative neither of his work nor of Japan, even if we loved it.

None of his films explain him better than *Dodes Ka-Den*, in which his piercing view of Japanese poverty reveals both despair in the face of harsh reality and a tender sympathy for the poor and disinherited. As for the famous *Seven Samurai*, one should not be misled: this film, in showing the frightened inhabitants of a village forced to turn to a group of warriors, reveals a realistic Kurosawa anxious to show his compatriots their stupidity. He is a painter with two sharply opposed views of Japanese postwar society; to him the Japanese can only be either samurai or pigs.

There could not be a panorama of the Japanese cinema, even a very incomplete one like this, without Kenji Mizoguchi. Tempted in 1941 by the ronin legend, he shot *The Loyal 47 Ronin*, but specialists in Japanese cinema are unanimous in saying that this film and the preceding *The Life of an Artist,* shot in the same year, mark the beginning of eleven years of artistic decline for him. Mizoguchi regained his old form with *The Life of Oharu*, which he himself regarded as his masterpiece. One should also mention the 1956 *Street of Shame*, a portrait of prostitutes, which had enormous success in Japan (it coincided with discussion in parliament about suppressing legalized prostitution). According to the producer of Misoguchi's chief masterpieces, the best contemporary Japanese directors have not found favor with critics in Japan. The big receipts come from abroad.

The Japanese cinema is a refuge of nonconformity. Better than any other art, it expresses the living drama of a society which is the prisoner of its ghosts and is incapable of shaking them off. Never have the Japanese myths declared themselves so forcibly; never before has a people been battered by so many truths about itself. The

Japanese cinema has at times been accused of sadism; it is, on the contrary, masochistic.

MYTH AND REALITY IN PAINTING

Curiously enough, it seems that the trauma of 1945 was necessary for Japan to find the path to freedom of expression, whether political or religious, intellectual or artistic. Traditional art has always been tied to power, and the close relations between the structure of art and of society were not due to chance when, in 1615, the most flourishing period of Japanese pictorial art began. It appeared in the form of the *ukiyo-e*—an expression borrowed from Buddhism to express the transitory nature of life—which characterized Japanese art for nearly three hundred years, coinciding with the historic period called the Edo, the last before the Meiji restoration in 1868. *Ukiyo-e* can be translated as "images of a floating world." There are several interpretations of this phrase, but it would be restrictive to confine the concept to the ephemeral nature of life or, even more, to the painting of pleasures. *Ukiyo-e,* like literature, was profoundly rooted in Japanese civilization. Utamaro, Hukosai, and Korin are specifically Japanese masters whose art cannot be confused with an art born of either a Chinese or a Korean heritage, or a religious inspiration that came from the Continent. After having been scorned, *ukiyo-e* finally acquired universal acceptance from about the middle of the eighteenth century.

It was at this period that the *bakufu* (designating the shogun's administration) established censorship of "printed materials." One of the two governors of Edo was empowered to ensure that nothing would discredit the government, and that public morality was always protected. The governor was also responsible for protecting artistic propriety. He had the power to inflict on offenders a whole series of graduated penalties, from warnings to exile for a given period. Authors, artists, engravers, printers, editors, and even censors, when their negligence was proved, were severely punished. The procedure appeared simple: the editor was required, before making the engraving or printing, to submit the artist's original drawing to the nearest censor, who if he had any doubts, had to take it to the governor himself.

One should recall that Japan's entire artistic production since its origins was not open to everybody, but was the monopoly of hereditary family corporations which enjoyed a certain social standing and were organized according to the same model as the various artisan professions. We have written proof of the existence of a corporation of painters which dates from the reign of the Emperor Yu-Ryaku (457–479), who invited craftsmen's families from Korea and China to exercise their profession in Japan. The conception of heredity in a family of artists was extended to adopted children or to those brought into the family by marriage. But they paid for the protection they enjoyed by submission to their patron; each time the patron changed, the artists' families had to adapt themselves to a new ethic or a new aesthetic in line with the desires of the man commissioning their work. Thus in the Nara period, which ran from 710 to 794 and coincided with the establishment of the centralized power that instituted Buddhism as the state religion, artists reproduced scenes from Buddha's life, and the Horiuji at Nara is the depository of what remains of the marvels of this period.

However, the golden age of Japanese painting came in the Heian period, from the ninth to the twelfth centuries, with what is called the *yamato-e*. This art, which employs a very strong line to draw contours, deals with secular themes, such as the four seasons, famous sites, and seasonal labors, although these themes are developed under the influence of esoteric Buddhism. *Yamato-e* painting also narrated court chronicles, as in the "Genji Scroll." Two different styles appeared in these works, one of which marks the debut of the tradition of humorous Japanese drawing. The other, introduced by Chinese immigrants, produced in the seventeenth century a refined painting marked by mannerism.

From 1615 on, the shogunate of Tokugawa, founded in 1603, succeeded in establishing once again a centralized government. It formalized the privileges of the aristocrats and military men (who received fixed revenues in the form of annual gifts of rice) and set up a precise hierarchy of three other classes: peasants, artisans, and merchants. The behavior of the aristocrats, the costumes of the samurai—everything was controlled by censorship. The peasants, grouped in clans of five families each, kept watch over one another and were responsible for the correct performance of their duties. Citizens were controlled by a system of corporations. Trips abroad were forbidden. Christianity, a foreign religion, was proscribed. Art participated directly in this politico-police organization.

How did *ukiyo-e* develop in such a climate, and above all how did an art so hemmed in and watched over in order to serve the objectives of the class in power rapidly become a popular folk art, almost an art of the masses, so great was its impact in the cities? According to Lubor Hajek, the only explanation is that the links between art and intellectual and cultural life were stronger than the links of art with power, in whatever form.

This period was marked by a long series of confrontations between the police and art, because art sometimes served the government but never the police. The themes of the *ukiyo-e* are concerned with the leisure-time pleasures of a certain style of life, but in reality they go further than simple representations of everyday scenes in the life of fashionable actors, or the pastimes of Japanese society.

The portraits of actors or the very beautiful women of the period evoke a theatrical art and have for us the value of documents. Moreover, in reaction against traditional amorous lyricism, which was a trifle affected, the portraits of famous geishas, comparable to those of our favorite actresses, were painted in a setting which must have seemed scandalous, in Yoshiwara—a district reserved for pleasure which has played an important role in Tokyo from the eighteenth century to the present time. These prints are often accompanied by inscriptions: Geisha So-and-So, from such-and-such a house; Masako, prostitute in this brothel, etc., with her address and price. *Asai Ryoi* (Tales of a Moving World), which appeared in Kyoto in 1661, presented a naturalistic explanation of the *ukiyo-e* world: "To live in the present moment, solely, to know and to be attentive only to the beauty of the moon or the snow, the cherry blossoms, the leaves of the maple tree, to sing, drink, be happy, and let oneself float along or simply be carried, to respond to the fixed glare of misfortune with sovereign indifference, to reject all discouragement and, like a straw, abandon oneself to the river's current, such is the ephemeral, moving world. . . ." This artistic movement thus appears to be tied to nature and its vitality, to the feelings of a man who identifies naturally with sexual power. It arises from the deepest sources of Japanese tradition. The blossoming of a form of art bearing the imprint of sex occurred about 1640, the date when the first paintings of courtesans appeared; it can be explained by the philosophical and religious current derived from Shinto. The two earliest compilations of Japanese history described the creation of the worlds by the gods in completely realistic language, as can be seen in this dialogue of the Izanagi-Izanami couple:

"How is your body made?"

"It develops everywhere but in one place. . . . And yours?"

"Mine, like yours, develops everywhere, but especially in one place. Would it not be good to put this excessive part of my body in this retracting part of yours? So then we would create some new countries. . . ."

All of Japanese mythology is saturated with sexuality, which explains the persistence of the phallic cult that today is still very widespread in the rural world. In the seventeenth century, the erotic print would find two sources of inspiration: the Kabuki and the brothels—truculent, fantastic, and violent Kabuki, glorifying passionate love, whose characters can be found again in the subjects of the prints; and the Green Houses, whose charms have been described by Edmond de Goncourt:

> The girls of Yoshima are brought up like princesses. From their childhood they are given a complete education. They are taught reading, writing, the arts, music, tea, perfume (the perfume ceremony sometimes resembles the tea ceremony: one mingles some perfumes, which are burned, and one must guess these perfumes from their odor). They

are all just like princesses raised in the security of a palace. Then why be concerned about an expenditure of three thousand *rio?* . . . Now, among these *daimiyo,* these literate gentlemen and these women who have received the education of great courtesans, the contact of two epidermises does not take place immediately. . . . Three visits were almost indispensable to arrive at intimacy: the first visit, which is only a gallant introduction to the woman; the second, which is a redoubling of the first, with the granting of a few familiarities; and finally the third visit, which is called the visit of "a matured acquaintance."

Yoshiwara was of great importance in Edo, for there was born and developed a culture that Japan integrated into the everyday life of its citizens. The creation of this reserved quarter was authorized in 1617 by the shogun. Anxious to have a means of bringing pressure to bear on the provincial notables, he forced his attendant lords to spend one year out of every two near him in Edo. Soldiers, men engaged in commerce, and unmarried servants lived in the capital as bachelors—hence there was a great disproportion of men and women. So Yoshiwara was at first frequented by warriors, rich nobles, established merchants. The girls came from the countryside. Their initiation, in marriage robes, was marked by a procession through the quarter, followed by great merrymaking. In this milieu of pleasure, in which, as in any Japanese institution, an etiquette reigned, the most accomplished prostitutes became high-ranking courtesans, *tayu,* famous throughout Japan. Gradually, however, Yoshiwara's clients changed as warriors and nobles were replaced by parvenu merchants. It was the end of the reign of Yoshiwara's courtesans. Other reserved quarters were created, frequented by the middle class. Visitors to these quarters, filled with memories and legends of Yoshiwara and of its rituals, made great efforts to revive it. This was the period of the *iki,* a sort of mental ambiguity, as only the Japanese knew how to create it, in regard to sexual matters. The *iki* style was imposed very quickly in the reserved quarters and survives in Tokyo by night. It was good form to be *iki.* It is worthwhile, if one goes often to nightclubs in the Japanese capital, to learn *iki* manners. Quite soon there was an *iki* art, an *iki* painting, which reflects the *ukiyo-e* of the eighteenth century, certain Kabuki plays, and the music of samisen.

Ukiyo-e, essentially inspired by eroticism, has gained worldwide renown thanks to a few names. It was Utamaro, the most famous in the West, who caught Goncourt's attention. Speaking of this artist's prints, he said:

> . . . the erotic pictures of this people should be studied by the enthusiasts of drawing because of the fiery passion and fury of these copulations, as if enraged; the jumbled heap of these ruttings which overturn the room's partitions; the entanglements of these bodies which seem melted together; the nervous movements of these arms, at once pulling

and pushing in the act of coition; the epilepsy of these feet with their twisted toes, beating the air; these kisses with mouth devouring mouth; these women's swoons, their heads flung back on the floor with the "little death" on their faces, their eyes closed beneath heavily painted lids; and finally, this strength, this power of line, which makes the drawing of a penis equal to the hand in the Louvre attributed to Michelangelo.

At the end of the eighteenth century and the beginning of the nineteenth appeared Hokusai, whose delicacy of line confers a kind of trademark on his work. He began his career with portraits of actors, but soon showed that he was more interested in the audience than in the players. Then, in a series called "Thirty-six Views of Fuji," Hokusai revealed his talents as a painter of landscape. His most famous etching shows Fuji emerging from the waves breaking on Kanagawa beach.

Korin, more academic, is distinguished by his very elaborate representation of flowers and plants. "One must speak of Korin's decorative art, but the true artistic value of the painter is due to this—that whether on paper, silk, or lacquer, he lets them sing out their beauty or deliberately keep their natural silence. . . . In his most beautiful works he presents them playing a solo." In this passage, Yone Noguchi, a poet, points to one of the fundamentals the Japanese aesthetic has inherited from Zen: the irreplaceable value of stripping bare, which sets off the unique object or central detail of a work.

Korin and Sotatsu, whose brush was capable of extracting the symbol or, if you will, the essence from reality, were preceded by the school of Kano, a dynasty of painters whose works can be considered the ancestors of engraving. Eitoku Kano, the most famous of the line, very quickly escaped the narrow confines of engraving, painting on silk, or decorating lacquer. He first made the large frescoes in the immense reception halls of Azuchi castle and later did the frescoes in Osaka. He used gold leaf to heighten the color of his paintings, all of them stamped with a certain majesty.

From Nara to Meiji, twelve centuries of seclusion forged an original art, both realistic and dreamlike, an art which, while owing everything to China, acknowledges in its expression a purely Japanese quality, at times harder, more powerful, more cruel, more stripped bare, at other times softer, sweeter, more complex. Contemporary Japanese painting—which owes everything to the West—has not yet discovered how to create a native art in this way. But what can contemporary art mean to a Japanese? Suzuki says: "Nothing. The abstract is finished." Himself a painter of Buddhist inspiration, Suzuki especially reveres the goddess Kannon, whose obsessive face can be seen through a field of reeds or in a floral composition. He is, in fact, an abstract painter who does not know it; in this sense, he illustrates the drama of the Japanese artist caught between having to make a choice as an artist and his revulsion in regard to taking any definite stand.

SCULPTURE

Taro Okamoto, born in 1911, came to dinner at my house together with some Japanese intellectuals to meet the French statesman and academician Edgar Faure. After the meal, Faure, discoursing brilliantly, as was his habit, on the American involvement in Vietnam, noticed to his acute dismay a small Japanese seated on a cushion in front of him and snoring away. He interrupted himself to ask: "Who is that?" All my Japanese friends burst out laughing, while Taro Okamoto woke with a start, got up, and left the house "in the English style." In the thirties, Okamoto was in Paris, where he met Breton, Miró, Picasso, and Max Ernst. He returned to Japan in 1940 for army service in China. In 1952 he had a show in France, then in the United States. His nostalgia for ancient Japan is brought to life in his book *The Japanese Tradition.*

In Tokyo, astonishment and perplexity overcame many passersby when on the south side of Sukiyabashi Square, at the entrance of the Ginza, Okamoto's sculpture *The Clock of Youth* appeared. (Okamoto is in the habit of saying: "Salvador Dali is the Taro Okamoto of Europe.") His immoderate taste for "modesty" can be seen in this monument of dwarfish scale, like a piece of a broken tower, its pedestal flanked by the horns of buffaloes or perhaps aurochs. The average Japanese stops, shakes his head—*"Sodes ne!"*—then casts a furtive glance at his watch, comparing his time to that shown on the clock, and continues walking.

Like painting, modern sculpture in Japan searches for a point of reference. Many Japanese artists live in America and Europe, or attend Western schools. More than a thousand Japanese painters and sculptors have settled in Paris, of whom none has attained fame. The drama of contemporary Japanese art inheres in the inability of its practitioners to find a creative compromise in the fusion of Japanese tradition with one or another of the Western movements.

In the Edo period—that is, before the opening of Japan to the West—sculpture, mainly at the beginning of the eighteenth century, betrayed the influence of the Ming dynasty in China. But truly great Japanese sculpture remains tied to the Nara period. The works are fashioned by a Japanese technique, perfectly mastered, that involves lacquer or clay. In the Toshodaiji temple at Nara, one can admire the portrait of Ganjin, the most ancient known effigy in lacquer; this Chinese priest who founded the temple in 759, served as a model for one of his pupils just a few days before his death. Also at Nara, at the southern entrance of the Todaiji temple, one finds the Kongorikishi, half-naked guardians sculpted in terra cotta in 1203, a reconstruction (in the Kamakura period) of the burned treasures of the old capital.

CALLIGRAPHY

Calligraphy is the only Japanese art that has not suffered from the inroads of time, maintaining its popular appeal and reconciling the preoccupations of today with yesterday's style. There are many schools of calligraphy throughout Japan and it is not unusual to hire a calligrapher to commemorate certain ceremonies (marriages, entertainments) or to solemnize certain acts (a donation, an adoption).

He prepares his instruments with great care, spreading out his ink and brushes on the tatami, then he cautiously unrolls his paper, which will absorb just as much ink as is necessary to ensure the desired thickness of each stroke. The master makes dozens of sketches, then suddenly, feeling that he is in form, with swift strokes of his brush he traces his poem or message. With a single stroke he reaches the end of each *kanji*, or ideogram. Then he takes out his seal, with which he will authenticate his work.

Hachiro Kanno, a Japanese painter who sought refuge in Paris, has abandoned canvas and gone back to bamboo pens and Chinese ink in a conscious and deliberate return to Japanese tradition. He says: "The absence of color is not a limitation, because one can suggest all the colors by shades of black and white."

MUSIC

Tokyo's Conservatory of Music was established by imperial edict on October 4, 1887. Since 1882, the method of teaching music had been copied from foreign systems. After the conservatory opened, Western music was given priority, and the teaching of Japanese music was not permitted until 1936. One can never say enough about the miracle represented by the enthusiastic adoption of Western classical music by all the people here. I witnessed this phenomenon during the first Japanese tour of the National Orchestra of the French Radio-Television network. Charles Munch was making his first big tour abroad. One night, during a reception in the garden of my house in Kakinokizaka, where all the important names in Tokyo's musical world had come to honor him, he told me confidentially: "I have never seen so attentive and so knowledgeable an audience. Here one finds a whole new breath of inspiration."

The infatuation of the Japanese public for classical Western music no doubt has contributed to the blossoming of talented composers like Takemitsu, Mayuzumi, Ishii, and such world-famous conductors as Ozawa. These votaries of great music, after having taken pains to produce works in the strictest dodecaphonic tradition, have, like the painters and sculptors, come to doubt the roots of their inspiration. Thanks to certain technical modifications, they think that they are much closer today to the creation of original, authentically Japanese works, and would thus be examples of a successful compromise.

The phenomenon of pop music is now evident in the street. Wherever there is a concentration of stores, one can find record shops, most of which sell imported records, "in the name of international friendship," but also to beef up the balance of payments. Indeed, the price of imported records is lower than that of records made in Japan. Japan's own record business has experienced a sharp drop in sales, because of the very small number of "hit songs" recorded in Japan in recent years. Of course, the two sisters who sing duets and are called Pink Lady are still successful. Nagissa Sindobado (Sinbad the Sailor) sold 950,000 records and earned $12 million, but this feat has never been repeated. Goro Noguchi appeared at the end of 1978 in a one-man show attended by a mob of adolescents. Western influence on him is still preponderant, and it is quite significant that Noguchi's best-selling album was cut at Polydor Studios in Los Angeles. But the palm still goes to imported pop music in the person of Bob Dylan. For ten years the Japanese negotiated to induce him to come. Finally, he arrived in February 1978 for a tour of ten shows; his fee of $1.5 million was largely covered by the fans. There had been nothing like this since the Beatles and the Rolling Stones.

Among the fashionable infatuations is the disco phenomenon. At Ginza, Akasaka, Roppongi, Shibuya, and Shinjuku, discotheques are increasingly crowded, since the age range of customers has broadened, including people fifty, sixty, and even older. The most crowded clubs are often carbon copies of well-known Western discotheques. At the start, a generation gap existed: those older than twenty-five abstained. Then people grew accustomed to the excess of decibels, and since in Japan one goes further than elsewhere, where people in Europe or the United States are content with sixty to seventy decibels, in Tokyo they have gone happily to eighty, even ninety.

A young audience for the classical concerts, a young audience for pop music, a young audience for jazz or rock, a young audience in the discotheques—this is the paradox of a demographically aging country where at each step one bumps into young people. Should one call the statistics real and regard as a myth this uninterrupted flood which engulfs visitors at Shibuya and Shinjuku? Where is the real Japan to be found? In this infatuation with music, whether rhythm or melody, I have always sensed a new "Japanese" duality: rhythm dominates the day, to be gradually effaced by melody as night falls.

III: REALITIES

3: The Japanese at Home

THE TRADITIONAL FAMILY SYSTEM

Japanese emotionalism inclines somewhat to a certain nostalgia for that past wherein the father of a family filled the role of patriarch, ordering around his sons and daughters-in-law, his daughters and grandchildren, and of course his wife. He received his authority directly from the emperor-god and exercised it within the framework of Shintoism, in which the basic unit was the extended family. Three or four generations lived together, in accordance with rules accepted by all. The *ié*, or family clan, has always been the foundation of the social order, and every Japanese individual defines himself in the light of two criteria: context and function. Context means locality, whether it is a matter of a village or town, a company or university; function indicates profession and title, and serves as a personal reference.

Consider the ubiquitous calling card: whereas Westerners glance first of all at the individual's name, Japanese give primary attention to that of the company. Further, the company for which a person works—the context—has more importance than his function in the company. It is more important to stress the fact that a person belongs to the Mazda Automobile Company than to indicate that he is the director general, although in this case the function is important enough to figure under the name. Quite often a Japanese who has a subordinate position has his name printed in small letters below the large name of the company. A Ph.D matters less than the university from which it was received, above all when the university is Todai, Kyodai, or a private university as prestigious as Keio or Waseda.

THE *IÉ*, FOUNDATION OF THE SOCIAL ORDER

The conception of the *ié* appears at all levels of society. By extension, today it expresses the reality of the group to which every individual belongs and so the context serves as a criterion for identification. Of rural origin, the *ié* is today a social group composed of members of the same family, including individuals who have been adopted into it, sometimes as fellow craftsmen or in exceptional circumstances such as war or accident or just chance. Interpersonal relations within the group are more important than any other. That is why a daughter-in-law, who has come from outside, will assume a more important place than the daughter who has left her family's house when she married. This extends to the son who leaves home and the son-in-law who comes to live with his wife's family.

Though the family system, linked with moral precepts dating from feudalism, is beginning to disappear as an institution, it remains morally rooted in each individual's heart. There exists in Japanese society a family law that, beyond all the vicissitudes and accidents which may modify it or alter the unity of the group, helps to establish complex bonds which death itself cannot break or cancel.

The progressive disappearance of the *ié* in its traditional form is chiefly the result of the change in its environment. The *ié* is disappearing at the same time as the rural world from which it came. Individuals can hold on to their romanticism, yet the society which surrounds them inexorably pursues a different course. Today it is more and more rare to experience in the cities the poetic vision of a wooden Japanese house deeply ensconced in a garden; in the past, the Shibuya and Meguro districts were adorned with many such houses. In places where some of them have managed to survive, large apartment houses a dozen stories high block the sun.

Old Madame U. has succeeded in saving her wooden house from demolition. In the last ten years, she has received offers for it from several construction companies, who want to put up a large new apartment house in its place. Someday, perhaps, Madame U. will no longer be able to turn down their offers. When she dies, her son will certainly be tempted to sell. If he resists this temptation, there is no doubt that her grandson will succumb. Madame U. was once a highly esteemed geisha. She loved to sit in her garden with strewn sacred rocks. A manicured green lawn surrounds a miniature lake into which a small waterfall empties amid reeds and pine trees. One approaches the lake on rocks placed at random; one false step will cost you your soul. Meanwhile one hears the plaintive notes of the shamisen, whose strings Madame U. plucks as night falls. In the minuscule lake, carp and red fish, symbols of immortality, swim in circles; they are symbols also of life's capacity to renew and adapt itself.

Although one can buy carp almost anywhere in Tokyo, and one can come upon them in aquariums on the fortieth floor of a skyscraper in the capital, it is hard to imagine that the rhythm of life of the traditional *ié* can survive in the setting of a modern apartment. In rural areas, the shared household helped maintain the cohesion of the clan's members, and this cohesion was reinforced by the relations prevailing among the members of the family, and by the house's spaciousness, which was enough to ensure the comfort of two to four generations. Each member of the family had an assigned rank; the order of precedence was systematically arranged from oldest to youngest.

It is said in Japan that tradition is dying because of the force of a devastating modernism. But despite the process of intense urbanization, it is quite obvious that the structure of the traditional family has been miraculously preserved. The *ié* is still the basic institution in society. Initially, the family clans, shifting from rural to urban occupations, maintained their structure and simply moved from the country to the outskirts of the cities. The *ie* could perpetuate itself all the more readily since Japan's idea of a city differs markedly from Europe's. Tokyo and Osaka still remain a conglomeration of villages, a mosaic of *iés*, as is apparent in the residential quarters. The true transformation appeared when the *ié* began to break up because of the proliferation of vertical dwellings. The Japanese with their *tokonoma*—sacred decorative niche—their *tatamis* and *shojis*, have made a great effort to keep the inner order of the traditional home alive in their apartments. But sharing by various generations has very quickly proved impossible for reasons of space, while relations with other people living on the same floor in a modern apartment house pose, according to the Japanese code of interpersonal relations, a problem that did not exist when one's neighbor lived in a separate building. But when this difficulty had been resolved, young couples do live with their relatives in apartment houses, still taking off their shoes at the apartment door, sitting and sleeping on the tatami. Sliding doors open on a garden arranged so as to give the illusion of depth. Yet the revolution in a system such as that which governs the family goes well beyond a style of life. The head of the family, while keeping the affection and loyalty of his close relatives, has seen their sense of obligation and duty gradually disappear. The moat between the generations has become wider here than even in the United States. If Tokyo has never been a hippie or punk capital, like Katmandu, Bangkok, London, or San Francisco, the *futen* (Japanese hippies) who until quite recently used to hang out around the Shinjuku railroad station have encountered their compatriots' almost complete incomprehension.

Nevertheless, a real challenge to the family has arisen, whether from the young or from certain sectors of society excluded from prosperity, or from a wide segment of those residents of rural areas (60 percent of the population in 1945, 16 percent today) who have been displaced and have not been able to find a decent life in the cities. Such pauperization can only lead to mounting tension and revolution. The beneficiaries of urbanization, above all the industrialists, enjoyed boom times in the sixties. They began to assume, within their firms, the authority which the father of the family could no longer wield. A kind of reconstitution of the *ié* began in the factories; in one, it was the hiring of all the members of the same family; in another, employment was found for a whole demobilized unit of the imperial army, which retained its old hierarchy. And everywhere employment for life was offered the employee, conditional of his total loyalty to the head of the company, who had in fact become the family father. This paternalistic approach was at times threatened by the rapid growth of the major companies, their size destroying de facto all possibility of any approach to management other than a purely technical one.

To understand the challenge to the family system, one must go to Enoshima, a small island forty-five miles southwest of Tokyo. At the beginning of the century it was a famous seaside resort, to which citizens of Tokyo would take a weekend excursion, spending Saturday night in a hotel. In the twenties going to Enoshima was exciting, all the more since one could take the train on the first railroad line built in Japan: Tokyo-Yokohama-Fujisawa. Today the island is no longer an island, since one can get to it over a bridge. A long street bordered with "by-the-hour" hotels and souvenir shops leads to the top of a hill, where a pine forest has been pretty much cut down to make room for an amusement park. The beach has been narrowed to accommodate a harbor for pleasure boats. But you ought to go to Enoshima, even though Enoshima today does not fill the social role it filled in the past. Only twenty years ago, a trip to the island enabled young Japanese couples compelled to be chaste by the lack of privacy in the *ié* to put a seal on their natural desires. They went to places like Enoshima following a kind of tacit convention.

Today other desires prompt a young couple to go to a hotel on Enoshima. It is no longer a question of evading the *ié* but simply of going to breathe some fresh air after a week's work or to escape for a few hours from cramped city dwellings. A change in the demographic structure has seen an increase in the elderly in proportion to the young, and young people now prefer to live by themselves. The relations between men and women have changed as a result of the liberalization of sexual customs and the status of women, who more and more often work.

Public Space and Private Space: Two Kinds of Behavior

Without going so far as to claim that the Japanese love myth and dream and hate reality, one must nevertheless admit that their natural predisposition is to prefer the dream. This is translated into the traditional house and also into the modern habitat. In fact, one might think that Tokyo, destroyed twice in a single century—first in 1923 by the great Kanto earthquake, then in August 1945 by American incendiary bombs—would have profited from circumstances to rebuild according to a careful city plan and the most modern architectural canons. If that had been done, one would not have the irritating impression, on one's first contact with Tokyo, of traveling through the streets of an immense shantytown. Yet this first impression has to be corrected in light of the concept of private space, as well as in terms of the refinement of the Japanese house. André Corboz, professor of architecture at the University of Montreal, has written: "The traditional Japanese house astonishes us by its 'modernity.' European artists first used it as a source—for the flat tints of the Impressionists and, a quarter of a century later, for the architectural advocates of functionalism who, in its geometric and graphic aspects, discovered the principles of modular composition and a high degree of standardization in a system that is more than just ingenious."

The concept of public space versus private space expresses the duality between which all Japanese evolve: on one side, everyday reality, hence a life in a context of duty, which one must share with others; on the other side, a life of dream, in a freely chosen context where obligations are no longer imposed. To each of these domains there corresponds a concept of space: the anonymous space of the street, of public transportation (which, paradoxically, produces a liberalization of behavior: in the street or subway one can do what one wishes, throw greasy papers or Coca-Cola bottles on the ground), and the space of one's house, one's office inside which one applies the rules of an inveterate aesthetic tradition.

The Japanese house has not changed much since the thirteenth century, when the samurai class became the privileged class and Zen prevailed as the ethic of conduct. The samurai house gradually copied the Zen priests' habitation, and in the fifteenth century a style of domestic architecture was born whose interior arrangement was defined by: the *toko*, the room's central alcove; the *tana*, a niche situated near the *toko* and provided with shelves; the *shoin*, a bay window open to the outside, facing which is a small table that permits one to write or read; the *genkan*, a kind of porch that leads to the entrance door.

This style of house, called *shin zukuri*, succeeded the more sumptuous residence of the Heian period, but differed, despite its simplicity, from the traditional farmhouse in the more advanced sophistication and the volume of the interior space. In the sixteenth century at Edo, they built more simply and on a more restricted scale. Today, whatever the size of the house, one finds the proportions of the ancient original, evolved by now into what is called the *sukiya* style—that is, a pavilion joined to a garden—the model for which one can visit in Kyoto, in the grounds of the Katsura, the imperial villa.

There are certain privileged places in the world where one is overwhelmed by a plenitude of beauty. Such is the shock of Chichén Itzá in Yucatán, when from the top of a Mayan pyramid one contemplates the forest which was gutted thousands of years ago to make room for the temples of a peaceful people. Such also, from the top of a stupa, is the view of the course of the Irrawaddy River in Burma amid the temples in the boundless plain of Pagan. And such is the breathtaking amazement which seizes one at Angkor, when at night, by the light of torches, the sculpted figures of the Bayon transfix the visitor with their gaze.

At Katsura, one experiences the same plenitude, but it is less stupefying, less grandiose, because it is better adapted to the human scale. It is a place where beauty penetrates one's being, to the point of transforming restlessness into serenity. One discovers harmony, the calming of all those conflicts which make man struggle with those around him or pit him against himself. There would not be a Japanese style without this harmony of house and landscape, which appear intimately made for each other.

I lived in Tokyo in a traditional Japanese house. From its entrance one was aware of the long hallways made of creaking planks. The rooms were enclosed by sliding partitions of paper attached to lintels of very light wood. One had only to pull up the shojis and the exterior space appeared, arranged so as to be looked at from inside. A few feet of depth gave the illusion of several yards, due to a technique of optical distancing achieved with the help of a reflecting pool. Very important is the sound which accompanies vision, and for this reason the Japanese never fail to contrive small waterfalls and arrange for the complicity of a few birds.

So idyllic a house, in addition to being out of reach for the great majority, also has certain inconveniences which have to be overlooked, such as the total lack of any heating system. Since it is obligatory to take off one's shoes at the entrance, the tatami proves rather cold in winter. In the twenties and thirties, the traditional houses often added a room floored with old-fashioned red bricks, which served as a dining room or lumber room—it was a concession in bad taste to the Western style of living. A house built on stilts less than a yard high reacts to earthquakes without much damage, but its sanitary facilities are rudimentary, nonexistent on the first floor, and the other rooms are often drafty. Discomfort is the other face of the aesthetic. To moderate this, the Japanese wear flannel vests and isothermic underwear. Winter clothes are padded with swansdown. A hole in the center of the room, covered by a low table, permits one to sit on the floor at table level, while benefiting from the stove that heats the cover fitted to the table edges.

The rooms are functional because they are like adjustable modules suited to multiple uses: living room/dining room/bedroom. When night falls, the mistress of the house takes the sleeping mats from the wall cupboard and spreads them out for the night. In the morning they are folded again and put away.

Vertical Versus Horizontal Dwelling

These habits have not been lost in transition from a house to an apartment averaging 40 to 80 square yards in a large housing development. Such apartments offer the same degree of comfort as that found in the houses that rent for moderate sums on the outskirts of the large industrial cities. But the Japanese complain that there is a housing shortage. Since what is rare is automatically expensive, apartment rents, even far from the center of town, are not within everyone's means. It is not the construction costs that are responsible for the inflated prices. It is the land: At the center of Tokyo, it is ten times more expensive than in Paris or New York. In Tokyo, as everywhere in Japan, plots of land are leased by their owners to a real estate promoter for fifteen to thirty years. The rents the promoters charge are high, especially in quarters where only foreigners in extremely comfortable circumstances can afford to live. I have heard of rents up to $3,000 a month for 150 to 200 square yards of space.

This situation chiefly affects young people. They must be satisfied with housing arranged by their companies, some of which have built dormitories for unmarried employees. Young couples may live two hours away from the center of town. The housing crisis cannot be solved except by initiating orderly apartment construction throughout the capital.

There are more than eleven million owners of real estate in Tokyo, out of thirteen million inhabitants. Some attempts at concentration have produced spectacular results in certain quarters, but in general, concentration is impossible. Countless small owners have preferred to transform themselves into promoters and build their own small apartment house. The site is so small sometimes that at Akasaka one can see an eight-story apartment house built on a plot no larger than 20 to 25 square yards. Each floor has only one room. These buildings are leased at very high rentals to Japanese companies of all kinds, which appear and disappear with stupefying rapidity. The owners have sometimes built only the exterior walls and negotiated the rest of the construction by contract with their future tenant. Certain companies even agree to install, at their own expense, the façades and the often luxurious decorations of the public areas of the building, on the understanding that those areas bear the company's name. One can thus often orient oneself in Tokyo in relation to Misubishi, Mitsui, etc.

The vertical dwelling has also invaded the suburbs, where many important companies have made a big effort to house their personnel. Mr. Horiguchi, chief foreman at the naval shipyard at Ishikawajima-Harima, lives thirty minutes from his work, in an apartment house built by the company and reserved for its employees. Buildings there are divided into apartments of two or three rooms, grouped around the same landing: employees who work in a particular job or department of the company are located in the same apartment house. Thus the homogeneity of the group is indirectly preserved.

Mr. Horiguchi's two or three rooms on the ground floor open on a very sophisticated garden. When the family has tea with the windows open and with their backs to the *tokonoma*, they look out on a labyrinth of greenery that gives the illusion of great depth. So Mr. Horiguchi can consider that his space has been rigorously preserved under the conditions of modern life, at the same time that his wife has at her disposal all the gadgets she needs. Of course Mr. Horiguchi possesses a color television set, which is used by his wife in the empty hours of the morning and by his two children after four o'clock in the afternoon, when they return from school. Mr. Horiguchi's colleagues are less favored. They live on the floor above and the space there is not the same. Although the buildings are well separated from each other and are not symmetrically aligned face to face, the fact remains that families living in these apartments have lost their traditional space and environment.

THE JAPANESE AND HIS GARDEN

His garden assumes an enormous importance for the Japanese. This can be measured by how much he pays for the services of a trained gardener.

One outstanding type of Japanese garden is designed to simulate, with trees, rocks, and water, the elements of a natural environment, in generally subdued haft-tints. The gardens of the imperial villa of Katsura are a model of the landscaped Japanese garden. And since adaptation to the environment also means miniaturization, the Japanese have brought to perfection the art of associating miniature representation with reality: a small spill of water looks like a large waterfall, a small heap of earth looks like a mountain. Sometimes, in another type of garden, the Zen garden, perfectionism attains abstraction. Here a boundary at right angles, like the wall of the Zen garden of Ryobji at Kyoto, can suggest boundless space, just as raked sand can evoke the sea.

This need for harmony and the extension of self in nature expresses the psychology of the Japanese, existing in a limited space and perpetually confronted by their surroundings. Hence the individual's quest for what lies beyond the barriers that hem him in, and his natural predilection for everything that avoids confrontation or conflict. Whether it be a miniature, copied from a model one would like to see around oneself, or an abstraction, the harmonious extension of man in his dream, the Japanese garden exists only in Japan's historic duality. Mythical Japan inserts itself into the reality of a dangerously damaged environment whose protection can be assured only by an arsenal of laws. In Japan, as elsewhere, what is needed is a change of mentality. House, space, and garden—these bearers of harmony are all dependent upon a renewed habitat.

The vertical dwelling has not been a success in any of the industrialized countries. Its development has coincided with an increase in insecurity, the appearance of such social scourges as drugs, and the flourishing of negativity and despair. The Japanese needs reference points to guide his behavior. He does not know his "etiquette" except in a certain number of familiar circumstances, but any new situation forces him to find a new ritual of behavior. This does not yet exist in the large apartment houses. A whole art of living must be relearned. Why else do the Japanese drop tons of wax paper, beer bottles, and jam and jelly jars on their beaches, whereas they visit Japanese gardens devoutly and respectfully, sit down on a bench, meditate, and rediscover peace?

THE SITUATION OF WOMEN

Although it is still to his own home that the Japanese man turns most readily for calm and serenity, since 1945 the change in the relations between men and women or, more specifically between husbands and wives has challenged the traditional family system. Until the war, the man had incontestably ruled, at least so far as everyone could tell. The Japanese woman traditionally cared for the house, reared the children, walked a few steps behind her husband in the street, lunched or dined alone after serving him and his friends. All this took care of "face," the public view. It was unthinkable that a married woman could betray her husband. In the *ié*, adultery was contravened by the exiguity of space, the vigilant presence of one's neighbors, the difficulty of escaping the watchful eyes of the family. Yet it did happen. The Oshima film *Phantom Love* describes very well how, during the Edo period, a young village wife takes a lover, with whose help she later kills her husband. But a much more significant reality concerning woman's place in the family should be noted. When Mr. Horiguchi, chief foreman at the shipyard, receives his pay, he hands it over to his wife, who every day gives him his pocket money before he leaves for work. Moreover, since 1945 many women whose husbands have died or disappeared have been forced to go to work. Here one encounters one of the most crying injustices of Japanese society, because although women have improved their situation inside the family, acquiring a new freedom and a veritable emancipation, in their relations to all other social groups there has been stagnation, and in their working conditions, even regression. The female blue-collar worker in particular is subjected to discrimination with roots in a distant past.

In a very well documented inquiry, a French journalist thus schematized their social situation: Forbidden (or almost) to women are regular status as a worker; seniority; well-paid jobs; and allocations related to the cost of living (indemnities for housing, financial help for the children's education, family allowances). Reserved for women are temporary jobs; work in small businesses; the lower level of the salary scale; and limited educational opportunities.

The Japanese have never refused to bring women into the world of work. The success of the economy, thanks to the high quality of products such as transistors and integrated circuits, is the direct result of women's work. Quantitatively, the Japanese work market absorbs a larger female work force than European and American markets.

In the restricted circle of the family, however, Japanese men are repelled by their wives' leaving for work in the morning. They believe that if work is a source of alienation for men, it would be paradoxical to consider it a source of freedom for women. Qualitatively, the highest positions and in all cases the majority of managerial positions are held by men. Equality of pay remains a goal to be attained, even if the law compels the employer to give equal pay for equal work. A woman will often be hired at the same time as other members of her family—for example, her husband. The boss then commits himself to ensuring them a family income for life. Thus the work of many women is subsumed in the traditional practice of a paternalistic society and in the mechanisms of an economy that does not obey, in its internal rules, the laws of classic capitalist economics.

Women's place in Japanese society can be much better appreciated, from the outside, when one takes into account her true social freedom. Even married women appear in public. One sees them using public transportation, strolling alone in the stores, going to the movies and to the theater with their friends—in short, leading a life independent of their husbands. This real independence, formerly hidden, is today openly reflected both in sex and in the attitude toward having children.

The Japanese attitude to sex has always been tolerant, even in regard to what are called deviations, such as homosexuality. A troupe of well-known French transvestites found themselves in Tokyo with a broken contract; they sold themselves to the highest bidders on the sidewalks of Akasaka, at prices challenging all competition, and were thus able to buy plane tickets home. Yukio Mishima told me during an interview: "Homosexuality forms part of the

Japanese tradition. It was the American missionaries who upset this tradition in the nineteenth century."

The Japanese, although quite discreetly, show a pronounced inclination for love affairs, which range from the at times tragic romance to the simple, agreeable pastime, and all without restraint or taboo. A minimum of three meetings are considered necessary before attaining a certain intimacy, but once the barrier of "protocol" has been passed, sexual relations are simply begun and simply ended, at least so far as the women are concerned. (Romanticism and a propensity to declare oneself the owner of the sexual "object" are masculine attitudes.) The Japanese woman's sexual freedom is comparable to that of women in any other country in the world.

This goes hand in hand with her freedom in regard to childbearing. Soon after the war, the use of contraceptives and then abortion spread throughout the country. The American occupier was not badly received, but the rejection of the GIs' bastards by Japanese society made women cautious. In consequence, abortion became widespread. However, Japanese doctors have begun to ask certain questions. On the official side, they are worried about the decline in the birthrate and its consequences for the country's future. The medical fraternity sees that in fact abortion takes the place of contraception. Dr. Sugiyama, one of the thirteen thousand doctors with a license to perform abortions, told American colleagues: "Forty percent of my patients have recourse to abortion as a method of contraception. On an average they have undergone two or three operations, but it is not rare to come across women who are at their tenth abortion. In one month I performed eighty abortions and delivered only forty babies. In terms of experience and the technique of abortion, the United States is an underdeveloped and Japan is a developed country." More than 99 percent of the abortions are due to the presence of two to four children in the household. The number of children is not regarded by the Ministry of Health as a sufficient reason for aborting, and most doctors perform abortions under the rubric "health of the mother." This is far from the *ie*'s tradition whereby a sterile wife would be dishonored and repudiated.

The change in the Japanese woman's status has spread everywhere. In terms of the permanent duality of this civilization, the woman incontestably reigns in nighttime Japan and in large part in daytime Japan. She is, one should not forget, at the origin of the myth of myths, which gave birth to the imperial lineage: the myth of Amaterasu, the sun goddess. She is the dream, at the end of a day's work, in bars which fulfill a social function. She maintains her supremacy in the home, in the reality of her control of its economic resources. She is present everywhere: the favorite consumer for advertising and the world of business; the inspirer of all the arts, in which she symbolizes life. Even the *dojo* (clubs of the martial arts) today number as many women as men in all their disciplines.

Today in Tokyo and Osaka, or in any large city, a woman can envisage living alone, going out alone, leading a totally independent life. Single women haunt the lobbies of the big hotels, cocktail parties, cafés, and even dinner parties, not to mention theaters, movie houses, and cabarets. This is a result not only of emancipation but of a tolerance for the coexistence of modern behavior and traditional attitudes.

When I met Sachiko, I was uncertain about her age. Was she thirty-five, perhaps forty? I had struck up a conversation with her at one of those gigantic parties only the large multinational Japanese companies know how to throw. In the grand Heian salon of the Okura Hotel, about a thousand guests crowded around tables garnished with crayfish, sauces, and typical Japanese dishes. In the press of people, she bumped into me and my full glass spilled on her blouse. Seized by a fit of mad laughter, she took a handkerchief from her bag to wipe my suit, which was not wet. "This party brings bad luck," she said, then, very naturally, she asked if I was free to go to dinner. So we went to the top floor of the Sony building. Although the subdued lights favored intimate confidences, she did not stop laughing and sniffing at her whiskey-saturated blouse. In an hour we had not exchanged three words. I remembered the advice of a Japanese friend: "Above all, don't talk a lot, and avoid all flowery language, for it indicates a lack of virility." So I had replied in the Japanese manner with a kind of belch: "AAAhhh!" making the *a* sound rise from the bottom of my throat, and then adding after a pause: "Sodeska!" Oh, fine! I had been belching since the start of the evening, when suddenly, point-blank, she looked me straight in the eye and said: "What do you think of a Japanese woman who offers herself to a man? Is it possible? But you can be assured, I am not making any allusion to our tête-à-tête. We business women are women alone; we must know how to take care of ourselves."

I wanted to retort: "Yes, you *are* a business woman!" but I was careful not to. After a silence, she went on: "You know that in Tokyo since Expo '70 there are bars in which the exclusively female customers are welcomed by young men who play the part of 'bar girls.' With a bit of money, it is very easy for a lady of sixty to leave with a young man of twenty-five or thirty. The French or German escorts are quite successful. But the French escorts *always* have a lot of success. . . . By the way, we have not introduced ourselves. *I* find that very improper." At these words, I stood up, bowed in the Japanese manner, and extended my calling card, then sat down again opposite her. She began laughing uncontrollably and managed to splutter out in English: "You are crazy." Inadvertently I had handed her the calling card of a Japanese I'd met at the party. After coffee, she asked me to accompany her to the taxi stand. In the street, she snuggled up against me as she took my arm, and I proposed taking her home in my car. Suddenly she twined her arms around my neck and kissed me, murmuring in my ear: "My name is Sachiko." I didn't have time to react. She had been swallowed up by a taxi.

Some days later, I received a postcard from London, signed "Sachiko." She was there on a business trip. The card mentioned her telephone number in Tokyo. The next day, I phoned. A secretary answered in perfect English: "Miss Sachiko is not in Tokyo at the moment. Do you wish to leave your name and telephone number?" The same reply was given to me three or four times and I got tired of calling. Then one day her voice sounded at the other end of the wire. We made an appointment for that very evening, in the Shinjuku. I promised myself that that very day I would get to the bottom of the mystery of women in business. Just as I was leaving, Sachiko phoned me. "I am very tired, I really have to go straight home. But if you want to accompany me, come and pick me up at my office." She was waiting for me on the sidewalk. She slipped in next to me and told me where to drive. I hadn't the slightest idea where I was going. She didn't seem especially worn out. On the contrary, she appeared to be in excellent shape. That evening at her home I got a revelation about women's "marginality." Her confession was exemplary, but as in all such testimony, the witness arranged things a bit and had a tendency to glorify her own role.

"My parents are very rich, but to my father's great despair I did not have a brother, only three sisters. I took over his import-export business because he was too old, but at the price of a thousand difficulties and amid the hostility of the company's employees. Five office managers have handed in their resignation to put pressure on me, but contrary to their expectations, I accepted them. All rebellion has been stopped cold. My father then got it into his head to marry me off. He arranged a meeting with an imbecile who always showed off his dentures in what he thought was a smile. I made a scandal by declaring that I preferred good lovers to a bad husband. My father then decided never to see me again. This has gone on for three years. My mother comes to the office on the sly from time to time, or brings me delicacies here. The company is going fine—that's what's essential. But I can never reconcile with my father unless I get married."

"Why don't you see it as a possibility?"

"Never. I am too old, I love my freedom too much, and yet if I were to do it all over, I would listen to my father. I think that he was right, because I am not happy."

So Sachiko was ashamed of her freedom, her deliberate choice of nonconformism. How much more time before she collapsed into loneliness? With terror she saw it loom up as a revenge by this society she had rejected.

When I left Japan, Sachiko's business was doing very well. She was hardly ever in Tokyo, and once or twice she sent me postcards from the United States.

The feminine model for the sixties was Princess Michiko. A commoner, she would marry Crown Prince Akihito, the future emperor, so something had changed in the empire. Unfortunately, it was a dream for a true confessions magazine. Michiko became Princess Michiko, and a young, spontaneous girl soon was transformed, under the iron yoke of protocol, into what a Japanese women's magazine called a puppet. The Michiko myth disappeared with her first pregnancy, and Michiko S., who collected her idol's photos, one day spat on the ground and became a militant in the ranks of the leftist Zengakuren.

Leftism, ecology, and feminism have always been good bedfellows. Michiko's militant feminism includes these classic ingredients, but she adds to it her rancor at realizing that one more role model had fallen into the trap. The fate, in fact, of even the nonconformist student who has to find a job, and behaves prudently. That famous day when three hundred students were barricaded in the library of the University of Todai and kept ten thousand policemen at bay, I succeeded in walking with a white flag up to the door that the police would take by assault twenty-four hours later. Michiko was the student who opened the door for me, but I had a problem of vocabulary with her. She punctuated her phrases with an English profanity which rang out "Tchitt." Each time she uttered it, she seemed to be sneezing too loudly, but this was her way of expressing disgust.

"I go to the University of Nihon and I study audiovisual techniques, or rather I studied them, because for the last two months we have barricaded the campus and all courses have come to a halt. The bastard fuzz were waiting for us to come out, but they had another thing coming. . . . Through the garden, from one house to another, we succeeded in creeping through their encirclement so as to come and give a helping hand to our friends at Todai."

"What do you intend to do?"

"Now, fight. Tomorrow? Fight. After that, I don't give a damn."

"Do you have a boyfriend?"

"This is a fine time to ask me that!" She burst into laughter. "Of course, I sleep with boys, if that's what you mean."

"Do you intend to get married someday?"

"Your question is idiotic; who do you take me for?"

Just then a student came in, wearing a helmet and a mask, and barked out an order. Without so much as bidding me good-bye, she turned her back and left to rejoin her firing station behind a barricade of books.

Emiko works as a secretary at a big newspaper. When I phone her boss, the two of us often have labored conversations. I said to her one day, disguising it as a joke: "You have a very sweet voice. Do you want to show me what it is hiding?"

"I get out at six. If you want to see me, come and get me!"

"How will I recognize you?"

"That's easy—I'll recognize you. I have the advantage of already seeing you."

At six o'clock, she came up behind me and took me by the arm. We walked a few steps to a very tiny coffee shop. I did not know how to start the conversation. She did: "Aren't you married? You don't wear a ring."

"Do you have to wear a ring if you are married?"

"Yes, in Japan. So I can consider you not married."

"And you?"

"Me, I'm engaged. I think my father has found a good match for me. I see him from time to time at my house. We went out together for the first time last Sunday. He took me to Hayama. Do you know it?"

"Yes, very well, but this isn't the season—I doubt that you went swimming."

"No. We had lunch in a club, then we played miniature golf. We took a walk along the seashore and went home like good folks at seven o'clock. My mother had prepared a dinner for us. But he refused and went home."

"Was that good?"

"Yes, Toru-San does not talk very much. But he has a sports car and drives very well. And also he knows a lot about the cinema."

"What is his profession?"

"He works at a marketing service, at Matsushita. It is a job with a future."

"I am happy for you, Emiko."

"I am boring you with my problems," she added after a silence, taking my hand.

She was charming. I asked her to come to dinner with me. She did not reply, but ran to the telephone. Returning she declared in careful English, "It's O.K."

Some weeks later, Emiko admitted that her fiancé had been an invention but her lie had become a reality and she was crushed. This time she was really getting married. And she got married and I like to imagine that she found happiness.

Yuki, who comes from a modest family, married a merchant who owned a souvenir shop for tourists under the arcade of a grand hotel in Tokyo. I lived in the hotel for a time, and every morning I bought my newspaper in this store. Yuki had an attractive smile, and since at nine o'clock she had practically no customers, she would engage in somewhat droll conversation with me, in fluent English, which could have lasted all morning if I had wanted to listen. Yuki had a clerk whom I hardly ever saw, since he was usually in the back. One day, Yuki asked me, "Could you get me a pass for the NHK TV studios?"

When the chance presented itself, I phoned Yuki and arranged a tour. Full of amazement, she walked from the room of videotape machines to the room filled with computers, and was very impressed by the robot studio, where cameras programmed by a computer operated without a cameraman. At the end of an hour, Yuki left suddenly; she absolutely had to get back to her store. Three months later, she phoned and invited me to dinner. She lived near Yokohama in an extraordinary traditional house. A young maid opened the door and led me into a large bare room with a tatami, a room of great beauty but unfortunately illuminated by a white bulb that hung at the end of a wire. I sat down on a floor cushion and observed what details I could; the shoji screens were all closed. Coming in almost immediately after the maid had poured the green tea, Yuki sat down on the other side of the low table and slowly drank the burning hot, rather greasy liquid. I had never seen her in a kimono, nor with her hair piled high to show off her neck, powdered white and tapering like a geisha's.

"You know," Yuki said, "I am a widow. Actually, I have a man in my life, but it's off and on. He is the man you've seen at the store. We are associated, he and I, or rather he was associated with my husband. He hesitated a great deal before working with me, but he hasn't the money to buy the place. So he preferred to stay with me. That suits me too, because I could not continue the business by myself. I would have been forced to sell. . . . I'm happy that you accepted my invitation. I was afraid that you would refuse. A woman alone in Japan is really very much alone. My parents are too old to be companions. My in-laws are dead. I had a woman friend who often came to share my solitude, but she finally married—an old man; rich."

"And what about you? You're going to marry again, perhaps?"

"The opportunities slip away with the years. My husband wanted children very much, but I refused to have them. Now it is too late. I'd like to travel. I've heard that there are very cheap charters for Europe. Yes, I should take a trip—this country gives me the creeps." She added, bitterly, "After all, I am a free woman, isn't that so?"

The maid pushed the sliding door to my right and the small salon was metamorphosed into a very large dining room. Another low lacquer table was covered with all sorts of Japanese dishes. I was by now accustomed to Japanese cuisine, although it had taken several months of effort to refine my taste and to eat something besides tempura. I swallowed raw fish without difficulty; I even went occasionally to restaurants that specialized in sashimi. I was fascinated by this cuisine for the eyes. The art of the presentation of dishes is so accomplished that just the sight of a Japanese table sets one's gastric juices flowing. That night I was astounded; never had I seen so sumptuous a banquet of colors. My eyes were immediately caught by the enormous half crayfish reconstituted in each dish. For each of us, there were about fifteen small dishes, round, square, oval, smooth or notched on the edges, blue or white, decorated here and there with ideograms, filled with foods that had been unknown to me in Europe. Yuki took great joy in guiding me through the dishes.

"You'd do better to eat the hors d'oeuvre," she said, laughing. "You could begin with the *tsukemono*, pickled cucumbers and turnips, then continue with the *himono*: it is a cured mackerel, boned, cut in two and salted; taste the tofu. That is bean paste served cold, which you must season with soy. Ah! Here are some slices of *kamaboko*; this is a cake of white fish, which should be seasoned with soy and horse-radish."

"And there, in the bowl—what are those reddish flakes?"

"We call that *kimpira*, a fried root mixed with carrots seasoned with sugar, soy, and red pepper. In the bowl there, still steaming, is *misoshiru*, a soup with bits of boiled fish seasoned with *miso*, a paste of fermented beans, then some vegetables and a little tofu."

"And this shellfish?"

"It is called *sazae*, a shell shaped like a crown. It has been taken from its shell, boiled, put back inside, and seasoned with a little soy and sake. I have also had them serve you some sashimi. But you know that already. It is pink tuna, very tender. Then I have a surprise for you—a seasonal dish, which most likely you don't know but which you will like, I'm sure."

Yuki sat opposite me, like a man, while the maid, Masako, came to fill my cup with sake, not giving me time to catch my breath. I kept trying to persuade her to serve Yuki first. To some remark of Yuki's, Masako launched into a tirade which I did not understand. She knelt next to her mistress, and they had the look of accomplices. When I looked at her, Masako blushed. Then she came over to serve me yet another cup of sake, and Yuki said to me, "Masako would like to take some too." I looked around, but there was no cup.

"You must offer her your cup," Yuki continued.

I offered it to Masako, who drank, washed the rim of the cup from a fingerbowl, and then handed it back to me, serving me once again. I looked straight into her eyes. She blushed even more, and I noticed that she was pretty and mischievous. . . .

"Well, what about this surprise?"

"Do you like oysters?" Yuki asked. "I think that French people eat them raw. Although it is early in the season, I have had them sent up especially for you."

Masako reappeared and put a dish on the table.

"Still another dish before the oysters? But I won't be able to taste the oysters! In France we eat oysters as an hors d'oeuvre, not as dessert."

"But they are the oysters," Yuki said, a trifle primly. "We call this dish *dote-nabe.* The oysters have been cooked in a special earthenware casserole with sweet *miso.* They rest on chrysanthemum leaves. . . . No, they're not a decoration, you can eat them. They are very good. Masako has also brought you this bowl of raw egg. You mix up the yellow and white—it will be used to season everything."

I asked for another cup of saké, winking at Masako; at the same time I offered her another one.

I do not know what happened next. I found myself the next morning lying on a futon in the same room, wrapped in a *yukata* (a cotton kimono for the night), my clothes carefully hung on the clothes horse. I had really drunk too much saké, and I swore—a little late—that it would never get me again.

Saké is treacherous. A 14 percent alcoholic drink, it must be drunk hot and it flows easily down the gullet, giving you an incredible feeling of warmth and good spirits. At first you begin to feel sleepy, then you are invaded by torpor, and then by a fine languor. You always gulp down another cup to regain your strength. You feel loquacious. Even the Japanese start to talk, but that lasts only a few seconds. First a flick of the whip, then another, and then suddenly you've been hit by a crowbar.

THE TEA CEREMONY

Whatever repast is offered, there is no hospitality without green tea, *o'cha.* The tea myth is no doubt the one most tied to everyday life. Bodhidharma, founder of Zen, had meditated for nine years. He was overtaken by so great a weariness that his lids fell by themselves over his eyes. Cutting off his lids, he threw them on the ground, and on that spot a tea bush sprang up. Bodhidharma's disciples, who came to listen to him, got the habit of infusing the bush's leaves in boiling water because it helped them meditate.

The Japanese have created around this myth a ritual evocative of peace, relaxation, and frankness among those who drink tea together. The privileged classes got the habit of setting aside a room for the tea ceremony, while the emperor and his lords went to take their tea in private pavilions in the middle of their gardens. When one enters a house or waits in an administrative office, or when one goes into a café, tea is immediately served. There is no ceremony. However, when a Japanese wishes to pay particular honor to one of his friends, he organizes the *cha-no-yu.* The Japanese have learned to conduct the tea ritual with precision; it forms part of their education. The tea is prepared in silence, in accordance with certain detailed and immutable gestures. It is drunk religiously, the participants having turned their bowls around three times before bringing them to their lips. The tea ceremony is an opportunity for the attainment of inner concentration, in preparation for the harmony which must reign between friends who meet, or between partners who must discuss. The influence of Zen is manifest in this custom. The Japanese regard it as very important, and it is far from being relegated to some folklore museum. I was invited to a tea ceremony less than three months after my arrival in Japan. A Japanese colleague asked me to come and have tea one Saturday afternoon. She lived with her husband in a traditional house. My hostess was dressed in her ceremonial kimono, while her husband had also put on traditional clothes: a dark blue kimono tied at the waist by a black belt. I took off my shoes, and was asked to go into a room with the tatami, empty save for a rack on which hung a dark kimono, intended for me. When I reappeared, Madame S. said, "I wanted you to put on a kimono because I am going to perform a tea ceremony for you." She had us sit down, her husband and I with our backs to the *tokonoma,* the household shrine, and then proceeded as had been taught by the professional tea master. She opened the tea box. Then she picked up the bamboo spoon with which she spooned up the tea powder, transferring it to a ceramic bowl. During this time, the water was heating on the portable coal brazier. She poured in the hot water, then began stirring powder and water together with a bamboo whisk until she had obtained a very thick green beverage. With a small piece of cloth, she wiped the rim of the teapot, then poured the tea into each of the bowls, each time taking care to wipe the rims. Custom demands that one turn the bowl around before drinking, and put it down carefully after having drunk. These gestures are meant to show admiration for the object, lacquer or ceramic, which is always very beautiful and very pure in form and in color. I remember my suffering that afternoon: first from my effort to keep looking serious and then from remaining motionless in the Japanese position—sitting on my heels—throughout the ceremony.

Afterward, though skeptical of using this discipline for purposes

of meditation, I admitted that one might use it toward attaining the
goals of Zen Buddhism. Yet I never felt that in this ritual the Japanese went beyond a formal aestheticism, or that it was really suited to
liberating the spirit.

THE MAGIC OF FLOWERS

Another expression of aestheticism is *ikebana*, the arrangement of
flowers. In more than three hundred schools, women are taught to
compose a bouquet in accordance with tradition. Hence it may seem
paradoxical that the renowned teachers of *ikebana* are men. One of
the most celebrated, Sofu Teshighara, has attained such perfection
that his art became world renowned. His skill is the consequence of
his intense communion with nature. Sofu, as he is known, is very full
of himself and conscious of his genius. In the 1970s, he made so
much money that he had difficulties with the tax collectors, but this
did not interfere with his success, *ikebana* or with *ikebana's* popularity: the schools suffered an insufficiency of teachers. To explain this
ancestral taste—flower arrangement was initiated in the fifteenth
century—one must invoke a term used to characterize both the tea
ceremony and the arrangement of flowers: *furyu no asobi*, distinguished pastime which refers to an art of living which Japanese feudalism invented to provide a counterweight to Bushido, the art of
dying.

Furyu applies to all activity connected with pleasantness, everyday living, and aesthetics—the art of the garden of everyday household objects, of everything signifying love and peace. This art of
living was inaugurated and maintained by the most famous samurai
of the feudal period. A mountain tree is considered in the West a
symbol of perfection; its Cartesian symmetry satisfies a logical mind
in love with rationality. In Japan it is asymmetry that is more valued,
for its uniqueness. In Europe or America, dishes on a table are always geometric in form. In Japan an infinity of forms and colors, an
infinite variety of materials, exists. This does not mean that the
Japanese fail to appreciate a symmetrical object: when it comes to
the arrangement of flowers, symmetry is called *sin*. Asymmetry is
called *so*. Between the two there is an intermediate style, *gyo*. These
three forms are the basis of *ikebana*.

Ikebana naturally belongs inside the house, in the special *tokonoma*.
Ikebana schools today teach two disciplines. The formal discipline,
founded on the principle "sky, man, earth," is called the *yo* or "masculine" style. If one uses a single branch, the main twig which rises
up toward the heights symbolizes the sky. One curves a shoot or
branch to the right: it represents man. Lower down on the left side,
one puts another branch which is curved slightly upward at its end.

This symbolizes the earth. In the "feminine" style, the three elements "sky, man, earth" can be represented by three different branches, which do not necessarily come from the same species. One sets them very closely: thus a bamboo will symbolize the sky, a pine branch man, and a bough of plum blossoms the earth. There are always an unequal number of branches because unequal numbers are considered bearers of good fortune. (Certain numbers are especially banned in Japan. In many apartment houses, the fourth floor is called five. One never sees an *ikebana* with four branches or four elements.) The *ikebana* must spread out quite broadly, since one uses not only flowers but shoots, branches, fruit blossoms. As the proverb says: The sky and earth are flowers, As are the gods and Buddha, While the soul of these flowers Lives in the very heart of men.

In a floral calendar, January is the month of the pine tree, which is wedded with the bamboo to decorate the entrance of houses at the moment of the new year, symbolizing long life and virtue. February is the month of the plum, whose white, red, or violet blossoms have the strength to resist the coldest temperatures of the year. In March the peach becomes queen. April brings the festival of springtime, with its famous cherry blossoms. The azalea perfumes the days of May, the iris the days of June; lotus flowers bloom in July. In August nobody can appreciate the beauty of summer if he does not contemplate the vivid colors of the *asagao*, the morning glory blues, purples, reds, whites, and yellows which have inspired so many *haiku*. September is famous for its *nanakusa*, the seven flowers which grow wild in all gardens. October is known for its fruits, the most popular of which is the persimmon. But with the first frosts of November, the countless varieties of chrysanthemum, the imperial symbol, decorate the homes. December favors the camelia, together with bamboo and *sasa*, a carpet of vegetation which grows even after a fire and in the shade of trees, while the all-white flowers of the tea bushes prepare to withstand the winter.

MARRIAGE

So family life is lived to the rhythm of flowers as well as of the seasons, in an environment both hostile to and protective of tradition, thanks to the well-established principle of duality. Both liberated and subjugated, the Japanese woman who has to take responsibility for herself does so. And even in traditional circles today there is development that has been translated into statistics by Japan's Ministry of Health. Of four thousand couples married on the same day, whose average age was twenty-four for the women and twenty-seven for the men, more than 60 percent married without recourse to an intermediary. Seventy percent live by themselves; only 13 percent with the husband's parents; the others live with more distant relations, uncles or cousins. But this statistic is offset by the stagnation of husband-wife relations. According to the same poll, to the question: What is your principal interest? Fifty percent of the married women replied: children, travel, or leisure-time pleasures; only 3 percent spoke of their husbands. To the same question, only 4 percent of the men mentioned their wives.

The Japanese couple faces the same dangers as the Western couple, as is proved by divorce statistics. The nature of parent-child relations—upon which the concept of the family rests—has been modified. Adultery has become common. Daughters-in-law often have problems with their mothers-in-law, and children feel themselves to be different from their parents. All this would be banal if tradition did instill individuals with guilt and move them to look outside the reduced family clan for the values no longer to be found there. The company has tried to take the place of the family, and adults of both sexes, as well as the young, find a family environment at the judo, karate, or kendo club, at school and the university, within the restricted circles of a religious sect, and at the *ikebana* school—wherever people gather to do something in common. Each individual finds a place in the hierarchy, a rule, a very precise behavior model, a code, and learns to act in relation to others. He is encased and buoyed up by a social structure.

THE GENERATION GAP

In the rapid transformation of his environment, the Japanese is instinctively impelled to search for every vestige of his moral and cultural heritage, drawing from himself the strength to recreate what the times have tried to wipe out. The generation gap, which was thought to be irremediable and extremely profound in the sixties, has narrowed as the young adapt to the new living conditions—habitat, transportation, work, and leisure. The hierarchical system places children in the lowest rank, but there is not the least paradox in the last preceding the first, the most exposed becoming the most protected. In fact, no country in the world lavishes more care and effort on its children than Japan, which is a veritable paradise for the child and preadolescent.

I had just moved into my new Japanese house in the Shimouna district. As custom demands, I bought a dozen boxes of *sembei*, the biscuits made with seaweed, and told our young Japanese maid to take one of these boxes to each of my close neighbors in the morning, together with my calling card. That afternoon, my wife was visited by a Japanese woman whose garden was next to ours. She had seen our children and proposed that she speak to the director of the nursery school about my son. In this way, Louis-Alexandre, three and a half, entered a kindergarten, or *yo-chi-en*. In a blue sailor suit and a small round hat, carrying a yellow briefcase, he did not find it too hard to merge with the group. But when he took off his hat, his blond hair stood out conspicuously among his new friends' black heads. There were about fifteen women to take care of a hundred children three to five years of age. As everywhere, the recreation yard was extended by a covered space under which the children could play when it was raining—which was pretty often in that part of the world. Throughout the day the teachers took turns so as to assure that there were many educational games. Nothing in all this distinguishes a Japanese kindergarten from its Western counterparts, except perhaps two characteristics: the teachers never raise their voices, and the children are respectful of authority and never disobey except by mistake.

In conformity with a duality which one could believe is genetic, Japanese children both obey and command, for nothing is refused them. Each year for centuries, on the fifth day of the fifth month, they have celebrated a boys' festival, *tango-no-nekku*, or the first day of the horse. This animal symbolizes the masculine qualities virility, courage, and strength. The celebration is also called the Iris Festival, since the long leaves of this flower are reminiscent of a sword blade. On May 5, above each house in Japan in which a male child lives, a pole bearing carp made of wax, paper, or cloth is hoisted to swell in the wind. The number of carp on the pole indicates the number of boys, while the size of the specimens corresponds to each boy's age. Carp can swim through the most violent currents. They are known for their determination to surmount obstacles, to writhe and twist and struggle until exhausted when they are caught on a hook. Therefore, carp are considered examples of ambition, strength, and will.

For young girls, the Festival of the Doll takes place each year on the third day of the third month, March 31. When a girl is born, her parents buy a group of dolls, and friends give dolls as gifts. These dolls, often added to others that have been inherited, are brought out of their boxes on the day of the festival. Exhibited in the *tokono-ma*, they are displayed for the admiration of the family and above all for that of the little girls, who wear makeup, and dress in the traditional kimono. Peach blossoms, symbolizing happiness in marriage, surround the dolls.

Boys are obviously more desired than girls in the Japanese home. Folklore is mixed up with this; how could it be otherwise? The most popular legend tells of Momotaro, the child of the peach. A long time ago there lived an honest woodcutter who went every day into the forest to gather sticks of wood, while his wife went down to the river to wash the linen. Suddenly she saw a floating object in the current. When she pulled it toward her with a stick, to her great astonishment she saw that it contained a big peach. She carried it to her house to offer it to her husband. Putting it down in front of him, she cut it in two and a baby appeared. They called him Momotaro. When he grew up, Momotaro, a great friend of the animals, conquered the earth and achieved the treasure of the ogres with the help of a dog, a monkey, and a pheasant, and he became rich and powerful. Momotaro's exploits enchant Japanese children. His adventures are told on television and in the comic strips. Momotaro's head decorates all the exhibitions of the boys' festival.

The Japanese couple lives by the rhythm of these festivals, which bring them together with their children. Even today, despite the formal breakup of the *ié*, mothers and fathers are concerned to transmit to their descendants the most sacred element: they have preserved filial piety, or *koko*. The *ko* is one of those obligations a Japanese bears from birth to death, that system of interpersonal relations which is a component of the "identity card" of a totally original culture.

Living customs and superstitions are another element in this "identity card," though often they are scorned. In a school that prepares Japanese for their contacts with foreigners, the employees of the Japan Travel Bureau have learned to speak of "folklore" whenever a custom or festival does not seem to correspond to the canons of Western conduct.

For a present-day Japanese family, the absence of all rules prevails in those situations of modern life which tradition did not foresee. In certain cases, they have transposed things effortlessly; the samurai of the automobile treat their "mounts" with great courtesy. When it comes to traveling in a plane or on a train, precedents of conduct are still being established. People are more at home in the subway, where the crowd is politer than it was ten years ago.

In the context of the family, how could tradition foresee that young couples would live alone, that the rules of neighborliness in a large housing development would be different from those governing the relations between adjoining houses? The house had a very well-defined space which served to place a family clan geographically. Therefore, the question has been to find out whether the concept of the *ié* can be maintained when several families with different outlooks live within one limited space. A dozen years ago, it was difficult to get families to live together in an apartment house without having first created among them a network of traditional obligations. Young Japanese couples of today are gradually adopting another mentality. Their preference inclines to anonymity, as in Paris or New York. There are quite a few other signs of these changes, which could really take effect only after several generations. Young couples walk side by side in the street and stroll with their children on Sunday. Rather than frequent the bars with hostesses after work, the men go right home to take their bath (the *furo*). Their wives dine with them. Afterward they watch television together or read the newspaper.

This change does not, properly speaking, constitute a change in attitude. It has obvious economic causes. On one hand, the young household has bills to pay after buying the consumer society's many gadgets, so less money is available for the husband's pastimes. On the other hand, the economic crisis, which has been felt since 1975, multiplying the failures of small businesses, creating unemployment for the first time in Japan's history, and reducing the incomes of salaried persons at all levels, has indirectly favored the men's abandonment of certain ancestral customs, a more equitable sharing of responsibilities, and the independence of the married woman vis-à-vis her husband's family and even her own.

CUSTOMS AND SUPERSTITIONS

If certain habits are being gradually abandoned, the Westernized routine—subway, job, bed—is offset through a kind of second growth of beliefs and superstitions. There exist traditional superstitions about direction: *kogaku*. The horizon is divided into twelve directions, each direction bearing the name of an animal—monkey, horse, dragon, snake, etc.—just as each day brings its beneficent and maleficent directions. When the direction "dragon-snake" is said to be maleficent, it would be prudent to put off one's trip or avoid the route. The direction northeast is always maleficent. It is called *kimon*, the devil's door. Other superstitions have been drawn from physiognomy: for this reason one shows photographs of one's wife-to-be to a specialist and asks his opinion. In the same way that each person has his own style (*ninso*), each house has its *kaso*, its good or bad fortune. One eats cakes of rice paste (*mochi*), because *mochi* can also signify "to have" in the sense of possessing good luck. One eats the herring's dried eggs (*kazunoko*) because this word means "plenty of babies." Beans, *name*, are synonyms for good health. The pine tree, or *chitose*, signifies a thousand years of life; the bamboo, *yorosuyo*, ten thousand. If you have been invited to dine in a Japanese house, it is polite to take a second bowl of white rice, because a single bowl symbolizes an offering to the spirit of a dead person. Between superstition and custom there is a tenuous frontier.

Seven days after its birth one baptizes a child, in the presence of parents, friends, and neighbors. A boy's head is shaved on the thirty-second day after naming, a girl's on the thirty-third. The baby is dressed in a small ceremonial kimono, and taken by the grandmother or nurse to the temple, where prayers that the child will grow up strong and in good health are offered. On the 120th day, after the first tooth has appeared, the ceremony of the first meal is celebrated. A bowl of rice, a cup of tea, and some chopsticks are placed on a small table. The mother holds the child seated before her on the table and demonstrates how chopsticks are carried to one's mouth. A child's first birthday is always celebrated by a banquet.

Adoption has been a widespread custom in Japan for centuries, for the extinction of a name has always been considered a great misfortune. Often a family without a male child adopts its future son-in-law, who is then considered a son. One can be adopted at any age. Old couples without children may adopt a young couple who agree to take their name, and are guaranteed an inheritance.

The family festival par excellence is the new year, *shogatsu*. Preparations begin in December with a meticulous housecleaning. The entrance is decorated with a cluster of pine and bamboo tied together by a cord of plaited straw combined with a broad ribbon of Japanese paper, the whole affair hooked onto the roof beams. The women fix special dishes such as the vegetables—*mochi* or *esechi* which today can be found prepared in the stores. On December 28, offices and factories close. At the stroke of midnight December 31, the bells of Buddhist temples begin ringing. They ring 108 times, to mark the 108 sins of man, which prayer will purify. Midnight also signals the moment for families to proceed to the sanctuaries. And December 31 is the day on which one lists projects for the coming year. On the morning of January 1, vows are exchanged. Children play with kites and receive gifts; adults play backgammon or trick-track. Women take advantage of the festival to wear their most beautiful kimonos. The *shogatsu* festival ends on the seventh day, on which the house decorations are burned. The night before, throughout the town, there are demonstrations in honor of the firemen, particularly spectacular in Tokyo.

BELIEFS

Shinto

Inside Japanese houses, it is not rare to see in the main room one or several photographs set on an altar among small receptacles containing a few grains of rice, some sake, or an orange. This is the Shinto altar, for use during family cememonies. Here the funerary urns are placed for a year, before they are taken to the cemetery, and when mourning has ended, the photograph of the person one has loved or honored is kept here. It is therefore the altar of the ancestors.

The Shinto religion can be traced back to Japan's mythical origins. Its two pillars are nature and lineage—every Japanese man and woman can claim a link to the foundation of the Empire of the Rising Sun, being descended directly from Amaterasu, the sun goddess. The pantheon includes innumerable gods, no fewer than eight million, including the gods and goddesses of the rivers, the sea, the wind, the mountain, fire, as well as famous warriors, certain faithful servants of the imperial household, and select relations and descendants of the emperors. It should be remembered that Japan was created by the couple Izanagi-Izanami and at its origin embraced eight gods. In mythology, the dragon whose tail was a saber had eight heads. But each element of nature has its *kami* or god, whether it be an animal, a mountain, or a tree. Nature is therefore filled with *kami* who play the role of protectors of their environment.

Thus Shinto is embedded in the history of Japan as worship of the emperor, family ancestors, and nature. It does not entail any moral sanction and it lacks an iconography, which explains the stripped bareness of the temples and their beauty. The orthodoxy of the cult was fixed in the annals when Emperor Temmu (673–686) had his scribes compile a history of the emperors since the creation of Japan by the sun goddess: in the Kojiki and the Nihonshoki can be found the canons of Shinto. Purification is of great importance; Shinto priests and the devout perform numerous ablutions to purify themselves—for example, after any contact with the dead or with human blood. Prayer is a means of invoking the protection of the gods against all kinds of demonic powers in nature: earthquakes, epidemics, floods, fires, tidal waves.

Traditional Shinto, born before the introduction of Buddhism into Japan and with its primitive manifestations linked to animistic beliefs, can be found among many Asian peoples. In Japan it was closely tied to the entity of the family clan and assigned the pragmatic function of protection against the prepotent powers which surround man. As certain clans became progressively more powerful than others, the protective divinities were gradually classified in the hierarchy. Thus the sun goddess Amaterasu became the supreme divinity. When Buddhism was imported from India to Japan by way of Korea and then China, a delicate situation arose. Emperor Kimmei received from the king of Kudara in Korea some sutras and images of Buddha, and soon priests, nuns, architects, and engravers came to the archipelago. The emperor instructed his minister to favor the new religion.

For almost two hundred years Buddhism competed with Shinto. Two great Buddhist priests proposed an amalgam of the gods of the Shinto and Buddhist pantheons: Dengy Daishi (767–822) introduced a new sect called the Tendai, while Kobo Daishi (774–834) created the Shingon sect of esoteric Buddhism. This "Shinto with two faces," as it is called, was in reality subordinated to Buddhism until the nineteenth century.

For almost one thousand years, it was common to see Buddhist priests officiating in Shinto temples, except for the temples of Izumo and Ise, sanctuaries directly tied to the myth of the sun goddess. Not only did Shinto adopt Buddhist divinities, but many Shinto temples became active centers for the study of Buddhist doctrine. However, Shinto did not deviate from its principal trend, keeping aloof from theological problems and remaining tied to earthly matters, while Buddhism tended to contemplation of the hereafter.

In the fourteenth and fifteenth centuries, under the influence of both Buddhist and Confucian concepts, the Shinto religion acquired a moral code, the identification of the emperor's "three symbols" with the moral virtues indispensable to everyday life. Under the Yokugawa, several schools revolted against the Shinto-Buddhist syncretism and developed the theory of the divine origin of the imperial throne. With the Meiji restoration, Shinto gradually assumed the character of a political ideology. After 1868, it became the instrument of imperial power to gain popular loyalty. Its preeminence was guaranteed by the 1890 imperial decree on education, which made the state's politico-religious structure official.

Japan is a country created by the gods and led by an imperial dynasty unbroken since its origin and descending in the direct line from the sun goddess. The state-family is the bedrock of national morality. In the schools, the army, and governmental organizations, an entire ritual of ceremonies of allegiance to the emperor and the state was established, foreshadowing the taking over of this apparatus by the militarists. In the thirties, *Kokutai No Hongi*, the essential principles of national unity, gave Japan the sacred mission of leading the world. The *kokutai*, or concept of the state, broadly understood by the people as a national sentiment, quickly turned into chauvinism and distrust of everything foreign. In 1946, the emperor renounced his divine origins. Shinto, put on a footing of equality with Buddhism, returned to its family significance and sloughed off certain ceremonies which, before the war, were used for mass indoctrination.

There are eighty thousand Shinto temples scattered throughout Japan. They are connected with a central bureau whose efforts are directed toward making Shinto into a popular cult endowed with a coherent theology and spreading a certain number of moral precepts. The public continues to participate in Shinto ceremonies as affirmation of its attachment to the national and familial heritage. The great majority of Japanese, even in the country, no longer believe in the supernatural power of the *kami*, which have nonetheless remained popular and continue to receive offerings. The *kami* form part of the everyday decor; they combine the individual's aspirations with the myth that drowses in the depths of every Japanese soul. The most valued gods are present in the country fields and the city streets. Thus Inari, god of rice and patron of merchants, comes down from the mountain in the spring and returns in the autumn. His messenger is the fox. At the entrance of Shinto temples, one passes beneath the torii and then, often, before two foxes carved in stone.

The seven gods of fortune are also very popular. A netsuke, a miniature sculpture in ivory, shows them as they sail the ship of fortune: Hotei, with swollen belly, the symbol of his good nature and greatness of soul: Jurojin, the god of longevity, with his white beard, lover of sake (but not to excess); Fukurokuju, whose narrow, elongated head encloses both wisdom and a long life; Bishamon, who combines the messianic and warlike virtues; Daikoku, the god of wealth; Ebisu, the hard worker; and Benten, the only goddess among the seven, who is associated with the sea and islands and whose favorite musical instrument is the corded *biwi*.

Buddhism

The Japanese is pragmatic. Attracted by myth, he nevertheless tries to bring his aspirations into accord with everyday reality, and he sometimes experiences great difficulty in reconciling these two tendencies. The question is decisively settled nowadays. One can at the same time be a Shintoist and a Buddhist. Six schools of Buddhism have been developed in Japan, forming numerous sects, the most flourishing of which are those that have been able to adapt their teachings to modern life. Some sects, among the most ancient, have today only a historical interest, such as the schools of Nara, Hosso, Kegon, or Ritsu. Their temples have been classed as national treasures. The Tendai sect on Mount Hei near Kyoto, associated with the famous temple of Enryakuji, attracted many priests who devoted themselves to study. But one of the most popular schools today is that of Amida, with its temples like the Honganji at Kyoto; Amida has followers in the United States.

Zen Buddhism is well known for its influence on art. Its principles of meditation and austerity have had a particular resonance in Japan's history, since they were the principles of the samurai caste. Their code, the Bushido, is more or less derived from Zen.

Returning the night before from China, I had begun, one early June afternoon, to sift through the pile of mail that had accumulated on my desk during my two-month absence. The sky, very clear in the morning, was becoming veiled, foreshadowing the arrival of the ritual rain, which each year at this same time falls for a month without stopping, until summer's great heat begins. The approach of this trying season makes one nervous. My secretary came to announce an unexpected visitor: Mr. Taro Banzai. I did not know who he was, nobody in my office knew him, but he insisted on seeing me. Why under these conditions did I agree to see him? Twelve years later, I can no longer recall. I remember only that a word aroused my curiosity: "I would like to have a talk with Monsieur Courdy about Bushido."

Silently he handed me a small book whose jacket was black and white, symbolizing sobriety and continence. The title, in Japanese and French, read: *Budo Shoshin-Shu*, by Daidoji Yuzan (1639–1730). *Elementary Readings on Bushido.*

"The cherry blossom in Japan is the symbol of the life of the samurai. It blossoms gloriously; its life is brief and it falls suddenly, without regret."

Having said this, my visitor showed me a cherry blossom at the upper right of the book jacket. Taro Banzai spoke correct French: "Have you heard talk about Bushido?"

"Of course, but I have never gone deeply into the matter."

"You were wrong. It is an idea that has guided Japanese life for more than seven centuries. One cannot wipe it out by a simple decree on the pretext that it is feudal and militaristic. . . . There are three periods in Bushido: The first extended from 1100 to the year 1600, which marks the end of internal wars and the establishment of the shogun's authority. Afterward, what we call reformed Bushido, an amalgam of Confucianism and Zen, lasted until 1868. Finally, there is modern Bushido, since the Meiji restoration."

"How do you define Bushido?"

"It is a code, a rule of life meant for warriors, which for a long time took the place of religion. In the period of the Bushido warrior, the rule formulated certain principles addressed to men bearing arms. It was a code resembling that of your knights in the Middle Ages. Its principles were: bravery when faced by danger and fidelity; loyalty toward the suzerain; a sober life; justice and integrity. Starting in 1600, the samurai were demobilized. They became peasants, functionaries, or ronin—that is, unemployed warriors. The *Budo Shoshin-Shu* transposes the code of the samurai into this new society, explaining Bushido from the Zen point of view. After the Meiji restoration, the pioneers of our economy applied the principles of Bushido to business affairs, and imperial edicts spread the code throughout Japan: an edict to the army and navy, an edict on education, an edict on sport.

"It was the spirit of Bushido that animated the pilots of the underwater torpedoes just off the American shores and the kamikaze airplane pilots. There were nearly no Japanese prisoners, except at the end of the war. After a single appeal from the emperor, combat ended.

"I believe that it is not reasonable to want to establish a morality outside national tradition. To establish a new morality on the basis of ancient customs and yet adapted to the present situation, that is Japan's problem today.

"What is at stake? Before all else, it is necessary that each samurai be intimate with the thought of death. It is essential to train him to use his weapons, shoot his bow and arrow, ride a horse. He must become cultivated—lack of culture cannot be justified. Filial piety is indispensable; it is the basis of the three moral precepts: the precepts of the loyal samurai, the just samurai, the brave samurai.

Taro Banzai stood up, wrote on the endpaper of his book: "To Monsieur Courdy, compliments of the author," then left without a word.

I never again saw the small, well-dressed gentleman who visited me unexpectedly in my Akasaka office that afternoon. But I kept his little book explaining the samurai's code of honor, the Bushido—from *do* (code or way) and *bushi* (warrior). This written code establishes in a rigorous manner the comportment of those who bear arms and who, because of this, occupy a privileged place in Japanese feudal society. Ancestor worship represents for the warrior the epitome of the precepts inherited from Shinto; fidelity to the reigning lord, even in death, shows the Confucian influence, while, as Michel Randon has pointed out in his book *The Martial Arts*, the qualities of mind and heart, the resignation to the inevitable demands on the warrior, are derived from the exigencies and customs of rural society. The "way of the warrior," one of the essential components of Japan until the most recent period, teaches one to face one's death with fortitude. The rite of seppuku is the consecration of this teaching, self-immolation as the supreme expression of fidelity.

What remains of this code today? To Yukio Mishima, who asked me this question with bitterness, I replied with astonishment: "But you are left, the Japanese, and your hierarchical society, your suzerains and your vassals, your complex ties and above all your taste for the martial arts." Pensively and as though talking to himself, Mishima said: "The Japanese are right to train themselves to die, since they do not have the strength to live as their ancestors taught them."

I have a very limited experience of the martial arts, but one cannot live in Japan without encountering the contagious infatuation. Strolling early every morning down the deserted streets in my district, I would observe young men stepping out of their houses, gliding into the street, and heading toward the *dojos*, the clubs for judo, karate, and aikido. In fact, half of the young men aged sixteen to twenty-five were in regular training in one of these disciplines. At seven-thirty or eight, those who had to start work at eight-thirty or nine left their *dojos;* they were replaced by those who started work later.

A Japanese friend took me to the aikido club where the master Ueshiba taught. Despite his eighty-four years, no one could beat him. He knew all the uncheckable moves to throw even his most talented students off balance. As for myself, I was quickly "dispatched": without his even touching me, I found myself on the tatami in a horizontal position. The master did not speak, but one of his disciples, with a great deal of modesty, tried to explain to me that what mattered most of all was concentration and strength of soul. Bodily strength and precision of movement were regarded as additional advantages. Karate looks more brutal, at least the sort taught by certain schools, in which skill, suppleness, and technical precision take precedence over the "mental" side.

When the mime Marcel Marceau came to Japan for the first time, he thought it indispensable for his art to study the martial arts' perfection of gesture. We went together to a *dojo* of kendo, which numbers more than two million practitioners in Japan. Children learn kendo in elementary school, and it is not rare to see them practicing in the school courtyards. First they participate in collective meditation and a kind of educational incantation, chanting their love for their parents, their teachers, and Japan, and swearing to respect their comrades. Then, rigged out in a helmet and a belt to protect the midsection, they practice in pairs to learn how to handle the baton.

My brief contact with the martial arts began in Tokyo. I have since returned to the Temple of the Thousand Buddhas, whose courtyard shelters one of the most famous archery schools on the archipelago. Everything in this art rests on Zen meditation. The pupils, lined up along a cord, execute a ritual of gestures and attitudes as firmly regulated as a ballet. When the arrows are shot off, they seem to bound toward their targets, as though propelled by a spiritual breath which guides them telepathically. Efficiency is not sought in itself. It is only the result of mental concentration, achievement of the inner void and perfection of the accomplished gesture.

New Religions

Since 1945, the Nichiren sect has had considerable success with the development of Sokkagakai. This very advanced and extremely structured organization has been misjudged as the resurrection of a certain kind of Nipponese fascism. In reality, its ability at organizing mass demonstrations, its great gymnastic festivals, its at times stern methods of recruitment, conceal a centrist political doctrine. It gave birth to the Komeito party, whose vague, undefined program merely advocates the path of the golden mean.

Sokkagakai today claims fifteen million followers. In its ultramodern temple, located at the foot of Mount Fuji, it organizes seminars, in which numerous foreign delegations have participated. They practice a kind of group therapy: American women dressed in cotton kimonos appear at an early hour in the common hall. They sit on the tatami. The man in charge mounts a platform and begins to shout: "How are things with you this morning?" "Good." "Louder!" he shouts, and they repeat in louder voices: "Good." "How are your things going this morning?" their trainer repeats again. Then, their lungs almost bursting, the three or four hundred women present split the air: "Good!" The observer wishes his hearing were less acute. Sokkagakai Buddhism has expanding swarms of followers in the United States and Europe, who carry out a policy of active cultural propaganda.

The Tenri-Kyo sect, whose center is in Tenri, near Nara, also possesses a vast influence, through its university, which has opened centers in the chief capitals of the world in order to teach Japanese to foreigners. Tenri has no political or social program, but its doctrine in some respects resembles that of Moral Rearmament. Its rites include confession or witnessing to musical rhythms, while the faithful roll on the floor.

But the 1945 vacuum favored the efflorescence of more or less serious religious sects. Seicho-No-Ye, the House of Thought, claims to forge a bond between Christ and Buddha. P. L. Kyodan, the Peace and Liberty Association, honors pictorial art. Its founder, Mr. Mili, possesses a rare collection of paintings by great masters, which is opened to the faithful once a year in a museum-temple near Osaka. This occasion is climaxed by a night ceremony crowned by fireworks: Happiness is found in the contemplation of beauty.

One of the most curious of the new religions is called . . . but in fact does it have a name? Sayo Kitamura, the wife of a farmer, one day discovered that a *kami* in the Shinto pantheon had entered her. She immediately proclaimed herself a goddess and began an ecstatic dance, the dance of the "not me." Men and women of all ages, lately more than 300,000, gather in a sumptuous residence in Tokyo in search of redemption. They dance, while tears flow down their cheeks as if they are hypnotized. Madame Kitamura loved to recall that she had received only an elementary education, but that the *kami* taught her modern techniques of cooking and bestowed on her the gift of predicting the weather with infallible precision. She died on December 28, 1976. A magnificent modern temple designed by the famous architect Kenzo Tange was built near her farm. Her daughter-in-law, who succeeded her, with the rank of "demigoddess," has recruited many followers in California.

Christianity

Among the religions that have been taken seriously, Christianity holds a relatively modest place, with a community of about 750,000 members, Catholics and Protestants of all denominations. Protestantism came in the fourteenth century with missionaries who accompanied the Dutch merchants, while Catholicism was implanted in the south of Japan in 1549 by St. Francis Xavier's Jesuits. The persecution and later the interdiction of the Christian communions led to the creation of sects like the "hidden Christians" of Nagasaki, who still exist but celebrate their cult as in the past, and are Christians in name only. Yet the influence of the Jesuits has been felt in contemporary Japan, radiating from the University of Sophia in Tokyo. Numerous important officials, journalists, jurists, and members of the liberal professions studied at Sophia, whose level of teaching, although considered below that of the great state universities such as Todai and Kyodai, is highly regarded among the private universities. The Protestants have opened more than a hundred schools and are active through the network of YM/YWCAs. Missionaries work in Japan against great difficulties, and those who are involved in social work do not always get support from the authorities.

Father X, a Catholic, lives in Kobe, in the most miserable section of the city. For ten years he has pulled a cart each morning through the streets of the richer districts and gathered things thrown out as junk, picking up an old iron, a transistor, a ball of twine. In his workshop, he collects young people who have come out of prison. He gives them work, tries to create a team spirit, but does not succeed completely. If one of his protégés leaves him, lapses once again into lawbreaking, and is arrested, Father X sees himself as guilty of not having done what he should. Father Y is a member of a contemplative community which earns its keep in the northern island of Hokkaido by making cheese. Father Z knows the Buddhist temples of Kyoto better than the cathedrals of Europe. They are his life, and he shows them off to his Italian, French, and Canadian friends as if they were his own home.

The Religious Sensibility

The Japanese reveal through their religious feelings one constant element in their character: the desire for coexistence among the beliefs and religions which history or circumstances have propagated around them. Some people see in this a spirit of tolerance, as opposed to Europe's crushing heritage of religious intolerance. Others see the inability to make a choice, inherent in the Japanese mentality. But most observers agree that it reveals the quest for a system of values adapted to an ever-changing social code. In fact, the Japanese often practice Shinto, participate in Buddhist ceremonies, and, sometimes in their homes, maintain the traditional religions side by side with Christianity—all this in the spirit of Pascal's "Don't trifle with religion; if it isn't real, you have lost nothing, but if it is, you have won everything."

The Japanese are not at all embarrassed about staking their bets on several religions at the same time. How far does this go today? A decline in Shinto and Buddhism has been noted, a renewed attachment to social values rather than metaphysical beliefs, but we can ask whether one has not been witnessing, since the sixties, a progressive abandonment of the codes which controlled the ancient divisions of

Japanese society and an invasion of Western concepts. The divisions between the samurai, peasants, and merchants seem gradually less important, while Japanese thought adopts, contradictorily, either Marxist or Christian attitudes, or rationalist or logical modes of thought. Here and there, metaphysical aspirations appear as a sign of the individual's permanent anguish.

The Japanese and Death

My friend Takashi Suzuki spoke to me of death: "There is no clear demarcation between life and death, except from the medical point of view. . . . Metaphysical anguish certainly exists in our country, but as a consequence of a historical syncretism of Shinto and Buddhism and, later, Christianity. The year 1600 produced Japan's 'Waterloo' at Sekigahara. Hideyoshi was defeated by Tokugawa, and some thirty years later Japan, which had begun to open up to Western influences, was shut tight for more than two centuries, until 1868. The fusion of Shinto and Buddhism occurred in the Heian epoch in the year 1000; by then the goddess Kannon had overlaid the representation of the Virgin Mary. Christian iconographic symbols were mixed up with those of the Shinto pantheon. The so-called hidden Christians of Nagasaki are a good example of the confusion that was at work. Todaiji, the famous Buddhist temple at Nara, is protected by Kasuga-Jinja and its Shinto guardian angels.

"The point of syncretism inheres in the Japanese attitude vis-à-vis the phenomenon of death, which invariably confers on death a sacred character. We say: 'One should not whip death.' Beyond this sacredness, a certain idea of death developed in our country on the basis of Buddha's teachings. After death, there is no punishment for some people or recompense for others, but death remains always very present for each individual, as a goal that one ineluctably attains.

"In *Kiro-I-Kao* [*The Yellow Visage*], by Shusaku Endo, a student commits suicide to find peace. Death, in his case, is an objective to be reached, and a certain pleasure attends one's getting there. So death does not have the fearful aspect with which it is endowed in Christian cultures. The kamikazes seem an aberrant phenomenon to Westerners—in other words, inhuman. However, one cannot speak of them in terms either of courage or of fanaticism. When a pilot flies his small plane loaded with one bomb with orders to crash it on the deck of an American battleship, there is simply an objective to be attained, which is realized in death. If the objective is accepted, there is no reason for the kamikaze to reject the idea of death. There is, on the contrary, enjoyment in approaching it, since it is tied to the goal of a sacred mission. The same thing applies to the suicides of children, of which a great deal has been said in recent times: a little nine-year-old girl in the Fuchu region hanged herself in her classroom because she received an unjustified reprimand.

This is but one example. In Japan last week there were three children's suicides. You feel that such deaths are an injustice. But all Japanese children have learned that death is not the end of life, and the idea of what we call 'the living death' has been inculcated in them from a very young age.

"In the West, the spirits of the dead do indeed intrude into the life of the living, but always in the form of malevolent spirits or wicked ghosts. In Japan, one summons the spirits of the dead, one keeps them as close to oneself as possible, in a place of honor in the home. One speaks to them during the festivals of the O'Bon. And on Osore Mountain in northern Tohoku province, old blind women, professional mediums, translate the will of the dead, delivering only beneficial advice for everyday family life. For a Japanese, metaphysical anguish has nothing to do with fear of the hereafter. It is born rather from uncertainty, that is, the disquietude of not having passed *politely* from one state to another. The Japanese, when they can, never fail to give instructions as to the ceremonial of their 'going hence.' The dead person stretched out behind the Shinto altar in the largest room of the house is hidden from the sight of his neighbors, relations, and friends, but his photograph dominates the altar. That is how the family receives the neighbors at the moment of incineration. The ashes will be preserved for a year in the house before being put in the ground or scattered. Thus the carnal envelope dies and the spirit lives."

"And what about suicide?"

In connection with the suicide of the little girl in Fuchu, the newspaper *Asahi* spoke of the loneliness of children. This was the case that same week with another twelve-year-old girl, who before dying left a message of regret at not having been able to get good marks in school, and with the young man of sixteen who burned himself to death before the gate of the Imperial Palace. All these suicides bear the mark of the loneliness of those who committed them, in a family milieu which no longer serves, as in the past, as a life preserver when the social environment becomes too overwhelming.

"Suicide is a way of accusing parents, teachers, the people in power, but it is also a way of attaining more quickly the goal that has been set in advance. The recent suicides of children are an 'example.' As for Mishima's suicide, which represented a philosophic-political act of rebellion, it would be unjust not to see in it evidence of the individual's frustrated search for a new system of values in our society."

4: The Japanese in Society

TRADITION AND MODERNISM: THE CHOICE OF A SOCIETY

In Japan, anxiety is expressed in the very laughter that marks the end of anxiety. This laughter, which the Japanese critic Tadeo Takemoto calls the liberating laugh, was the attribute of Zen monks who had achieved "illumination." It is often sought after, but can be found only in nothingness, the void. Most people are obliged to fall back on a system of values which reconciles the ancient and modern, and fulfills their hopes for an existence that finds its justification in certain national objectives appropriate to a country that would like to be first in everything. The oligarchy of the Meiji period established the objectives of national unity, international equality, and an accelerated modernism, without foreseeing the moment when these would become a problem for the thoughtful Japanese.

As long as no more was involved than adopting foreign techniques, coexistence of the traditional and the modern encountered few obstacles. Mastering Western technologies in order to survive entailed an insistence on efficiency, which is not at all incompatible with feudal values, and the updating of the samurai involved no fundamental change before 1945. But as an occupying force, the Americans did not only try to rebuild Japan's ruined economy. The efforts of MacArthur as proconsul were also aimed at the spread of democracy, equality, freedom, and individualism. The traditional became feudal, retrograde, unfashionable. Newspapers and radio were extensively used to spread the missionary ideas of the conqueror. This diffusion of an egalitarianism unprecedented in Japanese history created tensions between ancient and modern, and provoked crises of conscience by calling into question not only the accepted premises of politics and government but also people's acts and attitudes, and even more, their conduct of everyday life.

Adoption of a Western lifestyle was immediate and conspicuous. Students took to hanging out in the new cafés, where they discussed international problems or listened to classical music. Young couples danced to the latest tunes in cabarets or discotheques. Hippies, the *futen,* invaded the approaches to the Shinjuku railroad station, their

147

hair as long and dirty as that of their European or American counterparts. The girls of Tokyo and Osaka adopted the miniskirt. Baseball and golf are played, Western films and American television series watched. For protection against fire the Japanese do not trust merely in Buddha, whose image is still in their homes; they pay an insurance premium. In the countryside, the farmers participate in Shinto ceremonies to make it rain or ensure a good harvest, but they also make scientific use of chemical fertilizers. Do these new patterns of behavior signify a change in mentality? As to the essentials, this remains to be proven. Close observation tends to indicate the very opposite.

HANASHIAI AND RINGI: THE DIPLOMACY OF CONSENSUS

In a bilateral Tokyo meeting with a Western country, the Japanese delegation raises the question of import and export quotas. A difference emerges. The head of the foreign delegation tries to prove that his view is correct. The Japanese delegation listen attentively but show some embarrassment. The head of the foreign delegation thinks that his arguments are having an effect, that this embarrassment marks the first step toward Japanese recognition of facts he has effectively established. A day goes by. The Japanese attitude does not vary in the slightest. All of a sudden, the Japanese chief proposes *hanashiai*, a "corridor conversation," and breaks off the session. The Western delegation does not know what's happening. The Japanese takes his Western opposite number aside; over a cup of tea, he cocks his head and, mouth twisted upward, inhales loudly—a piece of miming intended to convey: "Look, I am upset." He then says, "I do not want to contradict you, but I am right; perhaps you are right too. . . . Please, let's begin by admitting this much and resume negotiations tomorrow." The Western delegate does not understand this signal, or rather interprets it as a show of force in opposition to the justice of his own position. The Japanese, however, must at all costs avoid the direct and open confrontation their interlocutors seem to be seeking, and save face by obtaining a concession in principle, even on a topic other than the one under discussion.

When disagreements persist, there is quite simply no decision. The process must lead to a consensus, even if that produces agreement on a point of no great significance. Paradoxical as it may appear, the person who makes a significant concession at the opportune moment could win in the long run, mostly because of the *giri* system of reciprocal duties and obligations between individuals or groups. This policy of consensus is normally and regularly applied through an institutional mechanism called *ringi*. Westerners sometimes ask where Japanese efficiency comes from; how, for example, does the shipbuilding industry, which involves competing companies, decide to build supertankers at a time when the market for them is not apparent since nowhere in the world are there harbor installations capable of receiving them? Not only is the decision taken in advance of the event, but it is made through the perfect consensus of competing shipyards.

How did the Japanese auto industry as a whole decide to break into the European market? How did the Japanese decide to sign the peace treaty between Tokyo and Peking? How, more simply, does a family accept a daughter's marriage to a young man whose family they do not know? *Ringi* is a process that takes place on several levels, all the more complex when the decision to be taken involves a great many groups or individuals.

Let us take the simplest example: marriage. The head of each family investigates the other clan, its social position, its financial circumstances, its origins, and above all, its reputation. The father will first consult his wife, then his other grown children, and finally his brothers and sisters, his brothers-in-law and sisters-in-law. If their advice indicates general agreement, he will then call together the members of the clan for a ceremonial family banquet, and will officially announce approval. If opinions differ, the reasons for the disagreement are sought. A further inquiry is made. If the problem does not seem too serious, agreement between the two families will finally be reached. But in the contrary case, the reasons against the marriage will be told the boy and girl in an effort to get them to change their decision. Even today not many young people decide to ignore these interdictions.

Let us take the more complex case of a government decision, such as the Sino-Japanese peace treaty. The China bureau of the Ministry of Foreign Affairs collects a dossier from the different groups who know something about the matter: Japanese diplomats in China, the ministry's technical services, the concerned ministers, the prime minister's cabinet, parliamentary commissions, commissions of the majority party, university professors, private research organizations, etc. A trial balloon is launched via the press, to test public opinion. The decision is then reached with the collaboration of all the factions of the majority party, including those opposed to the treaty because of their ties with Formosa. The actual decision took all observers by surprise. It was exceptional because of the relative rapidity with which it was achieved. If a consensus had not been reached, it might have taken several years of further discussion. A decision that is taken too quickly is suspect.

The System of Giri-Ninjo

In the case of the shipyards or the automobile industry, consensus is arrived at first between the representatives of the competing companies, after an analysis of the world situation and the changes in a specific market. Any consensus implies the abandonment by the parties concerned of some of their positions. When one party gives in on an important point, it is understood by the opposing party that some acknowledgment of this concession is called for. Schematically, this is the *giri-ninjo* system. It could exist only in a context of personal relationships.

The *giri-ninjo* system is complex because it involves duty, justice, honor, "face," respectability, courtesy, humanity, love, gratitude. It affects all classes of society, from the prime minister to the farmer or factory worker. Takeo Doi, of the University of Tokyo, who has written many articles on Japanese psychoanalysis for Princeton University, gave a relatively clear definition of the concepts of *giri* and *ninjo:*

"*Ninjo* is a term that the Japanese consider specifically Japanese (which means that Westerners either do not understand it or have their own *ninjo*). This term refers to the correct way of expressing *amaeru* vis-à-vis someone, or the correct response to another person's bow of *amaeru;* more simply, it is the correct manner of performing the bow, which is our way of expressing deep friendship or love, and the correct manner of responding to this bow when it is performed by another." *Amaeru* could be translated as "being strongly, passionately attached to someone."

While *Ninjo* applies to parent-child, husband-wife, brother-sister relations, *giri* refers to a series of moral obligations: relations with neighbors, superiors in the hierarchy, colleagues at work. What is essential is that the relations between two individuals, two social groups, or an individual and a group are not established on a basis of equality; one of the parties is always hierarchically superior to the other. To this we should add the concept of *on*, which involves the basic obligations contracted at birth vis-à-vis the emperor, one's parents, and, in the epoch of feudalism, the suzerain.

Advancing in life, one accumulates *ons*, or obligations. An entire life isn't enough to pay one's debts; each individual thus places himself in a permanent *giri* situation, which calls on his *ninjo* side. The Japanese are often imprisoned in this network of obligations, of which they are able to keep surprisingly accurate account: in the family, the business, the sports club. Every contact can create a *giri* situation. Thus it is not surprising that in their everyday life, the Japanese are very circumspect beyond simple superficial encounters. Two emotions prevail: one hesitates to enter on a personal relationship which can become a responsibility; further, one becomes aware of one's imperfection and is therefore cautious, so as to "save face" vis-à-vis an interlocutor who could become a "partner."

The Art of Adapting

If St. Francis Xavier and his missionaries had known these concepts, Japan might have stumbled into Christianity by virtue of another concept just as typically Japanese: *tenko,* the art of adapting to the ineluctable or submitting to a power that's demonstrably stronger. In the most commonsense terms, it is the Japanese faculty for adapting to an event. Japan has rarely let itself be surprised by evolution or revolution. Just as ants at work on a heap upset by a clod of crumbling earth or a stone placed in an unexpected spot circle around the obstacle or put chaos to rights and return the hill to its previous order, so the Japanese, troubled by the American decision to abandon the gold standard and let the dollar "float," or by the energy crisis, signal their distress and, after some months of vacillation, slowed growth, and a budget deficit, reascend the slope and reestablish their general equilibrium. It would seem that their chaos is not like ours, which has a tendency to amplify. One might suppose that theirs is programmed to return to order.

Tenko allowed the Japanese to accept the American conqueror and become his ally, to transform their economic structure through a successful technological takeoff, to negotiate the stormy cape of the seventies crisis—and now the specter of a crisis in the society itself has appeared. With Japan's political life reestablished, its economy flourishing, will *tenko* suffice to help Japanese society to evolve? The answer is in the process of being worked out. Yet one must go further and pierce the permanent substratum on the basis of which *tenko* functions. One remodels the house, modernizes it, adds a bathroom, repaints it, but the foundations are centuries old. That is how *tenko* functions, for it does not touch the substructure and would not exist without its permanence. Because *tenko* is not necessarily a flight forward, it can also be a return to the past, as in the case of those revolutionary students who fall back into the ranks when they sign their first employment contract. As a general rule, *tenko* represents a subordination of individual interest or inclination to the authority in the group.

THE JAPANESE LANGUAGE AND ITS AMBIGUITIES

In the Japanese language one finds the reflection of these complex systems of relationships. The same language is not used when one speaks to a superior or to an inferior, when a man addresses a woman or a woman addresses a man, when one puts through a business deal or chats with friends.

The structure of the Japanese sentence is the opposite of English or French. The sentence is cut up into small bits, the qualifiers or pronouns first, the nouns next, the verb at the end. A Jesuit missionary who returned to Rome after trying to win adherents in Japan put the Japanese language among the devil's inventions to hinder the preaching of the gospel. What foreigner in Japan has not experienced the misunderstandings that communication provokes! There was, for example, a sailor who lost all hope of being able to make himself understood by his taxi driver, either in Japanese or in English, when he asked to be driven to Yokohama, Tokyo's port. So he got the bright idea of drawing a boat. "*Wakarimas!*" (I understand!), the driver cried with a smile. The taxi began a mad race through the gigantic, anonymous labyrinth of Tokyo's streets. But when our sailor was due to board his ship, the port was still not in sight. The driver, smiling broadly, had taken him forty-five minutes from the center of town to a cabaret that had a boat on its sign.

The first communication problem in Japan is that of yes or no. When a Japanese says yes he rarely means yes, but rather "I understand" or "I have heard your question." I was invited by a big Japanese newspaper to serve on a prize jury that was awarding a scholarship for foreign travel. Our final discussion ended in a vote roughly like this: three votes for candidate X, two votes for candidate Y, and one vote for candidate Z. The president of the jury immediately announced the result of the vote: candidate X had won. I was stupefied when the president then announced: "Now we are going to give the grant for the trip abroad. We award it to Mr. Z." "But," I said naively, "Z got only one vote; therefore he is not the winner." The president continued: "Who is not in agreement?" I raised my hand. The president looked astonished and asked me to explain myself. No doubt I was visibly upset. Then, while tea was served and we chatted pleasantly, the interpreter took me aside and whispered, "It is true that candidate X is the winner since he received the largest number of votes, but it was never stated in the rules that the winner would get the grant. The president, after having declared X the winner, simply asked if one had any objection to the grant being given to Z." X was not denied his victory, but a semantic ambiguity took the grant away from him—the whole affair was simply a political deal. X and Y received very respectable compensations in proportion to their votes. I should have known that language and social relations are bound together in a permanent hierarchical matrix.

But the language is above all bound up with the Japanese preference for the vague, the "neither yes nor no." One of the fundamental difficulties of the language resides, according to a linguist, in "the number of empty words occurring as often as the number of words full of meaning, at times giving a sentence a rhetorical character which the Japanese call polite." I want, I think, etc., are claims whose formulation cause a foreigner to be regarded as uncouth, while for a Japanese such statements are unthinkable. One must have an inexhaustible reservoir of words to qualify and temper all affirmations. In any case, there is a major difficulty about affirming, because the way in which one does it indicates one's social standing or sex. Expressions such as "I am hungry" can have a very vulgar connotation if a woman uses the same phrase as a man. Whenever I

have asked a Japanese friend, especially a woman, to order my meal
in a restaurant, I have never been brought the dish I requested. On
the other hand, each time I have ordered my meal myself, with an
inevitable economy of terms, I have never encountered anything but
incomprehension. I cajole, saying that the honorable foreigner
adores the Japanese cuisine, that he would love to taste all the dishes,
that the fish seems to him particularly delicate but his stomach cannot stand raw fish, that he would therefore be satisfied with fried,
breaded fish (tempura). Then I am brought raw fish or perhaps both
raw and fried.

I have always thought that this chronic doubt of being understood by another represents not a failure of communication but the
possibility of a refusal to communicate. Each person can pretend not
to have understood or to have heard wrong and so nobody can feel
constrained by another person's words. The command can always be
interpreted, the hierarchy transgressed. Ambiguity comes to the aid
of freedom.

According to an eminent expert on Japan, Pierre Landy, "the
imprecision of the grammar, the syntactical fluidity, help to make
Japanese one of the least exact languages in the world for the statement of an idea. From the start of their intellectual development,
their language encloses the Japanese in a world of reservations, of
allusions, of shades of meaning." Written Japanese increases the ambiguous character of the spoken language. All linguists are in accord
in denouncing the complexity of the system of ideograms (kanji) in
Chinese writing. The Japanese infuse into this mode of writing their
taste for images. But, sometimes, what precision and what superiority in the ideas that arise from it!

In the hospital at Hiroshima, a woman of fifty, exposed to radiation thirty years before, is dying. The doctor knows that she has no
more than a day left or perhaps no more than a few hours; as is the
custom in Japan, he goes to tell her, so that she can, if she so desires,
make her arrangements and specify her last wishes. The doctor enters the sick woman's room and very quietly says: "Akirame." The
sick woman raises her eyes to the doctor, then rapidly with the index
finger of her right hand sketches on the palm of her left hand the
outline of the ideogram akirame, which means resignation. The doctor simply says: "Sodes" (It is that). A cloud passes over the woman's
eyes, furtively, then she gains control of herself and replies: "Wakarimas" (I understand).

COMPETITION AND THE SELECTION PROCESS

Resignation is undoubtedly the most accurate term with which to
describe the attitude of the Japanese faced with widespread despair,
a new scourge of their society. In the old Confucian ethic, whose

imprint on the Buddhist world influenced by China can never be overemphasized, one is resigned to fit into the mold, as if the personality could be shaped only at the level of its basic cell—the family. The recrudescence of children's suicides—could this not be a sign of the individual's revolt against the constraints of the group? Revolt today takes another form of resignation, the decision to die. Is it the fault of the one and only educational system? There is no quarrel between the supporters of "heads well made" and those of "heads well packed." Those heads have to be so fully packed that adolescence in Japan quickly becomes an inferno. And when one reaches the point where it is necessary to enter life as Mr. Everyman, very middle-of-the-road and a trifle depersonalized, one must also have a "well made" head if one wants to get on; the chosen are very few compared with all who are called. Such a situation often creates despair; so much so that the public has paid increasing attention to children's suicides.

At Kure near Hiroshima, a ten-year-old girl, Miyako, hanged herself from a tree with a stocking after having been reprimanded by her mother. At the start of one school year, at least one child between ten and fourteen committed suicide each day. A little girl of ten threw herself off the house roof because she was not the first in her class. A boy of seventeen hanged himself the same day because he was no longer first in his class. In 1977, 784 children and adolescents committed suicide.

A government report points an accusing finger at the examinations students must take to get into secondary school and later the university. So great the social pressure is that four times more young people under twenty commit suicide in Japan than in Great Britain, according to the London *Times*. Everything begins in kindergarten. It is important to get one's child into a kindergarten that will make it easier to get into a good elementary school, which facilitates the passage to a good secondary school. And that is essential if one wants later to enter a university, which will help one obtain an honorable job. The result is frantic competition, encouraged by the parents.

The government recently decided that the state universities would all use the same entrance exam, but in actuality each university follows a second admissions policy. The children's anxiety is equaled only by that of the parents, who make enormous sacrifices for their children, paying for private lessons in every imaginable subject. The children study as many as sixteen hours a day. A third of the children from six to fifteen attend a *juku*, a private school.

According to psychologists, young people today are entirely monopolized by their school, their sports club, and their families. They have fewer individual experiences and less and less opportunity to rebel. The weakening of the capacity for rebellion, combined with anxiety about exams, is one of the main factors that produce despair.

The more timid and docile students are the ones who commit suicide.

Competence, knowledge, and intelligence do not always suffice to open the doors of the university. At the University of Medicine in Nara, a third of the student body has for ten years been able to get admitted by the "little door"—an elegant way of describing acceptance as a result of a financial contribution. Moreover, during the last several years, the costs of education have accelerated: tuition, books, supplies, the *juku*, even lunches in school cafeterias.

In 1878, 75 percent of the students in the Imperial University of Tokyo belonged to the aristocracy or the military class; only 25 percent were commoners. In 1885, almost half did not belong to the nobility. Today new aristocracies have sprung from the public services or large industry, but there is also a still influential old aristocracy composed of the most famous regional feudal clans, like the Satsuma clan in the south of Japan.

Behind the great state universities, pillars of an elitist social system, another elite, that of liberal professors, is formed in the major private universities: Waseda, which produces important lawyers and the journalists most in the public eye; Keio, whose alumni include an impressive group of the highest state functionaries; Sophia, the Jesuit university, graduates of which occupy influential positions in all sectors and form a well-knit and active minority.

The separation of general and technical education when the student reaches the age of fifteen erects an almost definitive social barrier. Those who enroll in *kosem*—technical schools which one enters at fifteen for a five-year course of study—are aware that, according to the experts, they have given up their chances of further education.

The colleges and universities offer a superior education. Four years of study lead to a degree equivalent to an American B.A. Two more years qualify one for an M.A., three more, a PhD. For each of these degrees, one must have completed a certain number of lecture courses, each running one hour a week for fifteen weeks. A minimum of seventy to eighty are required for a B.A. These are either regular courses, or at the highest levels, seminars. This system, developed in imitation of the American, reinforces the competitiveness inherent in Japanese society. Certain universities receive thirty applications for each student admitted.

At this point we must make up our minds about education in Japan. We must recognize that since the Meiji restoration it has been the constant concern of the state as well as of parents and of teachers, whose methods are often old-fashioned but whose devotion and professional conscience arouse one's admiration and respect. The teacher, or *sensei*, is one of the truly important figures in Japanese society. After the emperor, he ranks beside the pater-familias in the hierarchy of obligations (*on*) which every individual assumes at birth. There are few or almost no illiterates in the country as prodigious, newspaper circulation and the prosperity of book publishers attest. Besides this there is the hunger for knowledge: no form of knowledge, whatever it may be, leaves the Japanese indifferent. We can meet the Friends of Shakespeare and the Friends of Pascal. Hemingway and Jean-Paul Sartre enjoy the same prestige as Robert Mitchum, Brigitte Bardot, or Alain Delon. The bad no doubt pushes aside the good, but the positive aspect of the Japanese education system prevails, despite all its defects, over all other considerations. It produces individuals ready for all of the mind's adventures.

The educational system is decisive in determining the hierarchical level an individual occupies in society. However, one must not consider rank as the supreme criterion of social comfort. More important is the feeling of harmony which prevails when everyone knows his place. In pre-1945 Japan, the military ranked high and enjoyed respectful, deferential, admiring consideration. The police were also advanced in the hierarchy, but the consideration from which they benefited was determined by the fear they could inspire.

THE POLICE AND THE YAKUZA

Following 1945, the military lost status and subsequently consideration. More than thirty-five years after the defeat, their status has palpably improved in proportion to the growing awareness of the importance of defense problems. But if the profession of arms no longer arouses an allergic reaction, it is far from having recovered the prestige it once enjoyed.

As regards the police, everything is more subtle. The Japanese remember the cantankerous behavior of these authorities, above all since the Meiji. Before 1868, the shoguns had no centralized police system. The people, especially in the countryside, were plundered and stripped bare by armed bands and subjected to the arbitrary rule of the samurai of the local feudal lord. After 1868, the police gradually became more effective; a rural police force was attached to each prefecture then, urban police forces were established, and were very soon involved in political affairs. Starting in 1900, the powers of the police were reinforced. First they were authorized to seize all firearms and to arrest, without warrant, any individual suspected of being a threat to public order. In 1913, the police extended their powers to conflicts on the job, public health, etc.; above all, they played a part in political surveillance and as guardians of orthodox thought. A special corps was called "thought police" (*kempetai*). It was directed during the war by a man who, after 1945, became one of the magnates of the Japanese press.

The Japanese public had formed the habit of servility toward the police. Denunciations were regarded as a civic duty. To facilitate their work, the police set up small units in each district and even surveillance posts in several sections of the same district. This setup continues today and has proved efficient: policemen know their district house by house, know those who live under their jurisdiction almost individually.

Nevertheless, the attitude of the Japanese has changed a great deal since 1945. Of course, there is spontaneous collaboration in the search for criminals, but individuals are sensitive today to everything having to do with individual freedom. Hence the police can count less and less on the public in any move against individual freedom. Time and again, American deserters sought by the Japanese police have been protected and hidden.

The Japanese police apparently arouse the envy of the world's police forces. In Tokyo, with an urban concentration four times larger than Chicago's, there are four times fewer murders than in the American city, four times fewer robberies than in Los Angeles, a negligible number of armed assaults on banks and other places. The average figure for crimes and serious offenses in the course of a year is five hundred greater in New York than in Tokyo. This exceptional situation can be attributed to the society's homogeneity, broken only by a minority of 800,000 Koreans. What's more, these Koreans are immediately considered guilty by the public and are under suspicion whenever a crime occurs. Psychoanalysts also see in the small number of crimes the influence of the traditional family system and education. This situation changes from year to year, what with the incidence of juvenile delinquency, notably among sixteen-to-seventeen-year-olds, the number of murders committed with firearms, which it is strictly forbidden to own and carry, and above all the increasing use of drugs. Here again one should put the facts in perspective: the drug phenomenon, since it is so severely repressed, is far from assuming the scale it has reached in Europe and, especially, the United States.

However, Japan goes in for a type of criminal behavior that is tied to its culture and tradition. The front page of one of the large newspapers one Sunday at the end of 1963 carried the photograph of a "gang" in the Shinjuku district in procession behind a banner, on the way to a nearby movie house to elect a new "boss." Astonishment was expressed for this unabashed and open demonstration, which occurred without police intervention. In reality, the tradition of Japanese gangs goes back to the seventeenth century and the organization of bands of unemployed samurai in a country gripped by civil war. Kurosawa's *Seven Samurai* effectively depicts a situation of this sort. Soon these men on the fringes of society who defended justice, the weak and the oppressed, became legends, like Robin

Hood. When the political confusion came to an end with the advent of the Tokugawa shogunate, some groups of young samurai, called *yakko*, became champions of the lost warrior values and formed bands roaming the streets of Edo and attacking passers-by and residents: these *hatamoto-yakko* soon found themselves faced by self-defense groups, the *nachi-yakko;* their brawls helped to nourish heroic legends. At the end of the seventeenth century, these bands disappeared, leaving as their heritage two kinds of gangs: peddlers and acrobats. These new bands, called *yakuza*, were bound together in accordance with the same principle of *oyabun-kobun* that is found in the family system or business. In exchange for the protection of the leader or group, each member pledged his loyalty and complete support. They had a code of behavior, a parody of the samurai's, and even obeyed written rules, a model of which is quoted by Devos and Mizushima in a study made for Princeton University:

1. You will not touch the wife of another *yakuza.*
2. You will not engage in any activities other than those of the group.
3. The secrets of the organization will never be revealed.
4. You will maintain the strictest loyalty to the *oyabun-kobun.*
5. You will never express yourself in common language but will instead use the language of the group.

Under the Tokugawas, the *yakuza* became a symbol of resistance to authority. At the same time, they justified their activities in the name of progress and social orders. One rediscovers these characteristics in the activities of the *yakuza* groups as they are organized today in Tokyo.

Yakuza today live on tributes levied from the merchants, a percentage of clandestine gambling—since gambling is illegal in Japan—and a cut of the profits from prostitution, which is also forbidden by law. No doubt, tacit nonintervention agreements exist locally between the *yakuza* and the police, as a result of which members of the gang escape police interference in instances of drunkenness, minor brawls or petty disturbances. A strong tradition tends to exempt the run of mortals from their aggression and to focus attacks only on other delinquents. There are said to be gangs that compel their members to abstain from raping a nondelinquent girl, a prostitute being by definition a delinquent. The *yakuza* also engage in political activities in certain circumstances.

It was to the superintendent of Tokyo police, Mr. Matsushita Kazunoki, that I went to learn about criminality in its most recent manifestations. "Originally, he explained, "the *yakuza* were divided into two groups: the *tekiya*, who had a racket in the temples, the peddlers' stalls, and the festivals, and the *bakto*, the group that got its money from gambling. Both groups, though organized separately, went in for the rackets, prostitution, and gambling. In the Kansai, they were organized in small bands of twenty or thirty and worked as doormen in cabarets, clubs, or hotels. They also supplied mercenaries to the companies that hire out guards. However, in Tokyo it was not rare to find gangs of six or seven hundred members."

"It has actually reached the point where the gangs hold public demonstrations," I said. "How do they arrange it so that the police don't intervene?"

"True, it is not unusual to see gangs celebrate the inauguration of a new boss, or the funeral of one of their men. But if none of the members is individually being sought by the police, the fact that they participate in a ceremony does not constitute a crime. So we cannot run them in. Yet we know that these ceremonies are a way of collecting funds. It is the custom in Japan to put a personal donation in a sealed envelope for those taking part in one of these ceremonies: marriage, burial, or simply an anniversary. The gangs organize several funerals and inaugurations for the same person, and each time they collect the contribution from more or less coerced participants. As for the rackets, some restaurants, cabarets, and various merchants have created informal associations to resist the gangs' basic demands."

"In Tokyo," the superintendent went on, "for months now a new kind of crime has been sprouting up; it is the work of perfectly organized groups, the *sokaiya*. They blackmail the presidents and directors of businesses. For months the gang collects the most diverse kinds of information about a company, if necessary getting jobs in it for one or several of its members: how it is managed, public relations, financial condition—they put it all in the hopper. A few days before the annual meeting of the stockholders, the *sokaiya* informs the management that they are privy to their business secrets and that they are going to tell them to the stockholders. Very often the stockholders meeting is postponed and the management ends by shelling out the cash. In order to put pressure on them, the *sokaiya* prints leaflets and threatens to circulate them.

The traditional *yakuza* have adapted themselves to an evolving society and Japan's prosperity has opened up new frontiers for them; they have extended their activities—in Asia and the Pacific. According to *Shukan Asahi*, they are established in Hawaii, the Philippines, Korea, and Thailand, where they carry on trade in women, guns, and drugs. As for prostitution, they quietly offer to satisfy the demands of their compatriots lost on these foreign shores or to provide Japan with exotic "consignments," such as Thai masseuses or the blond go-go girls who hang around after the discotheques shut down. The *yakuza* also show their "solicitude" for their compatriots by supplying them with guns and drugs. A .38 automatic worth $100 in Hawaii is sold for $10,000 in Tokyo. Tokyo Japanese can also visit Korea on a sex tour: the *yakuza*, using honorable travel agents as intermediaries, offer a weekend package deal. The men announce to their wives that they are going to play golf over the weekend. Each Saturday at the Narita airport, one can see them consigning to the baggage room their golf bags, which are picked up Sunday evening on their return from Seoul, after they have enjoyed themselves in the arms of a *kisaeng* (Korean geisha).

"This type of crime," the police superintendent said, "is relatively stable, but like all large capitals, we must confront gangs which are obviously not as well structured: gangs of adolescents or young people. In Tokyo there are about fifty such groups, with a total of a thousand members and such stylish names as the Black Emperors, the Killers, and so on. They gather in groups of fifty or sixty and hurl themselves down the streets in motorcycles very late at night, stealing, wrecking, or just making a lot of noise. They are obsessed with speed and freedom. In the daytime they go in for shoplifting or a few rapes, but they are always in a group. Individually, when they are arrested, they are rather pitiful, denouncing their comrades and making excuses for themselves. In Tokyo our police setup for protection includes a checkerboard of 1,200 police boxes: the city is patrolled by 600 squad cars and 800 unmarked cars, connected to an emergency center which receives about 1,400 calls for help a day. A helicopter service can reinforce these vehicles if there is need."

JUSTICE

The end results of effective police action against crime flow into the courts of justice, whose powers are defined by the constitution of 1947. Through profound transformations, the judiciary system has become supreme among all the organs of government; it is empowered to decide whether a law has constitutional validity and it has the right to promulgate decrees. Moreover, the constitution guarantees the judiciary complete independence. This has led to separation between the magistrates who preside over the courts and are responsible to the supreme court, and the examining magistrates and public prosecutors, who are under the authority of the Ministry of Justice. All special courts have been abolished, and there is no specific court to handle crimes against the state.

At the bottom of the pyramid are "summary" courts, which deal with minor violations punishable by fines, and which also handle civil suits, litigations, and claims up to one thousand dollars. At the district level one finds the family courts, on the American model, which deal with juvenile delinquency, the protection of minors, and everything that can endanger family life. A district court in each prefecture rules on all cases that the summary courts cannot handle. The high courts deal with appeals against verdicts handed down in the summary courts and district courts, and the supreme court judges the final appeals. It is also empowered to review all cases that raise questions on constitutional grounds.

Japanese prisons are not very comfortable, and discipline is quite strict. Prisoners are required to work at certain crafts. There are no leaves, but a prisoner can shorten his stay by good behavior. There is a death penalty, carried out by hanging. Publicity about executions is forbidden, and the newspapers cannot report them. Amendments to the penal code made on October 26, 1947, under the influence of the United States, are significant: abolition of the crime of lese majesty, revision of the laws pertaining to the right of the state to declare war, and the concept of the enemy and of foreign aggression. Until 1973, the law continued to make a distinction between murder within and outside the family, but this distinction has been declared contrary to the constitutional provisions for equality.

The new code of criminal procedure reflects Anglo-American influence, especially in its primary article, which ensures respect for the fundamental human rights of the individual and the maintenance of public order. To the Japanese, such a twofold purpose is not seen as contradictory. Aware that "one cannot chase two hares at the same time," they approach each case pragmatically, free of any intellectual bias and with a scrupulous respect for the evidence. Justice is powerful and modest.

THE MEDIA

Each year, Nihon Shimbun Kyokai, the Association of Newspaper Editors, organizes a national press week, for which a slogan is chosen. The slogan in 1968 (which could also have been used for national justice week) was: "Newspapers, Guardians of an Orderly Society." Indeed, the press tends to place itself on the level of the great national institutions and at the service of the kind of society that precludes any kind of dependence on a political party, a trade union, or a religious ideology. Japanese newspapers wield such effective power that they have a decisive influence on public life. With a circulation of more than 60 million copies each day, 37 million of which are accounted for by the largest newspapers, the press in the postwar period has become a power among the masses. There are 170 daily newspapers, divided into the categories national, regional, local, and specialized. The three great papers, *Asahi, Yomiuri,* and *Mainichi,* come close to or surpass a daily circulation of 10 million copies. *Sankei* prints about 3 million, as does *Nihon Keizai,* which specializes in economic matters.

National newspapers account for half the total circulation, which does not detract at all from the economic viability of regional papers such as *Hokkaido Shimbun,* which is sold all over the northern island, or *Tokyo Shimbun,* distributed only in the Kanto district of Tokyo. The specialized newspapers are also very well supported. Thirteen that deal with sports print a total of 5 million copies. There are also four dailies in English, with a very restricted circulation.

Japanese newspapers are delivered to home subscribers by exclusive agents, 22,000 of them, employing 300,000 persons, of whom 200,000 are boys on their way to school or home. The newspapers collect their information through a stable system of clubs grouped around sources such as ministries, public figures.

Radio and television have an integral share of media power. As a quasi-governmental institution, NHK (Nippon Hoso Kyokai), the national television network, with its two channels, one of which specializes in education, has the monopoly on rental fees. Japanese homes are 100 percent equipped with television sets, more than 92 percent of which are color sets. There is no national network for commercial television; instead it is divided up among 1,900 stations operated by a hundred companies and broadcasting on several channels. In Tokyo, one has a choice of seven channels; in Osaka, only four, which is about the average for the cities. NHK is administered by a council of governors. Its financial resources, based on the money paid for rentals, gives it a budget of over 150 million American dollars. The commercial companies belonging to NAB (National Association of Broadcasters) get their money from advertising. The Law compels them to devote 30 percent of their air time to cultural and educational programs.

In Japan, all organs of power have obligations. Thus the media have a code of ethics, extremely strict, which is established by canons of journalism. In a preamble to these canons, the Association of Newspaper Editors reminds us that the role of the press is important inasmuch as Japan is a democratic nation that loves peace. The same text speaks of its "mission." To appreciate this role, one should know some history.

The first Japanese newspapers appeared around 1860, at the beginning of the Meiji era; this was not long before Japan was opened to the West and the birth of modern Japan. But the new Meiji government suspended all newspapers; it soon realized the harm caused by rumors and false news. In February 1869, it created a system of licensing which regulated newspaper publication.

The first daily newspaper, *Yokohama Mainichi Shimbun,* appeared in 1871, and lasted until 1940. It was followed by *Yubin Hochi Shimbun* (today *Mainichi*), which was bought by the government. These newspapers were used by the Meiji government to make its policies known. The government also foresaw all the advantages of this means of mass education.

From 1875 to 1880, the government reinforced its control, imprisoning journalists and suspending newspapers. In reaction, the newspapers gave even more space to politics, and here again a parallel can be made between the convulsive birth movements of the 1860s and those of a century later.

The imperial ordinance of October 1881, guaranteeing the creation of a parliament within ten years, launched a political debate revolving around the constitution; the government wanted it to be based on the Prussian model, while the opposition preferred the English or French model. In 1883, the government, which was decreasingly getting its message across, began the publication of an *Official Journal.*

In the years that followed the 1945 defeat, political life revolved around the constitution proposed by MacArthur, and the Japanese again found themselves confronted by the choice between a democratic and a totalitarian model. It should be observed that at critical moments, the Japanese press has always sloughed off its reticence and finally ranged itself on the democratic side—a capitalist and antimilitarist democracy.

During the years that preceded the Second World War, most of the important Japanese press took a stand against the military and on the side of the *zaibatsu,* the large financial interests. For this the press paid a high price. The military imposed all sorts of restrictions on it and forced a certain number of newspapers to merge. In 1930, there were 1,200 daily newspapers in Japan and 7,700 periodicals in all; in 1943, only 43 remained. In truth, the Japanese press had to deal with censorship until 1946.

Information, Education, and Moral Obligation

It is evident that the Japanese press has not only taken on the task of purveying information. The educational purpose of the newspapers, radio, and television appears in their handling of information. Article One of the journalistic canon is entitled "Freedom of the Press." The press is free to report the news and to comment on it, provided that these activities are not contrary to the public interest or forbidden by law. Article Two provides for voluntary restrictions on this freedom and the context in which it is to be exercised: facts must be given in good faith and with precision; the journalist's personal opinion must not appear. The journalist must be aware that information can be used for propaganda purposes; he must treat the news in a way that avoids manipulation. Individuals can only be criticized if their dignity is respected. Partisan editorials must not stray from the truth; an editorial writer must not forget the public character of a newspaper.

The other articles of the canon stipulate by implication "the right of reply," tolerance of opinions contrary to those held by the newspaper, and hence "the obligation to quote" them, and finally and importantly, "decency," which acts to exclude scandalous or pornographic material.

These guidelines, adopted in 1946 during the founding meeting of Nihon Shimbun Kyokai, are in great part inspired by the rules that govern the American press, but their Japanese interpretation is at once more restrictive and more permissive. The association of editors is only a facade: it does not wield any real power. In any other country, the great options regarding professional ethics and the objectivity of reporting are the affair of the management of each paper. But in Japan, the big newspaper owners do not want to assume the responsibility for setting out national guidelines. They are at once judge and plaintiff, and they do not want to disagree among themselves or cut themselves off, in their search for a consensus of their peers and the approbation of their readers.

Every fundamental decision, whether popular or unpopular, is backed up by the ever-powerful authority of an anonymous management. Thus a newspaper's entire board of directors comes to an agreement on what is publishable and what is not. It decides against publishing, for example, material that might exert a bad influence on the young, or pornographic and violent stories. But the choice is difficult. Where does decency end and pornography begin? The association of editors constantly tries to reestablish the frontiers of what is "permissible." The Japanese claim that the press's increasing audacity regarding sex reflects the rampant liberality all over Europe, the United States, and now Japan. This invasion from outside has posed certain problems. There is, on the part of the Japanese media, a certain hypocrisy that permits large-circulation newspapers to justify, because of their readership, a moral strictness which they have perpetuated for the last twenty years. Japanese newspapers, yesterday as today, are behind the times in relation to the evolution of their society, which has always been more permissive than almost any Western society, even the Danish or Swedish.

Partisan journalism does not have the same significance in Japan as in America or free Europe. With the exception of the Communist newspapers, it cannot be said that a Japanese newspaper is defined in terms of its political line. Generally, the editorials represent a relatively broad range of opinion, but always within the framework of recognized and accepted ideas. No large Japanese newspaper advocates revolution or promulgates a fascist ideology. One must always keep in mind that the newspapers are conscious of performing a public service and also want to play a role of real importance.

The newspapers speak for nonconformists in a sea of conformism. They contribute to the evolution of the society but protect it from any hint of revolution. They ask the people at the bottom to take responsiblity for what has been decided at the top. They stir up tempests, but in a hermetically sealed container. The press is not the instrument of some higher power. It is a power and not subject to manipulation. So in this connection one can talk about the institution. The picture of Japan that it shows the rest of the world always conforms to the picture it shows Japan itself. It satisfies the most exigent, because each person can find in it something of himself.

The Japanese press as a whole recognizes the need for a technical revolution. It is a question of overturning the old technologies under the pressure of circumstances. During the last ten years, a race for technical innovation has accelerated in all newspaper departments—editorial, advertising, administration, transmissions, and distribution. Electronic equipment in particular has provided the big national newspapers with a solution to many problems.

Advances in the Japanese press have always accompanied a simplification of the written language. Despite the universities, the newspapers have been able to reduce the number of ideograms in general use and finally to limit them, so as not to become the exclusive preserve of a literate minority. The written language in newspapers, kept today to about two thousand characters, utilizes an alphabet which all Japanese know.

All the newspapers make a special effort in regard to makeup. The number of pages, the format, and the presentation are continually revised in order to stimulate the readers' interest. Computers are utilized, and the big newspapers make use of programming computers in composing the pages. New photogravure equipment can also be connected to the computers.

Eleven newspapers use offset printing today. The offset pioneer, *Asahi Hokkaido*, prints directly from plates made from a film transmitted in facsimile from *Asahi's* central office in Tokyo. It was the success of these transmissions that led *Asahi* to develop a similar method of distributing the newspaper to the home, anticipating the moment, a few years hence, when there won't be enough newsboys. In a country where 99.5 percent of the papers are delivered to the home morning and evening, this could become a matter of life or death.

For *Asahi Shimbun* in 1985, there will no doubt be enough home receivers to make a clean transition from the old system of delivery. With such a machine, the householder can receive, according to his mood of the moment, the sports page, the foreign news, or the personal notices.

Super-Television in the Year 2000

Innovation is also the order of the day at the television networks. Seven networks broadcast programs for six hours apiece, from six in the morning until midnight, or even later. Even if our capacity for astonishment has been blunted, our attention is still caught by the technological arsenal behind this flood of images. Thus at NHK, programs on videotape are taken from their shelves a few minutes before the broadcast, transferred to the room that houses the videotape machines, rolled onto the broadcasting apparatus, and broadcast without human intervention. The programming is on a computer. In a control room, three technicians make sure that the programs are set in place on the broadcasting apparatus at the desirable hour or, when the program is live, that the antenna is correctly linked with the predetermined studio or mobile unit. The same refinement exists at the level of production. Each producer has a computer terminal on his table and a chart of personnel. In this way, he can compose his program at will, and in a few minutes know the names of all the technicians, the sound team, the crew, the assistants, the scene painters and designers, etc., who will work with him. The dates and hours of studio time for rehearsals and for taping the show, the arrangements for exterior shots, and the total budget appear item by item. NHK has today become the foremost television setup in the world, the organization best prepared for the technologies of the year 2000 and the intensive use of satellites.

Television is also progressing at the other end of the network—for example, in the new city of Tama, where an event out of the year 2000 is taking place: cable television at the service of a community. Tama is thirty miles from Tokyo. In a wooded landscape with many deep valleys, concrete buildings suddenly emerge from among the trees. Leaving the railroad station, walking up one of the innumerable pedestrian arcades, I meet women on their way to the supermarket with their babies strapped to their backs. Tama could be a district in Brasília, a new town in the Paris region, or almost any suburban community in New Jersey. Nothing is specifically Japanese. The buildings, lined up on perfectly straight streets, indicate no architectural imagination. This bedroom city, which has 100,000 inhabitants, will house 300,000 ten years from now—that is, about 100,000 families. The average weekly income of each family is slightly higher than the national average—about 325,000 yen as against 290,000 in Japan as a whole. Each house has its cable television—in other words, it is connected with a centralized network of cables which will become the fulcrum of an information system—and pays a subscription fee for the cable hookup, just as people pay for their gas, electricity, and telephone service. The first problem posed at Tama is that of the terminal. What should be installed at the end of the cable, in the apartments, when they are connected with the local television station? A television set, of course. The cable hookup improves, quite markedly, the technical quality of reception from Tokyo's seven networks. But the cost far exceeds the importance of the service rendered, especially since the cooperative antennas atop the apartment buildings can, without harming the environment, provide the same service as the cables. You can add a receiver for the daily newspaper; you can also install a machine to transmit or receive documents if, for example, you are a subscriber to a library; and the same service is available for photography or television programs. In all, a dozen services are proposed experimentally, but one can foresee their extension almost ad infinitum, until the saturation point. The only problem is how to house all the necessary receiving equipment in a small apartment. But Tama's technicians keep searching for a comprehensive receiver.

MINAMATA: THE DISEASE OF POLLUTION

Osamu Takahashi is a name that is unknown in America and Europe. In Japan his name was greatly overshadowed by the work he created: a play telling the story of the Minamata affair. Written in 1969, staged often since 1970, it contributed significantly to the growing awareness of environmental problems at a time when accumulated data on the most deadly pollution in the world was being assembled. The Minamata disease is a form of poisoning that has progressively extended from fish to birds, from birds to domestic animals—cats, pigs, and chickens—and finally to the men and women who live on Minamata bay, mostly fishermen or people working in the chemical plant at Chisso, where waste materials from organic mercury thrown into the sea have been responsible for the scourge.

At the start, during the fifties, nobody could fathom the source of this bizarre disease which attacked the nerve centers. It was thought to be a variety of poliomyelitis, but in May 1956, an observation by Dr. Hosokawa, of Chisso, led to the discovery of the cause. In October 1959, proof that the mercury waste was responsible came as the result of experiments on cats. Soon after, the social consequences of the scourge made themselves felt in a general impoverishment of the communities that lived off fishing. The chemical plant did not collaborate willingly with the investigation; in fact, it actually increased production. The fishermen's association in turn tried to camouflage the illness, so as not to bring about a complete stop to all fishing. But the illness spread throughout the entire region. In 1960, all the symptoms were enumerated: disordered vision and other senses, excessive salivation, ataxia, difficulty in speaking. The Minamata disease became a cause for shame; members of families who had it tried to conceal it. It became the leprosy of the twentieth century, bearing the same burden of infamy. It was only in 1969 that the victims, who had organized a defense association, established their right to some sort of compensation from the Chisso plant.

Then the disease was discovered in 1963 in Honshu, in the Niigata region along the shores of the Japan Sea. The Showa-Denko company had been pouring organic mercury into the Agano River, although the company had been aware of Minamata. Showa-Denko was finally forced to pay a heavy indemnity to each person seriously affected or to victims' families. Similarly, Mitsui Mining was condemned for spilling cadmium into a river near Toyama, south of Niigata, and also on the sea coast. The resulting illness manifested itself in a painful erosion of the bones and a gradual general paralysis. Two hundred residents of the village of Fuchu-Machi died in ten years.

To combat the pollution of seawater and river water, air pollution and noise pollution, from 1970 to 1975 a whole legislative arsenal was created and reinforced on the initiative of the Ministry of the Environment.

But, the Japanese ask, can the problem be solved? Their everyday life may not have gotten even worse, but it has gotten no better. Alerted by the media to the acute, very serious consequences of pollution, they feel both concerned and impotent. The price is very high.

The department stores sell cans of oxygen which can be opened in the office just like a can of tuna fish; in the drugstores and in certain public places, you can breathe oxygen in a small booth by inserting a token. In a school in Kawasaki, the district of the blast furnaces, which is wedged between Tokyo and Yokohama on Tokyo Bay, I have seen the distribution of gas masks, the kind used in the First World War, to children so that they can play in the schoolyard.

A polluted Japan is not a new phenomenon. The priority given to industry, the dominant desire to become the leading nation in electronics, steel output, ship construction, etc., has inevitably called into question a whole way of life. But the misdeeds of industrial pollution represent only one item in a list of wrongs resulting from urbanization. In ten years, from 1960 to 1970, the Tokkaido line, from Tokyo to Osaka, has become the axis of the most densely populated space in the world. Since 1980, the cumulative effects of industrialization and overpopulation have brought man face to face with a straightforward problem: he will have to invent new patterns of transportation, of preserving green space, feeding the nation, and using the sea, or he will perish.

THE AGING POPULATION

Modern Japan is a relatively recent concept. The Universal Exposition at Osaka in 1970 marked the turning point. It became obvious then that Japan, the third-largest producer of automobiles, lacked highways; that the capital of the world's third economic power was virtually without a sewer system. The Japanese grew aware of pollution, the pleasure of paid vacations, the benefits of political protests and demonstrations, the possibilities of enjoyment in one's leisure time. (One such possibility is the very successful Tokyo-Guam charter flight, which offers the opportunity to "tan yourself silly"— though not as a European would. A Japanese does not pick an island with coconut palms and miles of beach on which to go around half-naked before returning home, roasted and broiled, to recuperation paid for by a health insurance plan. The Japanese chooses an island with coconut palms and beaches in order to take a stroll, which he does without taking off his ordinary clothes—the white shirt and the tie of the Tokyo summer or, if his social position is very high, a complete suit. His greatest joy is his return to Haneda airport, where parents and friends, behind the glass, watch the traveler as he unpacks his fresh pineapples and persuades the customs official to stamp them.)

This completely modern Japanese will no longer die of tuberculosis, but from a heart attack or cancer; the stress of urban life has led him to regard as possible a stay in a psychiatric hospital. The Japanese are no doubt up-to-date: their life expectancy has jumped to seventy years for men and seventy-five years for women, a level attained only by nations very advanced in medical research.

However, what was regarded in the past as a great victory has today become a great scourge. Thanks to a very high birthrate, human losses of the Second World War were replaced in two or three generations. Then Japan began to favor a policy of strict birth control, publicizing contraception and abortion in the sixties and thus transforming the old structure of the three- or four-generation *ié* into the modern family—father, mother, two children. By 1980, this had resulted in a predominantly elderly population, and sharply posed the question of a not too distant future when a heavier and heavier burden will fall on a decreasing number of young workers. The cumulative effects of this increase in the elderly combined with the falling birthrate made it necessary to appraise carefully a social-security and pension system which was integrated into the social structure only in terms of traditional family income. The retirement at sixty-five of an employee who is given severance pay equal to two years' salary involves additional compensation on several levels: hiring his wife if she has not yet reached retirement age, or a son or daughter who is looking for a first job, and finally, reclassifying the person who has retired, either as a part-time worker in an affiliated company or with a subcontractor whose salaries are lower.

The White Book on social security published by the Ministry of Health in 1978 throws into relief this particular situation in Japan when compared with Western countries. Of Japanese over age sixty-five, 74 percent live with families or relatives. Therefore, Japanese social projects take the family factor into account. Added to this is the desire to create an effective system of health insurance and to advance the retirement age by letting older people stay on the job as long as possible, while maintaining a policy of full employment. The White Book also emphasizes keeping the birthrate at its present level. A questionnaire has revealed a definite preference for two children as optimum for successful family life. Very few of the people questioned were concerned about the future of Japanese society. Experts in the field estimate that population growth will slow down around the year 2000 and that Japan will have 150 million inhabitants by the middle of the twenty-first century. At the same time, the Chinese will have gone past the billion mark and the Indians will be quite close to it. It is predicted that the working population aged forty-five to sixty-five will be more numerous than that in the twenty-five to forty-five group. Japanese aged fifty to fifty-five will increase from 4 million to 8 million by the year 2000. This situation will help to revolutionize traditional social presuppositions. Employers will be forced to renounce promotion by seniority if they do not want to create a situation of irremediable despair among young entrants into the job market. Demography has become the most revolutionary factor in social change, compelling everyone to rethink the educational system, the organization of companies and business, the question of job mobility, and the shape that careers will take.

MEDICINE AND HEALTH

Civilization breeds certain diseases. One is only too aware of how many Japanese wear glasses, how many are disfigured by bad teeth, how many have persistent stomach troubles, though of course these widespread ailments attract less attention than heart disease, cancer, or mental illness. It is barely one hundred years since Japan entered the era of modern Western medicine. And yet, as in music, a phenomenal assimilation has taken place at record speed, which has placed Japan among the first countries of the world in medical research.

At the Ninth International Cancer Congress in 1966, the world's leading doctors discovered to their stupefaction the great advances made by Japan in successfully developing a whole series of cancer-fighting agents, including bleomycin which, when produced commercially in France ten years later, was responsible for almost miraculous cures of certain forms of cancer of the throat.

Over the years, in fact, Japanese medical research has trailblazed in the most diverse areas. In 1890, Dr. Kitazato perfected a serum therapy for tetanus. In 1910, Dr. Hata discovered a specific remedy for syphilis. The same year, Dr. Suzuki extracted vitamins from the rice envelope, opening the way for research in this area. It was in Japan that the first method of contraception was developed, by Dr. Ogina of Niigata.

Japan has about 130,000 doctors, slightly less than one doctor per thousand inhabitants, which is the same proportion as in Australia, Sweden, and the Low Countries. Japanese hospital services, even when they are housed in old-fashioned, unsuitable installations, function with a remarkable efficiency, as I experienced firsthand. I was taken in the middle of the night to a Tokyo hospital and given a bed without going through any administrative formalities. An intern was attending me ten minutes after my admission, and the doctor on night duty examined me less than thirty minutes later. The administrative formalities were attended to in the morning, as is the case for all emergency treatment in this hospital. I was not treated differently from any Japanese. The physicians make less money than European or American doctors, yet they form a kind of guild which is deeply devoted to serving the public.

Owing to its importance, preventive medicine holds a place apart. Thus systematic checkups are available for pulmonary disease, and, what is more important and demands considerable effort, mobile units make systematic examinations for cancer in the provinces and the less favored cities.

THE EXCLUDED

In the summer of 1969, trying to reach the port of Kobe in my car, I got lost in a labyrinth of faceless streets lined by wooden houses and realized that I would never manage to find Osaka's main road to Kobe without help. I continued turning down one street after another until noon. The crushing heat had emptied the streets. The city looked dead. I finally decided to stop in one of those identical alleys, a trifle broader than the others, which led into an empty lot. The lot looked like what could have been left if it had been destroyed by air raids thirty years before and then abandoned. Perhaps it was. But my concerns lay elsewhere—in finding the right route to Kobe. My intention was to take the boat that crossed the inland sea to go to Beppu, the port of Kyushu. Beppu is famous for a hill inhabited by monkeys with red behinds and for its baths of colored mud.

I got out of my car and immediately noticed something abnormal: the houses, all built on the same model, had wooden balconies one floor above the ground, and the balconies were filled with freshly tanned hides.

I was among the *burakumin*, whose existence I had known of for a long time. I knocked on the door of a house whose garage space, beneath the balcony, was occupied by a small Toyota with a Tokyo license. In the other houses there were no cars and the garage's were filled with scrap iron and rags. A small, plump middle-aged woman came to the door, discreetly holding it open just a crack. I could see that she was dressed in the country woman's white apron buttoned up the back.

"Nan deska?" (What is it?)

I jabbered some excuse in fractured Japanese, asking to see the master of the house. But apparently she did not understand. Confronted by my strange language, she was silent. She then said to me, *"Chotto matte."* (Wait a bit.) Closing the sliding door, she left me standing there. I waited for a minute—nothing. Two minutes—still nothing. I was just about to go, when a man dressed in European clothes came out and said in correct English, "May I help you?" Moved by a reflex now well implanted, I took out one of my calling cards and handed it to him. He read it attentively, then asked me to come in.

I quickly removed my shoes, after having walked down a small crooked hallway and turned two sharp right angles, and the woman in the white apron opened before me the shojis of a room with twelve tatami. My host sat me down on a cushion with my back against the *tokonoma.* To my right, the half-opened shoji gave on a covered gallery which encircled the house. When I was seated, my host took a card out of his pocket and in his turn handed it to me: *"Dozo."* (If you please.) I read the card: *Masao Nemoto, Executive Marketing Department.* The card was printed in English on one side and in Japanese on the other; there followed the name of a company known for the success of its products in the West. The woman served us green tea and we drank in silence. He spoke first, without making any allusion to the reason that had led me to knock at his door. "Where are you from? Italy?" "No, France." *"Ah, sodeska!"* Nemoto then began talking about his company's European market. The year before, he had been in charge of a group of colleagues who traveled to Europe to learn how to set up a sales network for their products in the Common Market countries.

I told him that I was a journalist and that each time the international political situation allowed time, I would visit another part of Japan. I was going to visit north Kyushu, the region of Beppu and Mount Aso, and if I had the time, I hoped to go as far as Nagasaki, to the "Madame Butterfly" house. A question burned my lips, the only one that interested me now and which I hardly dared ask. I finally took courage and asked laboriously, "By the way, what are all those hides drying on the balconies?" My host had undoubtedly expected this question. He began laughing, as one does in Japan when an embarrassing question is asked, then, speaking in a clipped, slow voice, he said to me: "You are here among the *burakumin,* the outcasts. I am a *burakumin,* but if I admitted it in Tokyo I would lose my job. I do not know whether my wife might not divorce me, and I am not even sure whether my two children would continue to consider me their father. My sister, whom you just saw, has always remained here. I have another married sister, who lives in a house about two streets from here. It is my sister's husband who continues to sell hides, for my father and mother are dead."

"And what about you?" I asked.

"Everything has been very difficult for me. I decided to get out of the community, and from eighteen to thirty I led a vagabond existence. First I went to work in Pukuoka. I had a great deal of luck because I was employed in a company that rented cars. That left me a little free time and I could continue my law studies. After that, I went to Takarazuka and became secretary to a theater manager; then I worked at Nagoya for a small distributor of various products. I have lived in twenty different cities. Each time, I changed my name. Today, if I were investigated, if they tried to track me down, it would be very difficult to trace me back here, although I have heard that private detectives can do it because they search with such tenacity."

The case of the *burakumin* is a special one. They number about three million, living either as individuals or as groups throughout the country. More than half of them are in Mr. Nemoto's position. Since physically they cannot be distinguished from other Japanese, they can change their address ten, fifteen, twenty times, and, often, their names: they claim to have lost their papers, or that their birth certificates and other personal documents were destroyed during the war. When they achieve integration into ordinary society, they are still afraid that someone might identify them especially since a kind of witch hunt went on in recent years, after the appearance of an under-the-counter *burakumin* directory listing names and birthplaces, which was compiled through the patient work of private detectives hired by some large companies. These companies are guilty of discrimination in hiring, a completely illegal practice, since the term *burakumin* has been prohibited on birth certificates since the war.

These Japanese "untouchables" can be traced to the Nara period, when certain of the poorer classes agreed to do work that nobody else wanted to do: collecting garbage, cleaning out sewers, emptying cesspools, slaughtering livestock, tanning leather, making shoes, working as butchers, etc. Today these trades carry a social stigma which affects not only the individuals who engage in them but their families, ancestors, and descendants. About a million and a half Japanese like Mr. Nemoto are scattered through what is called *ippan* society, the society of the majority, and about a million and a half live in six thousand ghettoes (*buraku*) divided into villages or enclaves on city outskirts.

Those who have continued to live in these ghettoes have developed a group consciousness which, even before the Second World War, had become a political force. In 1946, wanting to forward their social integration, the leader of this minority met with Prime Minister Shigeru Yoshida, the father of contemporary Japan, and offered him the political support of the *buraku* in exchange for an active policy of liberation. Yoshida had a law passed with an antidiscrimination clause which forbade any mention of the *burakumin* in official records, but he was completely unable to change the old habits of thought. Disappointed, the *burakumin* gave many of their votes to the Socialists, the Communists, or the Komeito (the Buddhist party), denying the conservatives votes which they may someday need.

The campaign to liberate Japan's *buraku* gathered force at the end of 1977 under the prodding of Sueo Murakoshi, one of the rare *burakumin* to identify himself publicly as such. According to Murakoshi, who has ties with the Socialist party, more than a thousand copies of the directory listing *buraku* and *burakumin* are distributed yearly. One can understand Mr. Nemoto's fears and the fears of all *burakumin* who are hiding out in Japanese society. They run the risk of losing everything, even if they have supposedly been integrated for more than twenty years; it would take only a more than usually thorough investigation by future in-laws. If *buraku* origins were uncovered, not only would the marriage be called off but there would be great danger that the father would be fired by his company.

A Professor Cornell, of the University of Texas, has for years observed the life and behavior of a rural community of *burakumin*— the *buraku* of Matsuzaki, near the town of Okayama. He has tried to understand how these Japanese, whose situation during the Taisho period in the twenties resembled that of German Jews during the same period, regard themselves in relation with their neighbors in the larger society. The *burakumin* consider themselves superior to other Japanese in a number of ways, notably in their respect for traditional values. They also believe that they work harder and are less egotistical. They admit with a certain embarrassment that they are less adept in conversation, less educated and less well brought up, less well dressed, and that they have less rigorous hygienic standards; they also admit that relations between men and women are less harmonious than in the other society. Sometimes these Japanese "untouchables" are rich (mainly the butchers), but most often they are at the bottom of the economic ladder.

Having determined that Matsuzaki's *burakumin* as a group are eager to be part of the "other society," Professor Cornell asked their more privileged neighbors the reasons for this apartheid, since no physical characteristics distinguish one group from the other. Respondents began by replying: "It is very difficult to explain. . . . They are different, strange, dirty, unhygienic, without morals, disgusting. At Matsuzaki they speak in a vulgar way; they are coarse people. They lose their tempers very easily. They get insulted by the slightest thing. . . ." Most of them mentioned the eating habits of the *burakumin* as a primary reason for avoiding them. It is true that these communities were at one time the only ones in Japan to eat meat. And even though since the war the Japanese themselves have become "steak" eaters, they continue to regard as detestable and peculiar to the *burakumin* the consumption of liver, innards, and especially tripe.

Mr. Nemoto's fear is even more justified since, on the threshold of the twenty-first century, the perspectives opened up by technological development reveal more and vaster areas of darkness as regards man and his future. Mr. Nemoto sees his success increasingly threatened as the majority of Japanese become more and more afraid of losing their gains of recent years. If this occurs, they will be looking for someone to blame, and Mr. Nemoto knows that he could be cast in this role.

Just as with blacks in the United States, Jews in the U.S.S.R. and the satellite countries, North Africans in France, and Asians in Great Britain, so Japan's *barukumin* are tainted with the kind of original sin they can never collectively wash clean. Other minorities on the archipelago are in the same situation, especially the Koreans.

THE KOREANS

The history of Japan's Koreans goes far back in time—to a period when Indian Buddhism was introduced into the islands, coming from China by way of Korea. In our century, the relevant fact is that Korea was annexed by Japan in 1910 and became independent again only after Japan's defeat in 1945. The Koreans are to the Japanese what the Algerians are to the French. The same complex exists in both cases—the dispossessed colonist on one side, and on the other, the colonial anxious to reverse history and all too mindful of the mutual struggle.

I still remember the bitter sentence of General Park Chung Hee, the president of South Korea and signatory of the treaty for the normalization of relations with Japan: "Monsieur, you should understand us: They [the Japanese] wanted to take our soul." It is true that the situation of Korean residents before the Second World War was precarious. During the great Kanto earthquake of 1923, the Koreans were virtually accused by the government of having committed all the looting and vandalism which exacerbated the distress of thousands of homeless people. This official denunciation led to an immense pogrom throughout Tokyo.

Since the end of the war, the Koreans have been organized into two distinct communities: North Koreans, Communist in their allegiance, and those faithful to the Seoul anti-Communist regime, or at least to Seoul, even when they are opposed to the president. The followers of Kim Il-song are organized in a rigid hierarchy, and thoroughly regimented. These North Koreans have resisted every provocation on the part of Japanese authorities, in particular the police. They have succeeded in creating schools, where instruction is in their own language. Above all, they have succeeded in keeping these schools going even when confronted by existing restrictions on private schools. This colony numbers about 600,000, and North Korea refuses to repatriate them. The Japanese accuse them of espionage, holding no hope of establishing the identity of any member of the community, the size of the colony allowing the Communists to infiltrate Tokyo with their agents, when and as they wish.

Nothing resembles a South Korean more than a North Korean, and vice versa. However, the complaints brought against the South Korean colony, which numbers about 200,000 persons, of a slightly higher social status than their northern compatriots, involve not so much political as ordinary crime. There is not a rape, a robbery, or any crime whatsoever of which the average Japanese will not instinctively say: "It must have been a Korean." Government officials speak of the Koreans with contempt, and this feeling is returned in full. Yet they must live, and when one is aware of the reciprocal feelings, one can only be amazed at the scarcity of incidents. Both sides make great efforts to normalize everyday life. Today Japanese businessmen go to Korea, where they are welcomed cordially. The same goes for Koreans who visit Japan. Almost half a century of coexistence, even though forced, has eliminated linguistic barriers, and even a certain number of psychological barriers. Nevertheless, discrimination exists in social life and in employment. Koreans who live in Japan, even those from the south, cannot become an integral part of Japanese society. Whatever their degree of assimilation, they form a group apart, less ostracized, perhaps, than the *burakumin*, but emphatically kept out.

MOVES

For fifteen years now, since multistory housing has been promoted, the residents of individual houses, still numerous even in Tokyo, have, from one day to the next, seen themselves despoiled. Buildings of eight, ten, and more stories have robbed them of all hope of seeing the sun even for a single hour during the day, and signaled the end of rocks cunningly placed, sand finely sifted, dwarf trees judiciously oriented. Japanese space loses all its significance when one can no longer count on the play of shade and light to create the depth of field that evokes harmony in the individual, seated on his tatami, who sees life from ground level.

Associations formed in the various districts to demand the right to the sun persisted for ten years, until in 1977 this right was finally recognized by parliament, and complicated ordinances were enacted after consultation with the local associations. It is common in Europe and the United States to find regulations that limit the height of buildings, style of construction, and a building's orientation in relation to other apartment houses or nearby private dwellings. What is surprising about the Japanese ordinances is the fact that they established not obligations for the building owners but rights for the citizens, especially the right to the sun.

In the Minato-Ku, a business district in central Tokyo where one finds few residences, a new apartment house can cast a shadow not more than eleven yards beyond its property line, for not more than three hours a day. In municipal offices, mediators listen to the building contractors and residents' associations. When a contractor intends to construct a building of more than four stories, the authorities encourage him to collect written authorizations from the people living in the neighborhood. In return, the contractor indemnifies the residents in proportion to lost hours of sunlight. An hour of lost sun can be worth 500,000 yen. The state, too, must indemnify people owning property along a projected urban highway that will straddle house roofs, blocking out sunlight and increasing noise levels.

But money cannot replace the sun, and indignant citizens' associations have become active in local politics. Such movements are not new. What characterizes the best of them is spontaneity. Do the women working in a factory want to reduce the speed-up imposed on the assembly line? They have a meeting, make banners, flags, and caricatures, and the following Saturday they can be seen parading through the streets of Tokyo, preceded by a car equipped with a loudspeaker that blasts out slogans; eight or ten policemen follow, a kind of rear guard.

On the same day, on other routes, march householders of a certain district who protest the rise in the cost of rice. And another Saturday will see ecologists protesting against nuclear power plants. Parades through the streets of Tokyo have become a form of collective expression. They end up against police sawhorses in the streets of Akasaka, near the prime minister's official residence. A petition is submitted by the assemblage, and the demonstration disperses without incident.

Little by little, during the seventies, people passed from unorganized movements to more serious acts of protest, mobilized around several objectives: opposition to the big building projects; opposition to the construction and the subsequent opening of the Narita airport; opposition to the construction of nuclear power plants; opposition to nuisances and pollution; consumer protection. It should be noted that in Japan, as in all other industrialized countries, none of these problems has been integrated into the programs of the political parties, trade unions, townships, or districts. Of course, some attempts have been made at solving and controlling essentially local problems, but without success. Political decisions based on the principle of majority rule or elected representation have not always protected the interests of specific groups.

The grass roots movements have proved, however, that they can be complementary to the political parties, trade unions, or administrative structures. Just as an example, it is interesting to observe the impact over the last thirty years of the consumer organizations, which are almost all part of the women's movement. There is, for instance, the Kansai League of Housewives, which was responsible for the creation of a similar organization in Tokyo in protest against the manufacture of matches that did not light. Subsequently, an office was opened to test products in common use, and the league concentrated on denouncing defective products. Later, misleading or false advertisements were carefully scrutinized, and this led to a law prohibiting dishonest labels on merchandise.

A recent development is two-pronged. On one hand, consumer organizations choose more politicized targets; they do this under the influence of American movements like those of Ralph Nader, who came to Japan in 1971 to show them the ropes. There are also organized campaigns against the oil industry. On the other hand, the women's organizations have served as a springboard for the women's liberation movement.

Indeed, the conservative forces have understood the importance of these movements and have started to set forth a program of political action in everything that concerns the environment and consumers' rights. Here again *tenko* appears—the Japanese ability to adapt to a fluctuating situation, drawing strength from a tradition of political pragmatism that is unique in the world.

5: The Japanese in Business

THE "ECONOMIC ANIMAL"

Like all peoples, the Japanese have their national pride. They do not like to be insulted, and they do want to be understood. For some years now, they have had to bear with an insult from across the Pacific, from the United States. Was it said by the press? By a politician? I have not been able to track down the source; but that is not the problem. The insult remains. It has been picked up by Europeans, by Chinese and other Asians. The Japanese have been typed as "economic animals," and they are not so proud as they were before this affront. But they have let it go without a reply, awaiting the propitious moment.

There is some point to wondering what this epithet signifies and why the Japanese, who have created the most perfectly functioning economic machine in the world, do not want to be tagged with a particular image; it does, after all, pay homage, however crudely, to a genius no other peoples have been capable of emulating, even those who need it most. Yet, in the minds of all Japan's partners, to be an "economic animal" takes on a pejorative and restrictive connotation: "You take care of business matters, we'll do the rest. . . . You only know about commerce and money, so please do not meddle in high international politics—we will do it for you. . . . An animal possesses a limited intelligence, and an 'economic animal' should devote himself completely to the economic sector. Since he is in the position of running that game, let him stop there! Otherwise, he can ruin us all. At a certain level, economies become highly political; therefore, Japan must limit itself."

Now, the concept of an "economic animal" denotes qualities sufficient to cope with the immense problems confronting a country that is overpopulated and lacks raw materials. At the political level, it is the "animal" that got the best results from the miraculous upswing of the years 1965–70. Confronted by crisis, it has, since 1972, successfully solved the problems of balance of payments, of the value of its money, of a reasonable growth rate, and, gradually, of employment. But this success brought in its wake other problems, caused

179

precisely by an excess in the balance of payments, the increased value of the yen and too weak a growth rate, which was perceived as recession after a decade of growth at top speed—double that of Western industrial countries.

For the individual Japanese, "economic animal" means devotion to his company to a paternalistic system of management; limited individual ambition; discipline and esprit de corps; submission to a way of life altogether ruled by the company and therefore, when necessary, soft-pedaling some of his complaints and demands. And finally, at all levels, there is a heightened competitive feeling.

The sense of competition is produced by a state of mind: either one has it or one doesn't. The Japanese have it at all levels. Everything is organized so that they will be first: low salaries, docile employees who do not take vacations, undercutting prices on the foreign markets, the subordination of the quality of life to the dynamics of breakneck industrialization, close working agreements between the business world and the government.

Such characterizations elicited an indignant response from one of the directors of Nomura Research Institute. "Of course," he declared, "the Japanese government has worked in close liaison with private industry. Why shouldn't it participate in the cooperation necessary to rebuild an economy whose productive capacity had fallen by 80 percent? That does not mean that the interests of those in business and in the government are one and the same. It would say, instead, that it is the system of lifetime employment which has helped to ensure the fidelity and dynamism of a work force dedicated to national objectives. . . . Japan has the strictest laws in the world for the control of pollution. In 1977, parliament reinforced the antimonopoly law. The government has set up a special administrative council which exerts pressure in an effort to maintain exports at the level of the preceding year. Japan has wages that compare favorably with those of the most advanced countries. For the index figure of 100 in Japan, one must count 107 in the United States and 99 in the Federal Republic of Germany. . . . Japan is necessarily oriented toward exports in order to compensate for importing all its raw materials, to which end it must accumulate reserves of foreign currencies."

For the Japanese, the problem is not a mere redressing of the balance of payments. They know that it would not be enough for them to give up exporting a given quantity of some products. They are accustomed to demands of this kind. President Nixon did not hesitate to insist that the Japanese stop exporting textiles to the United States. He made it an affair of state. But the Japanese were reluctant to take part in a political maneuver of the Republican party, whose Southern voters were dependent on an archaic and doomed textile industry.

Something far more serious is at stake for Japan and the Japanese: it is the constant risk of seeing the entire structure of their society collapse. How, from one day to the next, can a system of job recruitment and thus a system of education be changed? How can one modify from scratch a system of relations between employees and management that has been forged in the course of a century? How can one ask those who wield power to give it up in an instant? Japan feels that the West is demanding that she initiate a revolution so as to safeguard the liberal, industrial, capitalist world. But although methods can be changed, structures modified or replaced, a national mentality cannot be changed. The challenge hurled at the Japanese companies is a challenge that goes against the grain of their patterns of thought.

The Western countries cry to the Japanese: "Watch out, your ship and our ship are sailing on a stormy sea. Our ship is sinking, yours isn't. So let's sink together and we'll keep each other company on the life rafts." Despite their occasional suicidal urges, the Japanese do not want to scuttle their ship.

Three Levels of Employment

Eiichi Kato, twenty-years old, spent three years at the University of Nihon, where he mastered the secrets of acoustics and tape recorders. He sent his curriculum vitae to all the television networks, as well as to the main manufacturers and distributors of audiovisual equipment. Only one firm kept his résumé. He was summoned to take a test—a written examination that must be passed before the company hires anyone. Out of a hundred candidates, about twenty would make the grade. Kato considered himself lucky to be among the hundred applicants chosen for the test. Would he be among the twenty?

I met him a few days later; he was radiant. Yes, he still had to get past a further weeding out, but he was sure of getting a job, and he also knew that the company had already blocked out the shape of his career. The chosen twenty would be recruited at the same level, whatever their aptitudes, and without their university degrees being taken into account. Two of the twenty came from the University of Tokyo, two from Keio, and one from Waseda, so that their chances of a good career would seem better than his, since Nihon does not rate as high as the others. But he had two strong advantages: he had been recommended at a very high level within the company (his uncle being a close friend of one of the general directors), and his second asset was his personality. Besides, most of the other twenty candidates had fewer academic credits than he.

Thus, these twenty recruits began at the same salary, and the personnel office marked out the first curve of their careers. At the end of a year, the two graduates of the University of Tokyo, as well as those who graduated from Keio, would have passed through three stages, Waseda's graduate would have passed through two, while Eiichi Kato would have passed through only one. After another year, all the others would be at the same level. At the end of ten years, the two graduates from Tokyo and the two from Keio would have forged much further ahead than their comrades.

Kato was enrolled in that branch of the university from which the company usually recruits, on the basis of recommendations by certain professors. Having finally negotiated the rough waters of interviews with several managers and the president, he and his nineteen comrades became part of the general pool of personnel. Secondary school graduates are directed toward the manual jobs; university graduates go into office work, and later have a chance to move into a higher classification, as administrators charged with different degrees of responsibility; they may even attain the highest level accessible to employees.

These three categories of personnel are found in practically all private or public companies. If an employee belongs to either of the two higher levels, the law forbids any trade union affiliation. It is at the middle level that one encounters a multitude of titles, of which the most common are department head and section head.

In the jungle of horizontal responsibilities, the Japanese themselves find it hard to recognize who is who. One day Eiichi Kato made an appointment with me at his office. Knowing that he had just been hired, I did not expect to find him in a sumptuous office with three telephones and two secretaries. The receptionist at the entrance announced me and directed me to room 504. On the fifth floor, a young woman was pushing a cart filled with newspapers, which she distributed from office to office; another crossed her path with metal teapots and small glasses, which she was bringing to each employee, beginning with the top men. The corridors hummed with incessant comings and goings, and here and there employees were engaged in animated conversation. I easily found room 504; it had the atmosphere of an examination room for Ph.D. candidates who wished to copy from their neighbors. About fifty clerks filled five parallel ranks of small metal desks set side by side and facing a partition, behind which were four offices, which sheltered the department head and three section heads. Each office was equipped with three telephones, one black and two gray; ordinary employees had to settle for one telephone for two people.

Quite soon I found young Kato in the second row near the window. He was busy phoning. Seeing me, he gave a friendly wave. When I went over, he told me that he wanted to introduce me to the head of his section. I found myself behind the partition. The section head rose with alacrity, handing me his calling card, which was relatively detailed, and invited me to sit down. I can no longer remember his name—I mislaid his calling card—but I remember very well what I learned from him about the inner mechanism of a Japanese business firm.

"Kato-san," he told me, "will remain in my section for about a year; thus he will learn everything about our affiliates and their relations with the mother house, because in this section we keep a record of the orders passed on to the affiliates. We follow the progress of their work and we keep track of the finished products they send us. Afterward, Kato-San will go on to the legal section, where he will become familiar with the firm as a whole. If he shows ability, he will no doubt move up and will become head of a section like me, or manager of a workshop if he is assigned to the technical side."

He went on: "In Japan, moving around within a company is encouraged, but not moving from one company to another. This is the opposite of Europe. The Japanese are employed for life, and since retirement starts at fifty-five, it is precisely then, as one of your singers says, that life begins. It is different for those on the highest echelon; they can remain on the job until sixty, and if one becomes president, he can stay on till death. . . . Ah, yes, presidents have the luck.

"But these three job levels do not form a pyramid of three superimposed layers. You must remember that our society is structured vertically. Thanks to communication among the three, each person can participate in the big decisions. This is called the *ringi* system. No decision we take can be imposed by authority. What counts is the *wa*—harmony. So, at each level, one can have one's say about opening an overseas market, or the right moment to start manufacturing this or that model, or changing a particular process, and so forth. When the president makes his decision known, he will have taken into account all the opinions and tried to satisfy everyone.

"We advance according to seniority—the *nenko* system—but unfortunately today one sees more and more young men too eager to get ahead. If we listened to them, we, the people around fifty, would be ready for the junk heap. Certainly when a young man is particularly brilliant he receives a flattering promotion that would have been unthinkable fifteen years ago, but the president is very careful not to disturb the people already settled in. We put young people in new management jobs that are created by the expansion of our markets, especially abroad. I think that in recent years, the young people have been getting their power from cliques within the company. It is not only a matter of the best-known cliques, like those of the alumni of the University of Tokyo, or Kyoto, or Keio. Each of these has at least a dozen members among the people in top management, and each of them protects younger alumni of their university. But other cliques have sprung up—small families within the large family."

Mr. Honda and "Familyism"

Soichiro Honda is known all over the world. His name, engraved on the frames of millions of motorcycles and thousands of auto bodies across the planet, may well evoke for a Westerner the vision of a tall, willful, determined, inaccessible man in an office with padded doors, guarded by an army of receptionists, secretaries, and executives. He is described as always working feverishly, rushing from one telephone to another, from board of directors to a meeting of his factory managers, here plying scissors to cut a ribbon, and a few minutes later ensconced in the back seat of his Rolls, watching a television show.

Soichiro Honda is not very tall. He is modest in appearance and is very lively and pleasant. Dressed in blue jeans, he strolls through his workshops, inquiring about the health of one man or the work of another. He does not have an office, for he pays managers to direct the work. He plays golf. He takes care of the business side and, so to speak, the soul of his enterprise: he is the person who keeps morale high. He believes, like the famous Meiji period businessman Eiichi Shibusawa, that the moral and mental conduct of each individual influences the entire country's productive capacity. The end of the *ié* and the consequent transfer of the father's authority to the head of the company has conferred on him a great moral responsibility in relation to his employees. A Japanese firm does not simply utilize a man's work; it *employs* the whole man. So there is not a purely contractual relationship between employer and employee, but rather a kind of "collective convention" which provides de facto recognition of the company union. This "familyism" is in no way different from what was foreseen early in the century by Shimpei Goto, president of the national railroads, whose motto was: "The railroad—your only family."

Such practices, derived from the application of the Confucian ethic to the work milieu, locate employer-employee relations within the traditional scheme that imposes the duty of protectiveness on one side and the duty of fidelity on the other. Obviously, in this context, the system of remuneration is in line with these obligations. Every pay sheet stipulates a base salary for each of the three job levels. To this is added a bonus for seniority—which, for the oldest employees, can represent a more significant sum than the base salary—plus allowances for transportation, family circumstances, lunch, etc., and a "bonus in recognition of good work," variable according to one's output, the nature of the service rendered, or quite simply, one's favor with the boss. There are also seasonal compensations, two months' wages frequently granted at the end of June and at the end of the year. Health insurance, pension funds, accident insurance, etc., are generally paid for by the management.

The Japanese attach a certain importance to salaries paid in cash. At the end of each month, one can see the employees of department after department filing past the cashier, who hands each an envelope with his name on it. What a joy to open it, but also what a disappointment if the bonus for "recognition" is not what was expected!

The President's Men

So the system at all levels does not simply encourage competence, but develops it through personal relationships between subordinates and superiors. These vertical relationships imply respect for *nenko*, promotion by seniority. They can flourish only through an older group to a younger one, or at least between classes of recruitment which differ in terms of age. A department head does not have to fear that one of his assistants might supplant him. Instead of distrusting his subordinates, he pushes the younger man to the center of the stage so that he can climb the corporate ladder more easily and quickly. Father Robert J. Ballon, professor at Sophia University, has stressed the role of the office of the president, a postwar creation in Japan. The big companies, such as Hitachi, Sony, and Honda, as well as the big newspapers and television networks, have created it, above all, to reinforce lateral coordination, which is often weak. All Western governments are familiar with this system; it is especially evident in the United States, where the President's men often have more weight than officeholders. In the modern Japanese company, vertical by tradition, the top executives have felt it necessary to establish powerful versions of this coordinating group and—a breach in the traditional system of promoting by seniority—have recruited young hopefuls from different departments of the company.

Alongside the traditional bosses, whose ages range from sixty to eighty, these "president's men" have come into being: a galaxy of young men, ambitious, unhampered by most of the social taboos, and often technocrats. The growth of their influence and power over the last fifteen years has been the most striking development and the most important factor for change the Japanese companies have experienced since the Meiji period. We have seen that the president's men undermine promotion by seniority; they also compromise the system of decision through consensus by concealing the views middle management or even top executives and directors might express, and by influencing the president to give particular consideration to their views. In the long run, the entire system of employment for life could be called in question.

In order to make up for certain promotions accorded the president's men, several companies have introduced opportunities for selective promotion by choice. Thus a development is under way that brings Japanese business policies into line with those in Western industrialized countries. All studies have stressed the originality of life employment, but in fact the Japanese system does not differ much from systems now in force in many European companies in France, Great Britain, and West Germany. Furthermore, according to certain Japanese experts, so-called employment for life embraces only about a fifth of the wage earners in the manufacturing industries.

In 1980, Japanese economists wondered whether employment for life would survive a continuing recession. The system, preventing recruitment of new talent and recourse to new blood, is obviously unable to satisfy the growing needs of innovation. It frustrates some workers who might want to move to another city or get started in a new profession. Despite these drawbacks, since 1974 the Japanese economy has evidenced maneuverability and adaptability which are much more important than might appear.

After five years of crisis, Japanese business and industry are doing well. To preserve their labor force, companies have carried through a policy of thinning out temporary personnel, cutting back on hiring, and turning to subcontractors only when things are looking up. The work week was reduced, as were some bonuses. In this way, when the crisis was at its height, otherwise surplus personnel were kept on the job. In fact, the objection to employment for life comes more from Japanese employers than from the workers. They point quite reasonably to an increase in their overhead. But they are not held back by this, as the dynamism, and aggressiveness of Japanese industry abundantly demonstrates. And the older leaders of business and industry very quickly grasped the importance of a permanent professional group. The best engineers in the electronics firms, data processing and computers, and especially in the industries that manufacture products for mass consumption (household appliances, cameras, etc.) are the "house" engineers. Finally, big business has avoided trapping the workers in a specialty in the name of stability. Instead, turning to new skills within the company provides a satisfying option for the person with a practical bent.

THE ZAIBATSU HERITAGE

After twenty years of an economic growth rate that has outstripped the rest of the world, and industrial growth that has led to an accumulation of capital that is exceeded only by the United States, the solid core of Japan's production apparatus still consists of the basic structures of the famous *zaibatsu*, economic-industrial concentrations set up at the beginning of the century. Indeed, one should not forget that Japan's industrial "takeoff" goes back to 1888, thanks to the impetus of intelligent government action, to clear and precise objectives, and above all to a generation of samurai converted to public service.

Until 1920, a largely female labor force was distributed among small companies. As industrialization progressed and was assimilated into the culture, despite modifications encouraged by the militarists, the basic structures did not change even when some small medium-size companies—Sony, Matsushita, Honda—acquired an international dimension. In 1945 and 1946, the *zaibatsu* were dissolved, but they began to reappear in 1950. These were not family trusts, as has too often been stated, but represented an affiliation among several related enterprises. However, it is true that at their origin, entire segments of an industry gave rise to family concessions, in the Japanese sense of the term.

The famous 1888 takeoff coincided with the government's decision to abandon industrial enterprise and transfer it to the private sector. The *zaibatsu* concentrated enormous amounts of capital in their hands, ably directed by appointed "managers" who cooperated closely with the government during the first stages of industrialization. They also came to the financial aid of the government and thus acquired impressive political power. In 1960, the reborn *zaibatsu* discovered another kind of power, and in 1963 the Mitsubishi group encompassed 21 industrial firms and 130 factories. The creation of Mitsubishi Heavy Industries in 1964 completed the process. Today the Mitsubishi organization includes about thirty companies; Mitsui and Sumitomo more than twenty each. Big business is still identified with financial groups, Dai Ichi, Fuji, and Sanwa, and with industrial groups, Nissan, Toyota, Matsushita, Toshiba, and Yawata. In addition, there are more than a few business organizations whose sales strategy embodies the techniques of worldwide distribution through a network of agents. They also have been the conduit for technologies imported into Japan. Their effectiveness is chiefly felt in the steel industry and in the manufacture of heavy equipment.

Big companies such as Sony or Honda have taken direct charge of the marketing of their products and reproach the smaller trading companies for using antiquated techniques, but these trading companies form an integral part of that public service which is the Japanese economy. And in that capacity they can, in case of a depression or a competitive struggle, favor the national products, even above their own immediate interests. Japan has passed into the final stage of industrialization. It has relinquished some of the profits it could gain from sending textiles, special steel, or other semifinished products to South Korea, China, and Hong Kong. Today Japan exports its technology and its factories; it even manufactures its own products in the countries of its competitors. For example, Japanese color television sets are now being made in the United States. The Japanese have become a redoubtable competitor of the European Economic Community and the United States in all the Third World markets, notably with what are called family computers: pocket calculators, mini-computers, etc.

The Qualities That Made the "Miracle"

To attain this, Japan has wagered and won against odds in a continuous miracle that ran from 1965 to 1972, the result of qualities which Herman Kahn listed as follows:

> Devotion to the common interest.
> Moderate increase in population.
> Commonsense judgment, motivation, and aptitude for organization both in government and in the private sector.
> High levels of education and technology.
> High rates of savings and investment.
> Liberal government and free enterprise adapted to Japan.
> Planning and government intervention skillfully apportioned.
> Aggressiveness in extending markets, with a definite orientation toward technology and the options of the future.
> No pity for unproductive economic activities.
> Economic growth serving as an "anchorage" for the West.
> A large available labor force.

The Men Who Fabricated the "Miracle"

The qualities necessary to the miracle are incarnated in the men who made it, the pioneer in this field being Eiichi Shibusawa (1840–1931). Possessing all the traits that distinguished the elite of the Meiji period, he helped transform the technological borrowings from the West and adapt them to the Japanese context. Shibusawa, the son of a rich tenant farmer, received the education of a samurai, learning swordsmanship, calligraphy, and Confucius. At the age of twenty-four, he participated in an abortive conspiracy against the Tokugawa shogunate.

But his hour had not come. A friend's efforts induced the shogun to pardon him, and in 1867 he joined the mission of Prince Mimbu, to the court of Napoleon III. This voyage opened up new horizons and helped to direct his political life toward business affairs. He was soon convinced that Japan's modernization could only be achieved through borrowing foreign technology. Thus, with the urging and authority of Emperor Meiji, he did what he had refused to do through political conviction: participated in Japan's opening to the West. Transferring his patriotism to economics, Shibusawa became an important public official in charge of reorganizing tax collecting, surveying, and standardizing units of measure. In 1872, he left public service and was elected general manager of the first national bank; he later became president of Dai Ichi Ginko (First Bank). He participated in the reform of the banking system, whose new statute permitted the samurai to pay for stock in the new banks with their pensions as feudal servants of the state. Whereas the merchants remained aloof and cautious, the samurai responded with enthusiasm and became owners of 76 percent of the capital of national banks; the merchant class took over only 14 percent. Shibusawa set about educating and training people to staff the new banks.

In 1877, the banker became an industrialist. Shibusawa took over the cotton industry first of all, then the railroads, but his name chiefly remains linked with industry and the modern businessman, which he personifies. Disappointed with the merchant class, he tried to launch and foster a kind of samurai merchant. The school he founded for this purpose has become the highly regarded University of Hitotsubashi.

A more contemporary Japanese economic pioneer is now in his seventies, and directs Nomura Securities, one of the most powerful financial organizations in Japan. The correspondent of the *Financial Times* of London, Henry Scott Stokes, has called him "a samurai in a grey flannel suit." Minoru Segawa was the fourth child of a modest family. His father was a schoolteacher, and he remembers selling charcoal in the street as a youth to supplement the family budget. He was a brilliant student at the commercial college of Osaka, and entered Nomura Securities in 1929, at age twenty-three. He soon was noticed because of his passion for work, his incomparable physical stamina, his calm, and his flair. As an agency head in the provinces, he brought in more business than any other agency, and outdistanced his competitors in all matters. The war did not affect him, since he was not drafted, and his refusal of a post in Manchuria prevented his rotting in a Soviet concentration camp. He awaited his hour in Tokyo. When the stock exchange was reopened in 1959, it had its ups and downs, and several times he saved his company from failure. Because of him, the Tokyo stock market became what it is today, and his work contributed greatly to the value of the yen. What is striking about Segawa's background is its resemblance to Shibusawa's: the same humble origins, the same energy in action, the same paternalism. Minoru Segawa shares a passion for baseball with his chauffeur and is concerned about the most insignificant of his employees.

One is in the presence of what Father Ballon, repeating the words of a Japanese economist, has called the "founder type": a success due to a boundlessly combative spirit, an unusually acute sensibility, a capacity for permanent innovation, despite a limited if not nonexistent university career. This has also been the case with Soichiro Honda and Konosuke Matsushita.

The "second-generation type" is characterized by men who have overcome the handicap of being "papa's sons." Often educated at the best universities, able, intelligent, receptive to new techniques, they have managed to win the confidence of directors who work under their fathers' orders.

As for the "high-level salaried types," these are men who have reached the top because of their abilities rather than their family connections. The oldest boss among Japanese bosses, Taizo Ishizaka, is one of these men.

The professional manager educated in the postwar school has been a spectacular technical success. It is this class of first-rate engineers, such as Ibuka Masaru at Sony, that is responsible for the glorious success of the electronics industry.

UPS AND DOWNS OF A DUALIST SYSTEM

With such a heritage and with structures so deeply rooted in the national consciousness, Japan should be confident about the persistence of its miracle. But discordant noises have been heard recently at several levels: business failures continue and everyone knows that Japan cannot go on living off the giants alone; unemployment is becoming significant for the first time and raises the possibility of a social revolution; changes in the companies' internal organizations because of the recent economic crisis open the door to a crisis in the regime itself—something even the Second World War did not bring about. This challenge is of course pointed out by the Japanese themselves.

In the flourishing period that preceded the crisis, business failures were featured every day in the press. One photograph became quite familiar to the Japanese: There were five, six, perhaps ten men, sometimes even more, wearing morning suits, gray trousers, swallowtail coats, waistcoats, black ties, high, stiff collars. They were bowing, their foreheads almost touching their knees, their hands dangling along the seams of their trousers almost to their ankles, and they were murmuring something such as: "We beg your pardon, it is our very great fault. . . . Pardon us for having led our company into bankruptcy." Facing them was an often stormy assemblage, shouting insults at some unnamed person. This sort of photograph appeared in the newspapers hundreds of times each month; after the crisis struck, it turned up more than a thousand times.

Who had failed? First of all, companies hastily set up in an attempt to profit from the boom. Thus, from 1970 until 1974, hundreds of companies selling old-master paintings and lithographs were set up and dissolved. Anyone with connections abroad could create a company and encourage investors to put capital into it. A television manufacturer would create an investment company, buy an apartment house here, a hotel there, elsewhere a high-fashion dress shop or even a farm, not to mention race horses, yachts, famous vineyards, country estates.

From one day to the next, the financial source dried up and these companies closed their doors. So did companies in the weakest segments of the economy. Ship construction was one of the hard-hit sectors, and today its survival is at stake. The most urgent measure, the specialists say, is to cut back on production. Small or large shipyards do not agree that they should follow the example of the textile industry, which simply destroyed its excess production. The Association of Shipbuilders asked the government for support and was granted special loans, provided it reduced production. The prediction is that in the eighties, Japanese shipbuilding will consist of the most important firms, operating at reduced capacity, three or four groups of middle-sized or small shipyards, and a few builders of specialized ships. The smaller shipyards accuse the large ones of having lured away all the orders. The big shipyards accuse the small ones of using outmoded technologies. The only consensus is in putting the blame on competition from South Korea or Hong Kong, encouraged by the rise in the value of the yen, which has made Japanese products 30 percent more expensive.

Big builders like Mitsubishi or Ishikawajima-Harima no longer work at more than 50 percent of their capacity. Japanese shipbuilding has already reduced its productive capacity by 35 percent.

All this calls into question the very structures of the economy. Furthermore, Japan is going through a crisis of change, since it is passing from an industrial to a postindustrial economy. That is why agriculture, silviculture, and the tanning industry are among the sectors in trouble. Failures have also hit big companies once thought to be solid, such as Nakamura Plywood and Kinsen Gosei Seni (synthetic fibers), now finding themselves in difficulties because of the sudden cutting off of bank credit, or liabilities out of all proportion to their assets.

Now Japan, the country of employment for life, finds itself with more than a million people looking for work. This phenomenon has utterly stunned the Japanese. Only the young brand it for what it is: "Down with the GNP," they cry. "It's a swindle."

"The young," an employer complains, "do not want to profit from the advantages they are offered. Even the girls who come from the countryside to work in Tokyo find it hard to accept the free lodgings we put at their disposal. They prefer to hang out all night with the boys in bars and nightclubs. They get to work in the morning with drawn faces, and some of them even go so far as to say that they want people to think we overwork them."

"These young people," another employer adds, "do not hesitate to walk out on us and go to work elsewhere. They are really unstable."

The ratio of wages to the total production cost in Japan is three to five times lower than it is in Western Europe or the United States. In fact, employment for life, ending at fifty-five and involving about one worker out of five, amounts to a smoke screen, concealing the poverty of the elderly. Eighty-five percent of Japanese workers are employed in small, subcontracting businesses and earn half the salary (if that much) of an employee in the big companies. Workers who are laid off have rights that are only window dressing—for example, social security provides benefits three times lower than the French equivalent offers twice as many workers. Housing, roads, means of transportation, sewers—all the public infrastructures are neglected. One could continue this list of inadequacies; it was corroborated by official sources in a White Book on Japanese life published in 1978. But the same source points out that individual income has increased fourteen times in twenty years, making it fifth in the world after Sweden, the United States, Western Germany, and France, and ahead of Great Britain and Italy. Japanese in responsible positions emphasize the advances in health care and increased life expectancy. They also note that almost all homes are equipped with color television and one household out of two owns a car. There are about five hundred telephones for every thousand inhabitants. Attendance at the upper levels of secondary school has risen in twenty years from 50 percent to 90 percent, university attendance 10 to 40 percent. The White Book reports lack of housing, inadequate sewer systems, the small amount of land surface devoted to greenery, the paucity of surfaced roads compared to Europe, the absence of long, paid vacations.

So where is the miracle? Is it in the statistics which support the facade of a society whose overall income comes second in the world after the United States and is ahead of the U.S.S.R. and West Germany, or is it in the preferential distribution of profits into the pockets of a few capitalists?

THE BURDEN OF RURAL SOCIETY

The privileged Japanese today are no longer those who were born samurai. But the existence of some privileged people and of some privileges is inherent in a social model deeply rooted in the past. The Japanese trade unions do not see anything inevitable in this. Influenced by Marxist ideas, they try to substitute for a historic analysis of the coexistence of classes a no less historic analysis of class struggle. But unlike what happens in the West, they cannot find support for this except in contemporary events; in vain they look to the past for precedents to bolster their thesis. In Japan's past as elsewhere in Asia, particularly in China, they collide with the rural world—the psychology of its family clans that have never experienced the industrial revolution but have parachuted into the industrial adventure as if they had been living on another planet, arriving with their hierarchy, their family, and their tradition of the closed society. Thus were born and developed the closed worlds of the workers in Japanese companies, set off from other workers and communicating only through the limited channels demanded by good neighborliness.

When one observes the ups and downs of those economic entities that break up today at a frightening pace but re-form with an incomparable capacity for innovation, one can estimate the overall effort they must make to maintain an equilibrium that will perceptibly reduce the illicit profits of a few. Japan imports 95 percent of its wheat, 99.5 percent of its corn, 100 percent of its wool and raw cotton, 100 percent of its phosphates, 98 percent of its iron ore, 100 percent of its bauxite and nickel, 98 percent of its manganese, 99 percent of its chrome, and 99.8 percent of its crude oil. No other developed economy in the world has to deal with such an array of imperatives. One can get a clearer idea of these constraints by carefully examining some of the sensitive sectors: agriculture, fishing, construction, housing, and public works.

SECTORS IN CRISIS

A recent White Book on Japanese agriculture lists the situations of which the farmers are victims:

> Economic depression, causing a decline in the consumption of food.
> Overproduction of rice and other agricultural products.
> The special situation of rice growers, who must find extra-agricultural forms of income and are consequently frustrated by the declining job market.
> A difficult equilibrium between food imports, indispensable to maintaining an acceptable balance of payments with China or the countries of Southeast Asia, and the not less indispensable tariff barriers to ensure the survival of the agricultural sector.

In Japan one sees a simultaneous decrease in the consumption of rice and an increase in the consumption of bread. That is why the government decided to reduce the production of rice to 1.7 million tons for the year 1979–80. Moreover, twenty-two agricultural products are protected from foreign competition, in particular beef, oranges, fruit juices, and the products of coastal fishing.

Japanese fishing is going through an unprecedented crisis and has now become a national problem. On all the world's seas, fishermen are terrified when the see Japanese ships arrive, and accuse them of literally emptying the waters. Outfitted with ultramodern equipment that permits treating the fish aboard ship, freezing their catches, and even canning them, they are floating factories. Confronted by competition they regard as unfair, other countries have extended their territorial waters from three to twelve miles and have created an "economic zone of two hundred miles." One after the other, the Americans, Canadians, Russians, and French have protested against "Japanese fishing." To the voices of the fishermen have been added those of the defenders of the ocean environment, for whom the Japanese serve as a target because of their pursuit of whales, most species of which are threatened with extinction. Japanese fishermen today demand a "more dynamic" diplomacy, which would permit them to discover new fishing grounds and new resources within agreements made with developing countries. They also want to see a new approach to the problems of coastal fishing through the establishment of a long-range plan for aquaculture. The fishermen's trade unions have called for improved port facilities, environmental protection of the fishing villages, and a more efficient utilization of the products of fishing, only 39 percent of which reach the food sector, while their quality needs to be improved.

Other sectors in crisis: public works and construction. A White Book issued in September 1978 pointed out that according to all forecasts, rapid urbanization will continue until the end of the twenty-first century. Thus there is an urgent need to thin out the congestion of mammoth cities like Tokyo and Osaka in order to develop the small or medium-size towns. Certainly the concentration in big centers has slowed, and if Japan's urbanization continues, the center of the city will tend to lose population to the suburbs. This population shift increases commuting, imposing hardships of transportation on the inhabitants and constant innovative efforts to resolve the typically Japanese puzzle represented by the twice-a-day displacement of six million commuters. In any event, the infrastructures remain insufficient and housing is not being built.

In 1978, the government concentrated on these problems. The result was a housing plan known as "Project 55," for the fifty-fifth year of Emperor Hirohito's Showa era—1980. This ambitious project called for very advanced standardization of materials and methods of assembly that would nevertheless allow for individual requirements, adapting the Japanese tradition of the individual house to three grand-scale housing projects.

Expanding Sectors

The talented pupil does not alarm anybody until the moment he reveals his determination to get rid of his teacher by proving that he can do it better. In the most up-to-date technological sectors, mastery has changed hands. Following the triumphs of Toyota, Nissan, Mazda, Sony, and Toshiba, we now have Tokyo manufacturers taking over the American computer market. Goal: to supplant IBM not only on the Japanese market, which has been done, but also on the American market. How, Americans ask, did the Japanese get ahead of them? The most powerful Japanese companies formed a consortium to develop research and adapt technology to a potential mass market. The pool of brains was supported financially by the government. As soon as the products were ready, they were either exported at a price lower than the competition's, or at a loss, or at tiny margins of profit. The official Japanese figures of computer exports to the United States show a tenfold increase from 1976 to 1978. Hitachi, Nippon Electric, and Fujitsu have attacked the IBM fortress. But although Japanese companies are completely competitive when it comes to hardware, Hitachi and Fujitsu, conscious of their inferiority in software, have perfected certain ultrasophisticated computers which can utilize the IBM software systems. Now the compatible system manufactured by Hitachi is priced at 10 to 15 percent less than the corresponding IBM models.

The Japanese display a cautious optimism in this sector. The relaxation of restrictions on foreign investments in December 1975 led Americans to acquire up to 34 percent of the stock of Nippon Mini-Computers, in the hope that this company, created by the Japanese Ministry of Commerce and Industry, would become the axis of the national mini-computer industry. Fujitsu, which is certainly the company best equipped to compete, hopes to realize 30 percent of its sales through exports in 1985. Yet the domestic market remains an essential objective. At the end of 1980, the number of computers in Japan was over 75,000. Thus, after the United States and almost at their level, Japan is the most computerized country in the world. Japanese industry has practically made up for its backwardness as regards software, which explains the anxiety of American manufacturers.

This campaign for foreign markets entails the danger of aggravating Japan's balance-of-payment deficit. The government announced that in 1979 this deficit had decreased 24 percent as compared with the preceding year and that the Japanese economy, in order to decrease it further, should orient itself toward a revival of domestic consumption. This decision was put into effect in 1980.

Government Measures

Measures taken in September 1978 and again in July 1980 were designed to attract the investing public to programs for educational and medical equipment, old age homes, and children's nurseries. In addition, the government is committed to encouraging individual home building through a system of loans and to setting in motion special incentives for employment. It also plans to advocate certain imports. Despite these measures, no industrialized country will think that they compensate for Japan's expansion into foreign markets. It seems more and more hopeless to ask the Japanese themselves to stop their "machine." Condemned to a flight forward, their dilemma is confrontation or suicide. The crisis did not lead to a break in the mechanisms of growth. It was vital for Japan to maintain growth at a high level—7 percent for fiscal 1978–79. This figure was maintained within a tenth of a point, despite a conjunctural inflation of 11 percent at the end of fiscal 1979–80, after prices were stabilized in 1978. Inflation, which had reached 20 percent after the first oil crisis, led on March 3, 1974, to the most important mass demonstration—more than 300,000 people, according to police figures—since those of 1960 against the Japanese-American Security Treaty. A popular council had been set up in January to fight the rise in prices and defend the standard of living.

TRADE UNIONISM AND WORK LEGISLATION

These almost spontaneous movements have not been carried forward in existing trade union organizations. In fact, union policies are paradoxical: inside their companies, union members vote an increase in the cost of their products; then, outside, they demonstrate against the general increase in prices. A further paradox can be observed both in internal union activity and in the relations of the unions to politics. In general, trade unionism continues to search for a path that avoids Marxist assumptions.

I was quite surprised one morning in mid-March when I arrived at a Canon factory. In the courtyard of this famous manufacturer of photographic equipment, about fifty people, wearing armbands, were listening attentively to a harangue being delivered from a flight of steps in front of the manager's office. "It is nothing," my PR guide told me. "Today is the beginning of *shunto,* the spring offensive." For an entire week, the employees would hold meetings in each unit of the factory. Wherever we went, the atmosphere was that of a normal workday, except for the omnipresent armbands. "Each worker in Canon," my escort explained, "belongs to a company union, and his dues are deducted from his wages as an obligatory assessment. Canon workers do not belong to an industry-wide photographic union, and their demands have nothing in common with those of the workers in Ricoh, Nikon, or Olympus."

More than 12 million workers belong to some 65,000 company unions. These unions are often affiliated with four large central unions: Sohyo, with 4.5 million members; Domei, with about 2.5 million; Churitsuroren, with nearly 1.5 million, and Shinsanbetsu, with a little less than 100,000. Trade unionism is dominated by Sohyo and Domei, the former almost unopposed in the public sector, while the latter mainly organizes unions in the private sector.

Domei, the Japanese Confederation of Labor, differs very little in organization from Sohyo. Sohyo has an executive committee with a president, secretary, treasurer, and four divisions: planning, organization, standard of living, and information. The executive committee has nine vice-presidents, representing the large federations that compose the central union. An annual convention sets the course for the coming year. Domei has the same structure, but has nine divisions instead of four. There all similarity stops, however, except for the fact that in both these organizations the central leadership is emphatically hostile to the Communist party. Sohyo's charter indicates its intention to fight for the coming of a socialist society, and its leaders believe that economic demands are inseparable from political struggle. Thus all its activity is tied to that of the Japanese Socialist party, and in particular to leftist elements in the party. The central office supports, both financially and with votes, everything done on a national scale. On the international plane, the watchword is independence, especially vis-à-vis the World Trade Union Federation.

Domei belongs to the International Federation of Free Trade Unions and maintains close ties with the AFL-CIO in the United States. Since 1965, the membership count of the two large unions has shifted, to Sohyo's disadvantage and a consequent weakening. There are more than 100,000 members in about thirty trade union federations. Sohyo, however, includes the million-member federation Jichiro, which greatly outnumbers all the others. Jichiro is the federation of employees of the local administrations, and has a far from negligible political influence.

If a certain number of federations have quit Sohyo, they have not shifted to Domei. According to one study, Domei's moderate ideology has no power to attract. The study attributes the disaffection toward Sohyo and Domei to their increasing bureaucratization, to the appearance of powerful autonomous federations, such as the Japanese Council of the International Federation of Metal Workers, and to the creation of trade unions as the result of the mergers of certain companies. The merger of Yawata Steel and Fuji Steel into Nippon Steel resulted in the organization of steel workers. To these changes of the economic scene is added a political factor—the growing influence of the Communist party, which tries, often successfully, to enlist Sohyo affiliates. Churitsuroren is a liaison committee of federations that recruits chiefly in the building trades, food industries, life insurance companies, and companies manufacturing electrical appliances. As for Shinsanbetsu, its small membership limits and localizes its activity.

Modern labor legislation gives wage earners important guarantees. Trade union rights are ensured in Article 28 of the constitution, which stipulates: "Trade unions must be organizations or federations formed autonomously, composed of workers with the principal goal of maintaining or improving the conditions of work or raising the economic status of the workers." The law further prohibits employers from firing anyone for union activities, rejecting collective bargaining with the workers' representatives, making any attempt at control of or interference in the union organization, and taking any sanctions against recourse to arbitration.

There are also collective agreements that have the force of law and take precedence over individual contracts. No punishment can be imposed in case of a strike, and employers cannot take steps against any trade union organizations or associations with regard to damages due to a strike or any other labor dispute. Job inspection and the investigation of working conditions determine employer-employee relations. An important role is given to arbitration as a means of ensuring that the laws are respected, in particular the law concerning standards in the work place. This law, which covers 35 to 40 million workers, established the minimal terms for work contracts, payment of salaries, hours of work, days off, paid vacations security, etc. Certain features are peculiar to Japan, such as providing for salaries to be paid in cash. Every company that employs more than ten wage earners is required to submit its work rules to the administrative authorities. There are fixed minimum wages, but they are usually exceeded, except in small companies which are at risk and less subject to the influence of the trade unions. Yet in all companies, whatever the union strength, custom demands that the duration of a strike be held to a minimum. Since 1974, the right of government employees to strike has been debated. People in the central administration can organize into associations, which are close to being unions, but they can neither bargain collectively nor have recourse to a strike. People working for the local administrations do not have the right to strike, yet they can bargain collectively.

Since 1973, Domei has raised the question of worker participation in management. A study committee set up by the employers in cooperation with the unions meets periodically; the employers from the start marked out the limits of what they can accept. In fact, in the large companies (more than 80 percent of those listed on the stock exchange), a committee exists for capital-labor consultations. One of these, functioning at Nissan Automobiles for more than twenty years, is cited as a model. But only 3 percent of the companies involved have a committee that functions regularly. This problem of workers' participation in management is also studied by the National Social and Economic Council, which brings together representatives of employers' workers and independent workers. However, this is all far from the agitation for workers' control of policy that in Europe preoccupies certain left parties and trade unions. In every case, the unions' objective is not a simple increase in wages. All Japanese labor organizations insist on a better distribution of the company's available resources, even going so far as to accept pay cuts when they feel the company is in danger. Thus the Japanese trade union world has distinct differences from American unionism.

Every November, the unions get together before negotiating with the companies about bonuses. In a period of prosperity, the bonus can go as high as four to eight months' salary; for certain particularly prosperous companies, it can equal the salary already earned. At the end of 1978, faced by demands for bonuses, various company managements retorted that layoffs were what was needed. But certain unions have also made annual agreements voluntarily limiting their demands to the 1977 level, or even below. According to the Federation of Employers Associations (Nikkeiren), the average demand for bonuses in fifty top-ranking companies was almost 3 percent lower than that of the previous year. In 1979 and 1980, the trade unions continued to present moderate demands, avoiding all demands for higher wages.

Dealing with the Contradictions

Japanese economists are in general very concerned about attaining the 7 percent growth rate the government has set as a goal. For ten years, the growth rate surpassed 12 percent, and not a voice could be heard that considered this development exceptional, let alone abnormal. Today, confronted by those who are anxious and nostalgic for the years 1965–73, other economists make a more accurate estimate of a situation which is the envy of all the great industrial countries. A director of Nikkeiren, did not hesitate to say: "The petroleum crisis has had a freezing effect on an overheated economy. In any case, we could not avoid this experience. It would have come one day or another. . . . In 1980, the revaluation of the yen, combined with a general cutback in economic activity and a reduction in the numbers of the unemployed, thanks to the massive encouragement of small and medium-sized companies, reversed the inflationary trend. The situation is therefore not too bad." However, employers, who, as a group, think less in terms of men and more in terms of structures, are preoccupied with the problems posed by sectors affected by the crisis and by competition, which have no chance of regaining their former prosperity. This is the case with textiles, shipbuilding, aluminum, and chemical fertilizers. "There is little hope for the workers in these sectors," says Ryuko Wada, a financial forecaster. "They can look forward to being laid off. Certainly the service industries are stepping up their activities, and so there are possibilities of absorbing the unemployed. But that will demand efforts extending over at least five years. Unemployment will become more serious than all the problems we now face. At present, there are about 50 million workers. The rate of unemployment is a little above 2 percent, as against 6 percent in Europe or the United States [sic]—that is, about 1.3 million workers are looking for jobs. One should also count about 2 million employees the companies keep on their payrolls although they are no longer needed. If these workers were laid off, the unemployment rate would then be comparable to that of Europe, especially France. Nippon Steel, the giant in steel, is going to close down five plants; it has a surplus work force of 6,500 employees. . . . Our economy must also carry the burden of the state's budgetary deficit. A third of the budget is covered by public loans and two-thirds by taxes. The income from taxes is not increasing significantly, and it will be hard to cut expenses. We cannot touch social expenses and we must continue to pay the interest on the public debt, and finally we must maintain the essential support programs to which the government is committed, such as support for rice, whose price is artificially fixed.

"Finally, we have within the context of our international relations this credit account in our balance of payments, which puts us in a situation of disequilibrium and of opposition to our European and American partners. Thus we are hemmed in by a series of contradictions we must do something about. To export less and import more would be to limit the output of our companies. . . . To reduce government expenditures would be to close off all possibilities of a revival thanks to public investment. So we have certain priorities: first of all, starting up again, then the reorganization of our industries that are in trouble. The other problems can then be solved one by one."

This analysis seems to me a trifle grim, if one takes certain positive factors into consideration. Restraint on the part of the trade unions, in return for management's efforts to maintain employment, has meant entrusting their hopes of achieving their goals to a plan for reorganization and conversion.

In a period of crisis, the concept of family income allows the Japanese to maintain their standard of living as a group, even if a depression lasts a number of years. Family enterprises, while often subject to failure, can more easily take their workers back, and so their maneuverability is greater than in companies of national or international dimensions.

The employers' outlook was somewhat less gloomy at the beginning of 1980, the fear arose of a labor shortage rather than unemployment. In two years' time, Japan had reversed the course of events by an accurate and rapid analysis of the situation, bolstered by a certain measure of employer-union agreement.

SAVINGS

In any event, the human factor counts for more than anything else. Talking to executives of employers' associations, I was conscious of not getting to the bottom of things. One can discuss the Japanese economy in the abstract or even concretely, figures in hand, but one will never approach comprehension without taking into account the man in the street and his behavior. In the past, one of the factors in the economy's rapid growth was the Japanese people's capacity for saving.

There was a young Japanese woman, on a train, Naoko, who wanted to practice her English. She struck up a conversation, but not with the ritual question: "How long have you been in Japan?" She said: "Do you live in Japan?"

"No, I live in Paris."

"Oh, you are French? I'm a student. To earn my living, I translate English into Japanese or I work as an interpreter. . . . Look, we are passing near my house. I live a half hour by train from the Shinjuku station. I intend to go to the United States and stay there for a number of years; as long as it takes to pay for my house. I live in an apartment with my mother and my sister, but I also own a plot of land on which I want to build a house. If I can save three or four million yen, I could get a loan and scrape together the ten million I need. I will rent my house while I'm in the United States, and the income from it will permit me to pay back the loan easily."

"How long will it take—first to save three million, and then to pay back the loan?"

"Not as much as you might think. I work a lot and I save a lot."

"Do you want to get married?"

"Not at all. That doesn't interest me. I want to travel and to have a house that I own."

A survey of six thousand households showed that in 1978, the Japanese saved 11 percent more than in the preceding year; their average annual income rose 6.5 percent over the year before. Savings surpassed the rate of income growth. In 1978, an increase in buying stocks was noted, attributed to the very low rate of interest on bank deposits. Moreover, 57 percent of the households took out loans to buy a house or a car. The interest rate on loans was very low, about 3 percent, but it increased at the end of 1979. The increase in credit is part of the anti-inflation plan, but at the same time, the increase in savings constitutes one of the bases of hope for an economy facing up to the aftereffects of the crisis. Each year in the cosmopolitan sections of Tokyo, one sees more and more luxury shops, better and better stocked with Japanese products and the imported goods that attract an ever-increasing number of customers. In the strictly native districts, those villages of wooden houses which cluster on the periphery of certain places such as Shibuya, Shinjuku, and the Ginza, the shops have not changed in outward appearance. But the houses have simple cooling systems, the wood is newer, the small electric appliance stores, the restaurants for sushi or tempura, the artisans' booths, and women's beauty parlors, present more attractive, more sophisticated display windows than in the past. I knew a time when the Japanese devoted his talents and his savings to the arrangement of his private space. Today everything facing the street also has its importance. They have planted trees on city streets; Tokyo's green spaces have undergone considerable extension at times; if present efforts are pursued, a model city will be born from an anarchic urbanization.

The attitude of the Japanese government, encouraged by the employers, and the response of the public to the state's taking over problems whose solution until now remained in the hands of private initiative, constitute a new fact which could very well be the beginning of a change in the respective roles of the public and private sectors. Another factor of hope for the Japanese economy is the psychology that underlies industrial conversion. There is general agreement, and not only on the part of the employers, to kill off those industrial sectors that are in trouble and regarded as having no future.

The evolution of the market, moreover, tends to put Japan in a superpower position compared to which Europe runs the risk of becoming a customer on the same level as any developing country in Southeast Asia. This evolution is not the result of chance but comes from a very precise choice, which Japan would not hesitate to rectify if it were proved that it had taken the wrong road.

CONCERTED ACTION

Who makes the choices and what are they? What are their consequences? The economic crisis has been studied carefully, and without smugness, by the trade unions. A company union has all the latitude and all the information required to evaluate the results. If these results are not satisfactory, the causes are lucidly analyzed. The company's prosperity is a constant concern of the world of work. What the Japanese call *hanashiai*—that is, the procedure that permits them to take a decision by consensus—is simply what the European trade unions call concerted action. Sohyo, the left-wing trade union "conglomerate," announced in October 1978 that its demand for a bonus would be moderate, after a "tacit" agreement with the employers. But concerted action goes much further than simple agreement on wage increases at the time of the "spring offensive," or on the end-of-year bonus. It is evident in the reduction in work days lost because of strikes. Compared to 1974, a record year for strikes in the private sector, with 9.66 million workdays lost, Japanese industry in 1978 showed a figure barely over a million. However, trade unions in the public sector have a tendency to adopt a different attitude and to resort more and more frequently to strikes. In the private sector, whenever circumstances demand it, the opposing parties come together in meetings organized by Nikkeiren. The employer's representatives join the leaders of the four big trade unions, and the results of these meetings often surprise the West. They are explained by the origin and education of the antagonists. On the employers' side, contrary to accepted notions, the big bosses of the eighties do not represent either a social class or the big family clans.

The success or rather the end product of concerted action is also explained by the internal organization of the company, which reflects the obsessive need for concord that brings together as partners employer, government, and trade union, in accordance with a conception of Japan that transcends all political ideology.

The Example of the Automobile

The results of this concord have been so spectacular and most of its decisions so judicious that everyone involved is led to attribute his own success to the establishment of harmony rather than to his victory in a confrontation. From this point of view, the history of the automobile industry is exemplary. Kiyoshi Takagishi, president of the Association of Automobile Journalists, has told the story in the newspaper *Asahi.* In October 1956, ten years after the end of the war, he points out, the report of the Watkins mission from America investigating the highway infrastructure in Japan concluded: "There does not exist a highway worthy of the name." Even national highway 1, connecting Tokyo to Osaka and almost wholly set aside for big trucks, was macadamized for only half its length. At that time Japan had 295,234 trucks, 493,389 utility vehicles with three wheels, and only 181,074 automobiles, mostly taxis or rental cars. The first true Tokyo–Osaka highway was finished only in 1970, a little before the opening of the Osaka Universal Exposition, and in that year automobile production exceeded 5 million cars; in 1972, it reached 6 million, and in 1973, 7 million. In 1974 and 1975, the recession pushed production back to the 1972 level, but in 1977 it moved up again and passed 8 million.

Mr. Takagishi attributes these surprising results to the obvious increase in individual income, to a growing desire to escape from the cities, to the efforts of Japanese manufacturers, but also to a certain stagnation in rail transportation. This has almost reached the limits of its capacity for expansion; its further development must be in the direction of improved service to suburban commuters. Thus the Japanese automobile finds itself today with a fully developed domestic market. In 1980, there was one car for every three persons. The manufacturers have certainly counted also on the foreign markets, American and European, and Japanese production superiority is increasingly affirmed. It should be noted, for example, that Toyota produces forty-five cars per worker per year, whereas Volkswagen produces nineteen cars and British Leyland only nine. As for eye appeal, Japanese manufacturers deliver well-equipped cars furnished with many sophisticated accessories. No European nor American industry can compare with Japanese car manufacturers when it comes to their efforts to adapt their cars' specifications to the needs of various countries. In Europe and the United States, they have set up solid service networks, and their advertising is widespread, incessant, intelligent, and in all languages. A crisis in the auto industry would have deep repercussions today. In fact, the Japanese registered a 6 to 9 percent drop in their sales in Europe and the United States in 1978, and the Nissan company saw an average 15 percent drop in its sales. But at the beginning of 1980, Japanese success was again confirmed on the European and American markets.

The specter of Japanese auto competition was particularly noticed at the beginning of 1980, when a wave of anxiety swept over America and Europe. Month after month, the big auto companies tried to perfect their strategy for stemming the Japanese invasion. American manufacturers even spoke of the "automobile Pearl Harbor." The Japanese minister of industry and commerce, caught between American threats of retaliatory measures and the dynamic exporting efforts of Nissan and Toyota above all, tried to gain time by making soothing speeches. He promised he would advise the two big Japanese companies to reduce their exports to the United States voluntarily and would suggest that they invest in the U.S. These promises had a short life, because Toyota informed the president of the United Automobile Workers union, Douglas Fraser, that it saw no point in investing $500 million to produce twenty thousand cars a month. Fraser returned from Tokyo without any illusions.

The industrialized West has raised many questions as a result of all this: first of all, the question of reciprocity. It is quite true that the automobile sector demonstrates abundantly the often insurmountable difficulties in breaking into the Japanese market. Japan takes in foreign cars with an eyedropper, while their entry is supposed to be free. But what American or European manufacturer will try to enter the Japanese market on his own without local partners, when he knows that, besides administrative vexations and duplicities, he must confront a stone wall on the distribution sector, which effectively prevents him from creating a serious service network that will function after he has sold his car? Toyota, Nissan, and Honda do not have this problem, either in Europe or in the United States. What's more, what would compensate the American manufacturer for the actual inequality in competition? Self-limitation? From the Western side they beg for it as a provisory palliative, while from the Japanese side it is looked upon as blackmail.

It is necessary, in fact, to understand that in the prosperous period, until 1973, all the industrialized countries were traveling in the same direction, the direction of an accumulation of wealth in a situation of frantic growth. The crisis, the warnings from such organizations as the Club of Rome, the byproducts of growth—pollution and nuisances of all kinds—have led in all the rich countries to discussions about the quality of life that have weakened their economic striking power. This is true in the United States and Europe, but not in Japan. Of course, there have been some courageous Japanese politicians who have said that an annual growth rate above 5 percent is not desirable. One was Saburo Okita, the former secretary of the Club of Rome, who was minister of foreign affairs in the Ohira government. But Japanese employers have never thought this way. They have always made every effort to attain the maximum growth rate, and the decade of the eighties is still dominated by the myth of growth—a less savage, more orderly, more qualitative growth, but a growth no Western country can hope to keep up with. It remains around 6 percent, when the most fortunate of Japan's rivals can barely reach 3 percent.

The Turn into the Eighties

Old habits have a way of becoming part of one. To give up the idea of growth would be, for Japanese employers as a class, the same as committing seppuku. Besides, ever since the price of oil soared, the Japanese employer has been less inclined to limit growth; he has felt himself forced to produce more and export more in order to pay the bill. Certainly, energy saving has been the object of a campaign aimed at instructing the people, and the results have been spectacular in respect of domestic consumption. So, too, have been the results of the effort at innovation and research in the field of renewable forms of energy. But oil consumption continues to increase, and most of it is absorbed by an insatiable industry. At the beginning of the eighties, significantly enough, when in all other industrialized countries growth tended toward zero, Japan was experiencing an economic boom. The rate of growth for the first three months of 1980 came to almost 8 percent, and the annual rate of growth for productive equipment reached 15 percent.

Yet the course of growth has its built-in limits. No Japanese household can indefinitely continue to buy television sets, refrigerators, washing machines, and automobiles. The same number of cars per inhabitant as in the United States would be enough to paralyze Japan. A decline in consumption will produce a reduction in growth, especially since the demographic curve of the last ten years shows a disquieting increase in the number of old people and the likelihood of there being too few children to ensure an increase in the labor force. Other disquieting signs: the decreasing number of farmers— yesterday they made up 12 percent of the working population; today barely 8 percent; 2 percent is projected for 1990. The service sector continues to expand, to the detriment of productivity, and the most pessimistic economists see signs of a future dearth of consumer goods and a scarcity of blue-collar workers which will compel even the highly educated to do factory work.

No one can give a definition of "Japanese" that would satisfy both a Westerner and a Japanese. Modes of Japanese behavior vary, anyway, like fashions in women's dress. The eighties are the years of the economy. Japanese minds have therefore become "economic" minds. One day at Sapporo, I watched the person in charge of baggage at the airport bus terminal. He had set about sweeping away the water in the gutter so that his customers would not be splattered. I wondered what filled him with so much zeal. It was nothing more than an instinct of solidarity with the interests of the company employing him, since his future depended on its reputation with its customers. In this sense, the Japanese have a more "economic" mentality than ever before.

Japanese economic growth has experienced three successive phases. The phase of the sixties, specifically Japanese and maintained at a very high rhythm, saw the development of big industries, supported by a dynamic home market. Quite soon the Tokyo stores selling bric-a-brac were transformed into luxurious boutiques selling consumer goods of the highest quality and thus favoring a rapid increase in inventories. To finance these inventories the companies did not hesitate to go into debt. Gradually Japan caught up with countries like France or West Germany and replaced imports with domestic products.

The phase of the seventies showed a Japan in the same situation as the other industrialized countries. The first oil crisis came down on it with a crash. A period of industrial stagnation began. Investments decreased. Capital became scarce and expensive. The rise in the cost of energy and raw materials chiefly affected the metallurgic sector, the basic chemical industries, and the shipyards. Small and medium-size companies were, paradoxically, less affected than the large ones. Female blue-collar workers became more numerous; people thought more in terms of wages than the job. But one must remember that the policy of the big companies concerning employment for life did not change because of the crisis—which explains the invariably low percentage of strikes (around 3 percent).

The phase of the eighties somewhat revives the state of mind at the end of the sixties, but with a shift which takes into account the lessons imposed by events:

Maintaining employment for life but speeding up industrial restructuring, with an emphasis on flexibility.

Small and medium-size companies benefit from the cutback in household consumption, bolstered by a campaign to encourage savings.

Channeling the fruits of higher wages toward productive investment in small enterprises.

Stressing the development of the goods and services sectors as opposed to the manufacturing sector.

In 1980, I went to Osaka, Japan's business metropolis, for the first time in ten years. At the superb Plaza Hotel, I was in walking distance of all the important business districts. Every trace of anarchy had been replaced by American-style urbanism. Where there were no buildings, there were construction sites. The whole town was on the move. The capital of the province of Kansai has benefited from the extraordinary industrial takeoff epitomized in the 1970 exposition. The entire future had begun to germinate in Osaka: the urban transportation of tomorrow, the overlapping of telecommunications and computer systems, etc. These days it is hard to find Japan in Osaka, except when boarding the suburban train that goes to the factories of the Sunstar group, a small industry born and reared in the strictest "family" tradition.

Sunstar's reigning family, Kaneda, came originally from Hiroshima. The company was created from scratch and set up in a suburb of Osaka. Today it employs two thousand people. In one room they manufacture brake bands for a Japanese car manufacturer; in another they cut up imitation leather for a whole line of suitcases. At the center of the building they make toothpaste (and put it into tubes), not to mention toothbrushes and, more cautiously, certain cosmetic products, face creams, and colognes of middling quality. The company is best known for its toothpaste.

I met all the directors of the company because I was accompanying my friend Victor Sarel, president of Washperle International, a Marseilles group that manufactures interior and exterior surfaces for buildings. President Kaneda and President Sarel met in the lobby of the Plaza Hotel. Point-blank, the Japanese asked: "What is your company's motto?"

The Frenchman was visibly caught short. He had thought of every question but this one. His reply was vague. "We are for human productivity. . . ."

The Japanese president shook his head disapprovingly. "President Sarel, what is your company's hymn?"

Sarel has a good product to sell, and faith in what he undertakes, but he does not have a hymn. A few days later, the French businessman was taken to the factory just when they shut off the power at the end of the day. Silence fell, almost a heavy silence, and than all the workers intoned the Sunstar hymn.

For the time being, as the metal industries decline, toothpastes and other consumer products are booming. Suitcases are designed in Italy, they make the raw materials in Osaka, but the suitcase itself is manufactured in Hong Kong, where labor costs less. Not infrequently, an intelligent skilled worker abandons his machine to become, after recycling, a white-collar worker. The Japanese worker is not affected by the "working class" myth that is a hangover from the nineteenth century. He is not tied to a specialization, and he does not think of himself as belonging to a class or category of worker. In the Sunstar company at Osaka, as in the majority of Japanese companies, an employee moves without apparent difficulty from one kind of work to another. It is the market that decides, although the hierarchical structures remain largely paternalistic. "Not so long ago," one worker told me, "a worker would not be given important responsibilities unless he had been in Hiroshima." Inside the company, the social context of interpersonal relations evolves very slowly. In other words, methods of work, organization, and the use of the most advanced technologies precede the evolution of the society as a whole.

IV: CHALLENGES

6: The Japanese and the Geijin

JAPANESE PRIDE

I am a *geijin*, we are *geijin*—all of us in the foreign colony in Tokyo, whether we be white, black, or yellow. At times smacking of discrimination, this term is always the symbol of a frontier between them and us. Whatever effort one makes to learn the language, to become integrated in Japanese society, to live as they live, one remains an outsider: the Japanese differentiate not between their citizenship and ours, but between their nature and ours. They are often astonished to find a foreigner who speaks their language fluently or who knows certain regions of Japan which they never visited or never even heard of. Sometimes they are flattered, more often they are embarrassed.

Visiting a Japanese friend, I told him enthusiastically about a marvelous trip I had just made along the coast of the Sea of Japan. I painted a picture of the old city of Kanazawa, the lively mercantile city of Toyama, the rice fields of the Noto peninsula. I had not gone to familiar places, and my listener produced a series of admiring gurgles. His tone changed, however, when I mentioned the island of Hekura, three hours by boat from the port of Wajima, at the very end of the Noto peninsula.

"And you went all the way down there? With your wife? Oh, oh. So!" He wagged his head with an incredulous air.

His incredulity turned into absolute stupefaction when I told him: "The island isn't inhabited, except from June to October. The entire population, with its divers, is transported there and lives on the fruits of its conch fishing. The women do the fishing and the men take care of the children and do the cooking. The women go about naked."

"And they are Japanese! Oh! So!"

My host stood up and our evening together was abruptly ended. He accompanied me to the door without a word, politely wished me good night, while his wife, who had served the meal and disappeared, did not appear again. I saw him several times thereafter, and each time he was cordial and urbane, but he always declined my

211

invitations and never again invited me to his house. He no longer took me seriously. For him I had become some kind of nut.

Presenting an Image

Each Japanese supposedly presents an image of himself and of Japan in which foreigners should be able to find the basic traits common to industrial, civilized humanity. Certainly they present a specific Japanese version of them. But this does not mean that the Japanese should be confused with some African tribe. Their sexual behavior is similar to that of Europeans or Americans. (In this area they have modernized less quickly than in technology; the topless bathing suit has not yet invaded their beaches.) They build airports, highways, skyscrapers, as is done in New York or Frankfurt; they even build them better. So how can a foreigner maintain that a resolutely modern and advanced civilization harbors a population that allows its women to work very hard as divers and go about naked in almost primitive villages, while the men take over the household work? There is obviously an inconsistency here. The honorable foreigner has confused Japan with some South Sea island. We admit we have a folklore: certain ways of life and communities that have escaped the sweep of progress and economic development and form part of those "smudges" we deplore and which must be cleaned up as soon as possible. Similarly, the French and Americans have their sects and their communes. According to the Japanese, marginal beings and beliefs should not survive unless they are linked to folklore.

But what one says and what one does are not always the same. No country in the world embraces so many marginal beings and so much diversity. The desire to present a homogeneous image prompts the Japanese to insist on historical continuity, but the history of Japan is in fact made up of discontinuities: discontinuous was the ambiguous revolution of 1868, which led to the restoration of the emperor and gave him the power to pursue an autarchic, isolationist policy while he was actually straining his wits to open the archipelago to foreigners; discontinuous again was the deliberate Japanese decision to imitate Western nations and become an imperialist country by annexing Korea in 1910; discontinuous the military's seizing power and the triumph of old generals like Tojo over the army's subaltern cadres, which had blazed the trail for feudal Japan; discontinuous the defeat of 1945; and finally, discontinuous the alliance and cooperation with the conqueror. What continuity can they have in mind?

Effacing the War

The Japanese make political, not historical choices. Hence they decided to not explain the period from 1930 to 1945, decided to speak of it as little as possible, and, if they did, to speak in lapidary phrases.

From 1963 to 1979, I did not find in the leading newspapers any examination of what happened in Japan during the Second World War. Whereas in the United States, all the shady aspects of McCarthyism, a not very glorious period in U.S. history, all the turpitude surrounding the Vietnam War, have been amply aired and examined; whereas French collaboration with the Nazis has been subject in France to debates and polemics throughout the mass media, in Japan one still awaits discussion of the *kempetai*, the thought police who had so potent an influence over the Japanese for so long. The Japanese do not willingly admit to the role they played during those dark hours of the world's history, except if one limits their responsibility to that of people carrying out orders. They did have a feeling of profound culpability, but all that does not count any longer because it is the past: the American tribunals sorted out the good and the bad, the bad have been punished and the good declared not guilty. So one should not talk about all that anymore. . . . They hide behind such vague formulas as: "Militarists were in power. We have suffered." They never mention the invasion of Manchuria and the Philippines. As for daily life in Japan from 1936 to 1945, there is no significant work on this period, either in literature or in films. Television has never shown or said anything about these years. In private and in dribs and drabs, one learns X was with the troops maintaining order in Korea; that Y was put in a work camp because he was suspected of leftist ideas and was lukewarm in his patriotism. It becomes a feat to succeed in reconstituting the life of a Japanese older than fifty-five, notably during the troubled years. Is this due to the old distrust of foreigners, or to a political attitude vis-à-vis the Americans? In any event, if the Japanese do have a kind of guilt complex about their military actions in China or in certain countries in Southeast Asia, where they are still reproached for their atrocities, they do not feel at all guilty about the Americans. It is Pearl Harbor against Hiroshima: zero added to zero.

Americanomania

Japan's relations with the United States were born out of a power equation between one state and another. Yet this must be considered in its emotional context. The two peoples are diametrically opposed: the easygoing attitude of the Americans is at odds with the seriousness of the Japanese. The United States does not welcome being defeated on its home turf of technological superiority. Both governments seem to have been chronically subject to intervention by their respective pressure groups. Yet these tensions could be reduced today. The geopolitics of the eighties in Asia are dominated by the Japanese-American alliance against the U.S.S.R. and Soviet expansionism, even if Japan assumes only a very modest part of the responsibilities of defending the free countries.

In both countries, the man in the street pays little attention to the regular, formal consultations between the two governments. Instead, relations exist at the level of personal contacts. Until 1970, Japanese who met a Caucasian presumed him to be an American and were astounded if they discovered him to be a Frenchman, a German, or a Russian. How often was I approached in the street by a young man or woman who asked in great excitement and without preamble: "Would you mind helping me practice my English?" A questioner who engaged me in conversation as though I were an American would openly show great disappointment upon learning I was French. Today the reaction is somewhat modified, and Europeans evoke friendly curiosity.

There is in any event a difference of attitude between groups and individuals. In a small café near the campus of Todai University, four or five Japanese students fraternize gaily with an American student, a blue-eyed young man with a shaved skull. They have returned together from a "demo" and are drinking a coffee, a Coke, an orange juice. At their feet lies a half-unfurled banner with the inscription: AMERICA GO HOME. In the seventies, this kind of situation was common, yet never have American businessmen made so much money in Japan as during the period of anti-American demonstrations from 1965 to 1970. There was not the slightest move made to cancel Eisenhower's trip in 1960.

If one wants to understand the reactions of the two peoples to one another, one must first recall the Americans' shock and indignation after the attack on Pearl Harbor. At that time, there lived in Hawaii a large colony of people of Japanese birth who were naturalized Americans. Immediately suspect, they were quickly taken from their homes and occupations and shut up in camps. They were not miserable in the camps, but for long after the war they nursed the feeling of having been unjustly treated; many of them gave up their American citizenship and went back to Japan. One of them, a photographer by profession, returned to the United States in 1978 to exhibit photographs that presented a day by day record of life in one of the camps, on the Nevada border.

Japanese reactions to the atomic bombing of Hiroshima were not more violent than America's explosion of anger after Pearl Harbor. A woman student, whose grandparents died on August 16, 1945, and whose mother, then ten years old, survived but was affected by radiation, told me in confidence:

"The Japanese sometimes wonder whether the atomic bomb has not been a punishment for the sins they committed."

"Yes," I said, "but why Hiroshima? Why innocent children and civilians blighted in this way for generations?"

"We are all Japanese," she replied.

In the eighties, Hiroshima's atomic hospital and its cancer re-

search laboratory continue to function on the basis of close cooperation between Americans and Japanese.

The feelings of the Japanese were again put to the test in 1956,
when the fishing boat *Fukuryu-Maru* was hit by radioactive fallout
from the hydrogen bomb exploded on Bikini atoll. The crew did not
notice anything and returned to Japan, where it was discovered that
the fish they sold were contaminated. The Americans, far from expressing their regrets to the unlucky fishermen, replied that they
should not have been where they were and should have respected
the ban against entering the area, which had been declared at risk by
the U.S. army. Yes, but the Japanese fishermen did not understand
English. The American authorities ended by admitting that the boat
was not at fault and that the radioactive cloud had been pushed by
unpredicted winds in an unexpected direction.

To this feeling of rancor, which has been exploited by the
Japanese press, is added resentment of the American presence,
which, despite the end of the occupation, remains important and
conspicuous. The Americans' general headquarters are in Akasaka,
at the Sanno Hotel, in a very busy district that is both an entertainment and a business center, close to the big hotels, the ministries,
and the prime minister's official residence. In 1970, my office was in
a building right across from it. In 1979, despite negotiations which
had stretched over more than ten years, the Sanno Hotel was still set
aside for the American military. Yet the apple of discord has lost its
"prestige" and the "demos" do not even bother to boo this vestige
of an old historical-political confrontation.

The big U.S. installations, such as the recently abandoned base
at Tachikawa, the northern base of Hakodate, the naval bases of
Yokosuka and Sabebo, and the impressive installations at Okinawa,
offer proof, among other things, of the permanence of American
military activities in Japan. Of course, one no longer sees American
soldiers in uniform on the streets of Tokyo and the American officers are very discreet. When, in 1957, the "love affair" between the
Japanese and the Americans was still going on, an enlisted man,
William Girard, killed a peasant woman who was collecting some
shell cases on the border of a firing range. The national press demanded that Girard be tried by a Japanese court, but the U.S. authorities replied that he had to undergo an American court-martial.
This affair indirectly brought about an agreement between Prime
Minister Kishi and President Eisenhower on the time for the withdrawal of U.S. land-based troops.

In 1960, the Japanese-American Security Treaty, which had
been signed in 1951, was finally amended as the result of a massive
protest movement that verged on revolution. Prime Minister Kishi
had anticipated that the new treaty would be ratified on May 20, the
second day of President Eisenhower's projected visit, and the Liberal

Democratic Japanese leaders had carefully prepared their maneuver.

Earlier in 1960, at the time of the renewal of the 1951 security treaty, the Kishi government had ably negotiated an agreement by which the United States was committed to defending Japan if it was attacked and to consulting beforehand with the Japanese if it was felt necessary to introduce nuclear weapons into the archipelago's territory. But the opposition of the Socialists and Communists spoiled the ruse and made mincemeat of the political cunning of the liberal democrats by brandishing Article IX of the constitution, according to which Japan "renounces forever war as the sovereign right of the nation." The Japanese left—that is, the united left-wing political parties and trade unions—set the masses dreaming of a disarmed Japan in a disarmed world. Thus an unrealistic pacifism, carefully kept alive by Moscow and Peking, was transformed into a great anti-American movement. Ten million Japanese signed petitions denouncing the security treaty. Sohyo, the left-wing trade union, organized an illegal strike of railroad workers. The Zengakuren students' association threw shock troops wearing plastic helmets into the streets. The prime minister was asked to hand in his resignation. On June 7, James Hagerty, the White House press spokesman, was attacked on his arrival at Haneda airport by a Communist-controlled crowd of several thousand. The Cadillac in which Hagerty and United States ambassador Douglas MacArthur II were riding was taken by assault, its tires punctured, and its windshield shattered. Under a rain of rocks, the two Americans ended up boarding the helicopter that had come to save them. On June 15, a young high school student, Miss Kamba, was killed in a counterdemonstration organized by right-wing extremists. Police brutality was charged. The upshot: 341 policemen and 459 demonstrators were hospitalized. A wind of revolt was rising all over the country, provoking strikes in all economic sectors. All the islands were in the grip of an intense agitation in which anti-Americanism was mixed with political confrontationalism.

Kishi had acceded to the demonstrators' demands—Eisenhower did not go to Japan—and, interestingly, the privileged ally of the United States has never managed since then to create conditions favorable to the visit of an American President while in office. (Despite all this, the elections of November 1960 were easily won by the candidates of the Conservative party.) The Vietnam War continued to agitate further the highly charged Nipponese-American relations, especially as the Japanese people's feelings became aggravated and revived by the delicate question of Okinawa.

I had gone to Naha, the capital of Okinawa, at the time of the forced sea landing of the Apollo XIV capsule. Carrying out an extensive inquiry into the island's ties with other islands of the archipelago, I immediately noticed the gulf separating Japanese opinion in Tokyo from that expressed in Okinawa. A young Socialist professor told me: "I am for the return of Okinawa to Japan, unconditionally. We are Japanese like the others." There precisely was the problem. The inhabitants of Okinawa were dependent on the U.S. military bases and the American army for 80 percent of their income. They benefited from numerous economic and tax advantages for imports from Japan and the United States. "To whom will we serve food and drink?" the owner of a bar-restaurant asked me. "They should make these Americans go away. I don't want these horrible B-52s staring me in the face right in front of my house," said a Japanese woman, who then invited me to stand on the terrace of her house because from there one could photograph the B-52s and watch everything that was happening on the base. The powerful black birds, their eight jets expelling trails of exhaust, were taking off uninterruptedly from Okinawa for some ultrasecret mission over China, the U.S.S.R., or Vietnam. I had asked permission for my crew to film them, but the press officer told us that it was forbidden, while indicating with a wink of his eye and a sly hint that there was a place at the edge of the base, off limits for the soldiers, which would let us see the monsters just as they left the ground. From our position as we lay in a ditch, the bombers taking off skimmed less than three hundred yards above our heads. Yet when Okinawa is given back to the Japanese, many of Naha's inhabitants will miss the American administration. Meanwhile nothing has changed, except for an American presence which is more discreet though still sizable; an entirely Japanese civil administration, and Okinawa inhabitants' complaints about Tokyo's fiscal pressure.

Japanese-American relations are no longer burdened by the problem of the American military presence, and only rarely does Japanese opinion question the installation of nuclear arms on their territory. The object of contention has been eliminated. People living in the northeastern suburbs of Tokyo were relieved to see the base at Tachikawa disappear, and the nuisance, noise, and pollution of a few military airports were not political pretext enough for anti-American agitation. Demonstrations are now very rare.

Not so long ago, while Richard Nixon was President, the Japanese-American economic dispute suddenly became shrill and bitter, due to the pressure of lobbyists for American textile producers who found themselves competing with imports from Japan. More recently, Japanese textiles have been supplanted on the American market by textiles from Seoul, Formosa, Southeast Asia, and, increasingly, Peking, but the Japanese are now upsetting America by taking over the electronics and even the computer markets. Yet despite the consequent tensions, the two countries are dependent on each other for 30 percent of their foreign markets.

On the American side, American-Japanese relations are closely watched in the realm of security above all. That is why the Pentagon expressed its anxiety in November 1978 when the Ishikawajima-Harima shipyard sold the U.S.S.R. an immense floating dock to be anchored off the coast of Vladivostok. This, according to the American military, would permit the Soviet Union to deploy its naval forces in the Pacific more easily and would make it possible to repair in the water airplane carriers of 40,000 tons, as large as the *Kiev*.

On Japan's side there exists a certain hesitation and modesty about parading its friendship for the Americans. Yet for twenty years now, the bilateral cultural ties have only become stronger and closer, and there are no longer any spheres of activity in Japan where one fails to find at least one and often several preeminent figures who have stayed in the United States for purposes of study or research. Whether it be in literature, films, or art, technology or economy, law or the sciences, medicine or space, the Japanese know and appreciate the work of the Americans. All the American universities are "stuffed" with Japanese; modernism and the future are viewed in Tokyo through the American prism. The Americans are not as saturated with Japan, but the Japanese challenges that look to the year 2000 cannot leave them indifferent.

Nor have the Japanese in turn been able to remain insensitive to the faith Americans have in the principles of democracy and liberty, of which they have become the earnest proponents. The Japanese newspaper *Yomiuri*, with a daily circulation of close to ten million, joined with the American Gallup Institute to ask the same question in Japan and in the United States: "What in your country are you proudest of?" The Japanese first mentioned their technological potential and their feeling of innovation, plus their "economic power," and it appears that they are particularly proud of the high quality and large number of automobiles they manufacture. As for the Americans, they speak first of their freedom, their democratic government, and the human resources of the American people. They are also very proud of the equality of opportunity for each person, whatever his economic condition might be at the start. Scientific progress only figures eighth in their list of occasions for pride. *Yomiuri* judges the Americans as follows: "Their faith in freedom remains unshakable. Since their creation, more than two centuries ago, the United States, a melting pot in which all races have mingled, has always needed symbols of unity for the different ethnic groups. Each citizen feels the need to experience the tie of belonging that attaches him to the community. Among these symbols are the star-studded flag, the President, incontestable leader at the summit of the hierarchy, and freedom. . . . In 1960, President Kennedy declared that he was ready to fight any enemy and defend freedom at any price. Immediately after this, United States power underwent a long eclipse with the failed invasion of Cuba, the war in Vietnam, and Watergate, and over the years the Americans have lost all their illusions and their faith in progress and traditional values. These factors are at the root of their present skepticism about 'their own economic strength and their scientific and technological advances.' "

As for the Japanese, *Yomiuri* wrote: "Today the Japanese are more American than the Americans. They are optimists concerning everything that pertains to their country at present and in the future, just as Americans were until recently. . . . They believe that they can surmount the economic recession if they continue to work hard. The Japanese certainly lack a firm moral foundation. And this newspaper regrets that the constitution cannot serve as a common spiritual denominator for the Japanese people."

I report this joint inquiry because it has significance in terms of the exchanges between and the mutual interpretations of the two cultures. If it fails to stress the attachment of the Japanese to a certain form of individual freedom imported from the West, that is perhaps a consequence of not paying serious attention to what one sees every day. Never have I heard so many people admit to giving up bits of their freedom for the community's advantage and interest as during the course of my last visit.

In this connection, the Japanese newspaper noted that the devotion of the individual to the community or nation might well arouse the suspicions of other peoples "as to the real or imagined threat they might represent as economic animals." And it is true that in 1980 the Japanese menace was seen as more dangerous than ever before. The procedures resorted to by the Nixon administration developed even more rapidly under the Carter administration. American anxiety was manifested in a warning in the *Wall Street Journal* by Ezra Vogel, professor of sociology at Harvard, an esteemed expert on Japan. "Japan," he wrote, "surpasses the United States in all spheres; these are irreversible movements unless we react swiftly."

Yet Japan's progress has not been either sudden or dazzlingly brilliant, but has instead been regular and progressive since the fifties. First there were the textiles produced by cheap labor and of a quality comparable to those produced in the West. Then the market for watches was taken away from the Swiss, the photography market taken away from the Germans, and the market for radios, television sets, computers, and automobiles taken away from the Americans. Many additional manufactures—pianos, ski equipment, motorcycles, pottery, glassware, calculators, photocopying machines—have become the particular specialties of the Japanese.

The result for Japan has been significant cash surpluses. The Japan–United States balance of payments is heavily weighted in favor of the Japanese, and until 1979, the Japanese financed the increased costs of petroleum out of their cash surpluses. At the end of 1979, the situation was modified because despite expanding foreign trade, the Japanese balance of payments shifted into the red, and the increase in their exports could no longer compensate for the vertiginous increase in their petroleum bill. In 1978, Japan's balance of payments surplus was $18 billion. In 1979, the corresponding deficit rose to $12 billion.

The Chill from Siberia

America has just recently become aware of Japan, whereas Japan has been aware of America for a long time. In Japanese polls, the United States consistently tops the nations most loved by the Japanese, whereas the U.S.S.R. comes last.

No, decidedly the Japanese do not much like the U.S.S.R. Historical rancor goes hand in hand with current political rancor and popular resentment. Japan failed to become Communist after 1945, when five hundred Soviet "advisers" laid the foundations for a popular revolution (only the energy of General MacArthur prevented the country's "domino" fall). On April 13, 1941, in Moscow, at the end of an unusual trip, Foreign Minister Matsouka had signed a treaty of neutrality with the Russians. Earlier, in Berlin, he and Hitler had signed a mutual assistance treaty. He had then flown directly to Moscow. It was the April 1941 treaty that was broken by the Russians on August 9, 1945, after Hiroshima and Nagasaki were bombed.

The Russians' declaration of war shocks the Japanese each time it is mentioned, even if it was the direct consequence of the agreements at Yalta, and the feeling of having received a stab in the back after being laid low only serves to deepen the old rivalry that originated in the Russo-Japanese War of 1905. At that time, two imperialisms confronted one another. The imperialism of the czars, confident of its history and power, had underestimated Japanese expansionism and Japan's determination to equal the imperial powers of old Europe by creating, in accordance with their example, privileged spheres of influence, notably in China. Since 1945, no peace treaty has been concluded between the Soviet Union and Japan: the Russians have refused to sign the treaty of San Francisco. Currently, the basic dispute between Moscow and Tokyo involves the southern Kuril islands.

It is true that the protectorate of the Kuril islands has legally been entrusted to the Russians, but the Japanese have solid legal arguments to back up their claims to regain control of Habomai and Shikotan, less than three miles from the coast of Hokkaido and technically not part of the Kurils. The Soviets have on several occasions agreed to listen officially to the Tokyo government's complaints, but they have always refused to discuss the merits of the case. They see Japan as an essentially militaristic state, whose aggressive tendencies are rooted in the samurai spirit. According to them, this intrinsic militarism coincides with and is supported by European and American capitalism. They maintain that Japanese militarism, though vanquished, has not been rendered harmless; the Japanese economy has not been demilitarized; Japan's economic potential can support the resurgence of militarism. This Russian analysis has created a barrier of distrust between the two nations. Thus the Russians vetoed Japan's membership in the United Nations until 1956. After this, their attitude is reflected in two kinds of behavior: on the one hand, an attempt at economic barter, offering Japan the unexploited riches of Siberia and luring them with rare raw materials, such as the reserves of copper in the Chita mountains, which equal the presently known reserves throughout the world. On the other hand, the Soviets have made an attempt at a military-diplomatic reconciliation, with the renewed offer of an Asian security treaty that would consecrate the U.S.S.R.'s ambition to become a fully accredited Asian power. The Japanese have been expert at steering clear of this diplomacy with both firmness and a smile.

After careful study of the Siberian problem, the Japanese have stressed their lack of capital to make the necessary investments for significant development and have presented Moscow with counterproposals, offering to bring the Americans into the negotiations with the idea of a joint venture.

Until now, none of these great projects has come to anything. On the military plane, China's evolution, viewed in the long term, and Japan's obligation to maintain its disarmed neutrality, as the Socialist opposition has proposed, have made the conservative government reflect on the advantages of a cheaply bought defense, assured by the Americans and more to be trusted than the treaty proposed by the Russians. Today the peace treaty between Tokyo and Moscow appears as far off as it was thirty years ago, and disputes have been added to disputes. Periodically, the Japanese minister of foreign affairs goes to Moscow. He manages to get a few contracts signed, but whenever he mentions the Kurils, he sees that he is entering a plea in an unfriendly court. This scenario has continued for twenty-five years. As for Mr. Gromyko, each of his visits to Tokyo is punctuated by a conversation on the subject, but he has never been authorized to discuss it.

This diplomatic stalemate has had its effect on the economic life of northern Japan. On Hokkaido, one can already feel the impact of the state of latent conflict. More than 50 percent of the region's economy depends on the Russians and on commerce with the nearby Kurils, three to twelve miles from the Japanese coast. Sakhalin is twenty-two from the Japanese port of Wakkanai, on the other side of what Europeans call the Strait of Perugia. In this region, much less populous than the rest of the archipelago, two things stand out. First of all, the population feels somewhat cut off from the main Japanese community and easily develops an isolation complex, above all during the winter months. Moreover, involved as it is in a network of daily relations with the U.S.S.R., it feels trapped between the reality of its economic prosperity and the fundamental demands of Japan and the Japanese.

Mr. Hashimoto is a young schoolteacher in Sapporo, Hokkaido's capital. I met him one November evening not too long ago in a souvenir shop, where he was kind enough to act as my interpreter. The streets in the center of Sapporo were straight as a die. Sidewalks were lined with shrubs, and neon signs drew all sorts of abstract forms in the shadows. Mr. Hashimoto accompanied me to the bar of the Tokyu Hotel, where I was staying.

"The Russian colony is not very numerous at Sapporo, but you can meet a few of them. Their consul general is very important and engages in a great deal of cultural, diplomatic, political, and military activity. They do not mix with us very much, but they do their shopping in the city and don't live in cloisters. Individually they are quite pleasant, and most of them speak our language. They are involved in many business affairs here. For example, they sell us lumber for construction. At Hokkaido we sell them a lot of canned fish, but there lies the problem. From one day to the next, they could deprive the Japanese fishermen of every chance of going on with their work. Our government is constantly engaged in negotiations about fishing. How can one apply the twelve-mile limit to territorial waters and two hundred miles to the fishing grounds? At the last negotiations, the Japanese lost 30 percent of their fishing grounds as a result of quotas Tokyo had to accept. The fishermen in Nemuro are not satisfied with these arrangements. But there is something worse: thanks to these regulations, the Russians often seize our fishing boats. They board them in so-called Russian territorial waters, which are really Japanese territorial waters. Hardly a week goes by without an incident. The boats are sometimes given back only after three months."

"And the fishermen?"

"They are very discreet about living conditions during their enforced sojourn. I think they're afraid that if they reveal certain things, they will have difficulty resuming a normal life as fishermen."

"Why?"

"Tokyo does not consume enough of Hokkaido's fish and the Russians absorb much more."

"Aren't these exchanges an occasion for useful contacts on the military plane, given the strategic importance of Hokkaido?"

"I don't know anything about that. That's something you should ask the military men."

"Are you for or against Russia?"

"That is not how the question should be posed. Japan's relations with Russia will never be good, because of the Japanese-American Security Treaty. The Russians have never had a friendly attitude toward us. Ten years after the end of the war, they were still keeping many of our men in prison, especially men from the Manchurian army—According to rumor, about ten thousand. Wherever we turn, we are caught between the world's two great atomic powers. We don't want the atom bomb. Why should we throw ourselves into the arms of the Russians, who are much less friendly than the Americans?"

The Japanese have always been careful not to get mixed up in the quarrel between China and Russia. That has not stopped the U.S.S.R. from intervening violently in relations between Tokyo and Washington and continually issuing warnings, and this harsh stance disposed Japanese leaders to look toward Peking when the time was ripe.

Since 1972, the date of the signing of the treaty of peace and friendship between Tokyo and Peking, the Russians have stopped lavishing warnings on Tokyo, feeling that the treaty's anti-hegemony clause refers directly to this. When, at the end of October 1978, the Chinese deputy prime minister, Deng Xiaoping, visited Tokyo, Moscow was infuriated, not least because Tokyo showed a rare unanimity about such a public event. The shouts of welcome for Deng were so many jeers for Brezhnev. At least, that is how the Russian officials reacted to it. And perhaps that is how the Japanese people unconsciously wanted it to be understood.

The Smile from Peking

I was in Tokyo during Deng's entire visit. It was all spontaneous. Nobody restrained his feelings, either on the Chinese side or, with greater reason, on the Japanese side. Television gave us, as always in such cases, insufficient information about the emotional dimensions of the event. My time in Tokyo was limited, but I could not help but gaze every evening at the flood of images that were unleashed by the seven television networks, chronicling every step Deng and his wife took as they trod Japanese soil. Madame Deng visited a grammar school in the Tokyo suburbs. Children ran to her and smothered her with flowers, an official gesture followed by a marvelous free-for-all, all of them wanting to touch her and be kissed. Those who brought a poem or a drawing just dashed off were rewarded. Their teacher managed to establish order by getting them to sing the song they had prepared. And Madame Deng could not hold back her tears. In Tokyo, Deng surprised the Japanese officials when he declared: "I want to see Kakuei Tanaka." Very cautiously it was explained to him that the former prime minister was no longer in an official position and above all had been having difficulties with the Japanese courts regarding a certain "Lockheed scandal." But Deng insisted. "I do not want to meddle in Japan's internal affairs," he said, "but I want to greet Mr. Tanaka, without whom my visit today would not have been possible." On Tuesday, October 24, the former prime minister stood before the door of his private residence with his wife, Hana, who was dressed in her ceremonial kimono. The couple was surrounded by representatives of Tanaka's clan, his daughter and son-in-law. As the press, herded together by the police, invaded the street, Deng's car arrived. A security helicopter circled overhead. Deng grasped Tanaka's hands for a long time, while the photographers clicked away; Tanaka did not release Deng until he was sure the photographers had done their work properly.

Deng Xiaoping's visit to Japan in 1978 involved more than a mere state visit. From the day of his arrival, a significant historical reaction was triggered. A century of war and rivalry was coming to an end. The Japanese people could finally give free reign to their instinctive enthusiasm for the source of their culture and beliefs. The intellectuals, press, business circles—everyone (with the exception of the Taiwan lobby)—induced in the government true remorse for having followed Washington's policy vis-à-vis Peking. Since 1945, the Japanese had developed a guilt complex in regard to China because of military behavior, especially in the thirties. On their side, the Chinese, since Mao, have never lost interest in Japan.

Tokyo's new relations with Peking have geopolitical significance. The balance of forces between the Communist world and the free countries is now totally altered. Once again the U.S.S.R. sees disappearing into the distance the objective it had expected to attain: the status of an Asian power in the full sense, which China has always denied its old ally and ideological tutor, feeling that Asian affairs should not be mixed up with those of the two superpowers.

China's rapprochement with Japan seemed consolidated by the visit of Prime Minister Hua Guofeng to Tokyo in 1980. Guofeng was an easy guest. His stay rolled along without mishap, though it lacked the emotion of Deng's earlier visit. The political content was serious, and the leitmotif was "Distrust the Russians." Those damned Russians—one tries as hard as possible to forget them, but certain incidents in Hokkaido remind the Japanese government that the armistice does not signify peace, and Moscow has never endorsed it.

On the economic plane, all goes well. The Chinese are ready to import all the Japanese technologies the Japanese will agree to sell them in exchange for promissory notes. These notes have nothing in common with the notes behind Russian loans at the beginning of the century. The latter were never redeemed. The Japanese are apparently gambling on the future. They have credit and confidence. This time China will be grateful, unless some of their leaders get the idea that what is in question is a "repayment" for past injuries.

A "HISTORICO-FOLKLORIC" KNOWLEDGE OF EUROPE

The Japanese lavish affection on each separate country in Western Europe. They love Goethe, Wagner, Beethoven, and Stockhausen. They never tire of watching Swiss cows at pasture, the grass growing at the foot of the snow-covered mountains that dominate the cantons. They love those extravagant Frenchmen, who are so witty, who portray sex to perfection on the stage and in popular songs, whose literature and philosophy are rooted in a civilization as old as Japan's. They envy and copy stable British institutions. They do not detest Belgian fried potatoes or Amsterdam's hot streets, and though they may distrust Roman pickpockets, they cannot help but stop on the Piazza di Spagna and savor—noisily—a plate of spaghetti. Spain has not yet been programmed in the circuits of the tour operators, but it hasn't escaped the businessmen from Honda and Sony.

Today Western Europe and Japan have discovered their divergent economic interests, while recognizing that they are both in the same ideological camp—Japan and Europe are much closer and more mutually concerned than headline stories might lead one to suppose. Japan maintains continuous bilateral relations with all Western European countries, it has equal footing in the EEC, and it maintains commercial relations with Europe. Europeans reproach the Japanese for their balance of payments; they pressure their Asian partner to restrict their exports voluntarily. The Japanese reply: We should not be penalized because of the high quality of our products and the efficiency of our commercial services. We welcome foreign investments; only imports are subject to tariffs: beef, leather, and certain agricultural products. The Japanese invasion of Europe is insignificant: e.g., for Western Germany, the most important market, only 3 percent of its foreign trade involved Japan, and for France less than 2 percent.

As for the opening up of Japan to European products, the problem posed is partly political but largely technical, a problem of distribution. Few European industries are capable of adapting to the Japanese market; the commercial officials at the embassies seem unable to find sources of potential profits. Japanese administration is mysterious to many Europeans; the problem is compounded by ignorance of one another's practices and the lack of verbal communication—the Japanese language provokes misunderstandings. Today Japan seriously competes with Europe in third world countries—China, Vietnam, Malaya, Indonesia, etc.—and the Japanese have succeeded in spectacularly modifying their image in those countries. Even at the height of the Vietnam War, the Japanese, although allies of the United States, were sending commercial missions to Hanoi.

They also became competitors in Africa and South America (their move into Brazil has been extensive), and Iran and the countries of the Middle East and of North Africa, above all Morocco, have become favorite areas for Japanese commercial ventures. Certainly, Tokyo often enters these markets after agreements with Paris, Bonn, or London, but the competition can only become progressively keener, and it is impossible to see how Japan's objectives for the year 2000 could tone down the rivalry.

FROM CULTURAL TO POLITICAL RECEPTIVITY

Japan's cultural receptivity toward Europe, the United States, the U.S.S.R., and China deserves to be analyzed in Marxist terms. The Japanese people, whose reasoning is often tinged with emotion and whose dialectic confuses subject and object, curiously make a distinction between theory and practice. Cultural hospitality exists in the domain of the practical—it never engages the individual. How could it, if the individual is incapable of making a choice? On the other hand, all hospitality disappears when national objectives are at stake. Tokyo's diplomacy toward Peking is revealing: the Japanese have transformed a reversal, a loss of face, almost a gesture of contempt into an offensive weapon, permitting them to take a decisive step toward the realization of a unanimously approved objective.

Herman Kahn defined part of this objective when he wrote: "Japan will one day supplant the United States in Asia." I met Herman Kahn at the Hudson Institute in 1970. On Croton's greening hill in Westchester County, north of New York City, he was the animator of several research teams, notably on Vietnam and Japan. Kahn was fascinated by Tokyo's dynamism and convinced that this could only result in a drive for political and military power. Two years later, I met him again in Paris, at the Hotel Plaza Athénée, which then housed Hudson's European offices. Kahn, reflecting the opinion of the Hudson group, now went even further, claiming that Japan's rearmament was inevitable.

The Japanese were surprised when President Nixon announced his intention of recognizing the Republic of China. The prime minister at that time, Eisaku Sato, received the news a few hours before its official release. Japanese politics was not prepared to take this leap. A powerful lobby inside the conservative government supported Taiwan. The route of Japanese world leadership did not pass through Peking. Washington's tutelary shadow was a convenient screen behind which they could reach the center of the stage without upsetting anyone. Now the premature raising of the curtain suddenly exposed Japan in all-out economic ascension, confronted by an important political decision. The Australian journalist Wilfred Burchette, a Marxist and a great friend of the Chinese, translated Peking's thought as follows: "It is the attitude which the present Japanese leaders will adopt toward China that will reveal their real plans. It will become clear whether they aim at peaceful coexistence or whether they want to launch their country on the path of military expansionism." In fact, Tokyo analyzed the situation quite differently. They found themselves in the presence of two triangles: a triangle of power whose poles were Washington, Moscow, and Peking; and an economic triangle, of Washington, Europe, and Tokyo. Faced with China's recognition by Nixon, Tokyo's approach remained pragmatic—to increase its influence in the triangle in which it was implicated. But the Japanese also glimpsed the possibility of inserting themselves into a triangle of power, in line with their historic ambitions. Zbigniew Brzezinski, President Carter's special adviser on foreign affairs, spoke of a new triangle of Washington, Peking, and Tokyo. So Peking has been, willy-nilly, the agent of a new kind of relationship between Japan and the United States. Tokyo was no longer a vassal of Washington; it would now play a determining political role in the north-south problem by contributing directly and effectively to the economic growth of developing countries in Asia.

What was the upshot? The question was posed in the seventies, as it is still posed in the eighties. Will Japan's economic and industrial power be translated into military terms, as it has already been translated into politico-diplomatic terms? If one takes the evidence of history, says history professor T. C. Rhee at the University of Dayton, the response is affirmative. According to Rhee, certain parallels can be established between economic realities and political aspirations. He points to the Sino-Japanese War of 1894, after an initial attempt at control of Korea; the rivalry with czarist Russia, still in connection with Korea, ending in 1905 with the defeat of the Russian fleet in the Strait of Tsushima; the question of Shantung; the twenty-one demands; the Manchurian crisis; the setting up of the puppet state of Manchukuo; the militarism of the thirties; and Pearl Harbor. All these actions took place within the context of building an industrial state, and Professor Rhee sees the same process shifting into gear with the upsurge of nationalism. It is a good idea to leave responsibility for this view with him. The Japanese defend themselves vigorously. Those among them who have demanded a change in the constitution so as to move freely in that direction are cut off from the mainstream, and their audience among the masses is nil. The spectacular suicide of Yukio Mishima gave rise only to a feeling of sympathy for a courageous traditional gesture—it did not provoke any disorder or even a discussion of ideas.

Japan's relations with the outside world are not always based on "reasons of state." Unless vital economic interest are involved, Japan is a pearl-bearing oyster, developing in itself a wealth that it offers only to the most persevering, those who have the daring and nerve to win its friendship. Thus Eisenhower's visit to Tokyo was canceled in 1960, but Deng's visit in 1978 was a great popular success. Neither the Russians nor the Europeans have yet understood that sentiment is an important aspect in the overall Japanese behavior pattern.

KOREA, THE OLD COLONY

The American ambassador in Tokyo recently expressed conviction that by now an American phase-out will not have disastrous consequences for the free world in Asia because the "politico-military translation" of economic power flows automatically and no longer depends on specific political aim. There is, however, a flaw in such American logic. It is South Korea, the strongest military power in non-Communist Asia. Tokyo and Seoul belong to the Western camp, but in a context of relations whose normalization has been difficult. It is little more than an hour's flight from Tokyo to Seoul, yet one steps down into what seems almost another continent. Sky and earth have more marked contrasts; the light is cruder; Japan's cotton-muffled atmosphere gives way to sharp, high sounds. At the entrance to the city, as one comes from the airport, a few old traditional houses are swamped by new apartment houses.

Seoul has grown at a vertiginous rate: while the Japanese have had a growth rate per year of 12 to 14 percent, the Koreans, their pupils, have gone as high as 16 percent, using factories delivered into their hands by Japan to manufacture competing products.

During my first stay in Japan, I went to Seoul a number of times. I was concerned about two questions then in the news: the question of the demilitarized zone along Korea's 38th parallel, and that of Korea's relations with Japan. "We want to normalize our relations with Japan," Premier Chung Il Kwon declared, "but we want negotiations between equals—we never again want to fall under the Japanese rod." Japan, following in the footsteps of European colonial empires, annexed Korea in 1910. Korea regained its sovereignty only in 1945 with the Yalta agreements, but at the price of partition of the North (Moscow's sphere of influence) from the South (Washington's sphere of influence).

South Korea was devastated by the war of 1950–53; forced to take on excessive military expenditures, it stagnated in backwardness.

Then the first Japanese industrialists arrived in Seoul. They drove their Toyotas, then their Toyota assembly lines arrived, and finally complete Toyota factories. Other brands and other products followed.

I was in Seoul at the start of this evolution, and I asked President Park Chung Hee: "What is the reason for your difficulties in normalizing relations with Japan?"

"You must understand that during their occupation, the Japanese wanted to take over our soul."

Premier Chung Il-Kwong clarified this: "We lived under martial law during the Japanese occupation. We couldn't even speak our language—it was no longer taught in our schools."

And a university professor told me: "Japanese patrols listened to conversations in our houses. When they heard people speaking Korean, they broke down the doors, made brutal arrests. People taken from their homes simply disappeared."

Today Japanese businessmen come to Seoul and are treated well. Economic realism prevails over memories of the past. South Korea is no longer in the absolute sense a developing country, even if it remains one due to the unequal division of the country's resources and the heavy burdens of defense assumed by the Koreans despite American aid. And the United States has begun a process of disengagement in Korea, similar to the procedure they followed in Japan.

Obviously Japan is directly concerned in everything that happens in Korea. The forces present in this part of the world are impressive, both for their size and for their armaments. Russian foot soldiers—that is, the North Korean army—number more than 400,000 men facing more than 600,000 in the South. On the sea, the two superpowers confront each other head-on. This was quite apparent in the *Pueblo* affair in January 1968, when a U. S. spy ship containing extremely sophisticated equipment was boarded and seized by North Koreans in the sea off the port of Wonsan. At the moment when the ship was about to be towed off and its crew taken prisoner, its captain destroyed secret documents as well as equipment that permitted direct transmission to Washington. Now—surprise—some frogmen were already busy around the American ship. They were not North Koreans but Russians. The eighty-two sailors and their captain remained in detention for almost a year.

I followed the entire affair, which made a lot of noise at the time, and witnessed the liberation of the prisoners. The American press officers had eliminated the representatives of French Radio-Television from the pool of journalists because that organization was at times considered subversive. (I had on several occasions sent it documents of North Vietnamese or Chinese origin.) Yet I managed to find myself at the right place at the right time thanks to the friendly complicity of the United Nations commanders. My announcement of the freeing of the *Pueblo*'s crew on France-Inter some hours before the official communiqué put the U.S. embassy in Paris in emotional turmoil. This serious affair also caused the Japanese cruel embarrassment. The *Pueblo* was actually based near Tokyo, at Yokosuka, in one of the bases granted to the Americans. A colleague from American television who, with his crew, had hired a fishing boat to go out on the open sea near Okinawa suddenly found himself within shouting distance of a submarine which had surfaced. To the stupefaction of the American journalists, it was a Russian submarine. My colleagues got the fishing boat to sail over to the submarine so that they almost touched sides, and threw them a pack of cigarettes. In exchange, they got Russian cigarettes. They chatted for a few minutes, when suddenly a brisk order rang out on the submarine and the crew vanished as the ship prepared to dive.

Telling about this episode, which seemed incredible, one of the journalists heard a high-ranking American officer reply that it was quite normal: Russian submarines reply to greetings from American submarines they encounter by chance in the ocean off the Russian coast. The tacit nonintervention agreement between Russians and Americans has been ignored by North Koreans. Each time an incident takes place, the Japanese are aware of their impotence: directly or not, they are in effect geopolitically concerned by an event that occurs in their territory, along the seacoast, or on the nearby continent. What is at stake is nothing less than Japan's survival, which is based on the security of its supply routes and the independence of its islands.

7: The Japanese and the War

A VISIT TO THE ARMY OF THE NORTH

Japan has not completely weighed the consequences of taking its place among the democratic industrialized nations. Neither have the Japanese people, or the intellectuals, or the politicians, save for some rare exceptions, realized the strategic meaning of an overlapping of power. In reality, it is no longer a question of translating politico-industrial power into politico-military power. The Empire of the Rising Sun has passed the point of no return, beyond which any economic triumph has politico-strategic consequences. The Washington-Europe-Tokyo triangle, instead of simply representing an economic relationship, in fact determines the entire policy of an industrialized country in respect to the countries that produce raw materials, including the rich producers of petroleum. As for the Washington-Peking-Tokyo triangle, which has for the moment no military thrust, it cannot be thought of except vis-à-vis Moscow, which consequently implies—right now—the redistribution of the balance of military power in Asia.

Japanese military men are very cautious on this subject. They do not make any statements and prefer working in silence. So I went to visit them in order to see for myself what Japan's economic power signified in military terms.

At Sapporo, capital of Hokkaido in the north, it was twelve-thirty in the afternoon when I arrived at the Tokyu Hotel. I found a message saying: "You have an appointment at three o'clock with General Kobayashi, chief of staff of the Army of the North. Mr. Hasei, an interpreter, will come to take you to the general's headquarters." Five minutes before the set time, I was in the hotel lobby. A man about sixty-five years old, with the manner and style of a retired officer (I would learn later that during the war he was a school principal), accosted me with lively, sparkling eyes. He spoke correct English and told me as he proffered his calling card that he had been assigned by the Foreign Press Center at Tokyo to accompany me to General Kobayashi.

"Do you prefer to take a taxi or the subway?"

I opted for the subway, Sapporo's pride since the 1972 Olympic Games. We were just on the outskirts of the city, at the edge of an immense park. Facing us were the mountains, barely a few miles away, not yet capped with snow although a cold breeze announced the winter.

We could not go far in the subway because the line swerved away from our destination. So we hailed a taxi to general headquarters in the suburbs outside Sapporo. The rectangular brick building, built between 1930 and 1940, with a central terrace supported by two columns, was one of the few remaining military or civilian buildings of this sort in Japan. As is the custom in Japan, the general did not receive us from behind his desk but sat down with us around a low table. Tea was served. The general then gave us an account of the troops under his command: four infantry divisions, plus four brigades: armored cars, artillery, antiaircraft defense, and engineers—fifty thousand men supported by two squadrons of planes. In the eyes of the general staff, the enemy was the Soviet Union. Japanese military strategy is clear on this point. Coordinated with the strategy of the United States, its objective is to protect itself against any violation or invasion of Japanese territory.

"Our problems are different from yours. Your defense is simplified by the existence of NATO, even though France is not part of it. We have no regional military treaty. Two matters demand our attention: the problems raised by the two-hundred-mile fishing zone, hence the protection of Japanese fishermen; and the violations of our air space—180 cases in 1977, and just as many, if not more, in 1978."

"Do you have contacts with Soviet authorities?"

"Of course! At Sapporo the U.S.S.R.'s consul has quite a large staff. But contacts are all made north of the Wakkanai base."

"Is it true that the Russians approach people directly to obtain information?"

"The Russians do in fact try to get some of the fishermen to give them information in exchange for permission to fish."

"Do the fishermen respond to these overtures?"

"I should imagine so."

To another of my questions, the general replied: "It is true that we try to encourage our demobilized soldiers to come and settle in Hokkaido. We ease their changeover to civilian life. If an emergency arose, we would have a hard time. We practically cannot budge without an order from the prime minister. We would find it hard to contain a nuclear offensive. It is something else again on the conventional plane. It is only thirty-five miles from Sakhalin to Wakkanai, but the Russians would have trouble landing their famous T-72 tanks, which we can confront with our Mitsubishi T-74s. To head directly for Sapporo, they would have to land twenty-eight miles from here in the Bay of Ishikari; in that case, the road from Sakhalin is longer, and we would have time to intercept them."

On the training field, the Mitsubishi T-74 was astonishing; accompanied by General Imada, commander of the First Artillery Brigade, we watched the tank go through its paces: weighing thirty-eight tons, it can go faster than thirty miles an hour and can ford water more than six feet deep. It is equipped with a 105-millimeter cannon, an automatic rifle, and a machine gun. Its turrets can turn the full 360 degrees. Thanks to a laser it can fire very accurately at night. Its maneuverability seemed to a layman like me slightly superior to that of analogous French or American tanks.

It began to rain just as we reached the training field for the R-30 rockets. But everything had been foreseen. While we waited in General Imada's jeep, soldiers put up a large tent. There we were sheltered as we sat in sizable chairs, with a table in front of us to facilitate note-taking. Colonel Misobe, commander of the R-30 group, clamped the plan of his maneuver on an easel. Then he took a microphone out of his pocket. As his voice resounded in the tent behind me, I noticed with surprise that two loudspeakers had been installed; his voice also reached the various vehicles carrying rockets, as well as the mobile radar station half a mile away. As Misobe issued his orders, I saw radar antennas under the trees at the edge of the forest point up at the sky to check on wind direction, indispensable knowledge for accurate firing. Two vehicles, carrying three launching ramps each, faced us and pointed their tops above the rim of trees, while an antiaircraft surveillance half-track equipped with special machine guns stood ready to intervene. The order to start firing was given, and the countdown began.

All the military men I met at Hokkaido agreed on two points: The Self-Defense Forces will serve to stave off real Soviet pressure. In case of a conflict, everything possible will be done, but in the best of cases, the Japanese army could contain a Russian invasion force for only a few hours, just long enough for diplomatic negotiations to get under way.

Back in town, I asked my interpreter about the possibility of an encounter with Russia. Mr. Hasei said, "Wait, I'll show you something."

He went to the newsstand and bought the magazine *Qualité*. He then proceeded to translate for me the second installment of a work of fiction in the form of an on-the-spot report of a Russian invasion: "The Japanese-Soviet War in Hokkaido," by Kaoru Murakami, a military critic. It was subtitled "The Life of Hokkaido's Inhabitants Becomes More and More Miserable."

The end of May 198— . . . Soviet forces have landed at Wakkanai. The Japanese Self-Defense Forces try in vain to push back the invaders.

Losses are heavy on both sides. From Moscow, the commanding general of the Soviet armies phones a message to congratulate his troops on the success of the Wakkanai operation. The Russians have proposed that China remain neutral. This operation is not directed against her, but if she sides with the United States she will suffer the consequences—the Russians will not hesitate to use missiles with nuclear warheads. China estimates that the collision of the U.S.S.R. and the U.S.A. can only confer on her a great increase in power, if not world leadership.

The Soviet fleet has entered the Strait of Perugia, encircled Hokkaido, and occupied the Strait of Tsugaru. Television has shown the arrival of the Russians in Wakkanai. In panic, Japanese housewives rush to the supermarkets, for sugar, soap, and toilet paper, but in three days all the most necessary commodities have disappeared from the stores. Countermeasures have been taken to send reinforcements to Hokkaido so as to preserve communications and ensure accommodation for refugees. The Diet has passed an emergency decree calling on the President of the United States to invoke the security treaty and launch an immediate American intervention. Surprise has been total. The American satellite alert system did not detect anything abnormal. Traffic from the island of Honshu to Hokkaido has been interrupted by the Soviet blockade, which has sealed off the Straight of Tsugaru with floating mines. The Chitose airfield has been damaged. Civilian laborers wear headbands with *Keishitai* [suicide corps] inscribed on them: they are sacrificing themselves to work in the front lines. Despite the blockade, arms, ammunition, and a small trickle of provisions have gotten through. The Self-Defense Forces have regrouped around Sapporo. At Wakkanai, almost the entire population of 56,000 inhabitants are now under Soviet control.

Sapporo is still unoccupied, but there is gunfire at Chitose, Eniwa, and Ishikari. Fires are burning everywhere and the people are taking refuge in the forests. At headquarters in Hokkaido, the heads of the military and civilian services are in permanent session. They have asked the directors of the television networks and newspapers to join them. The chief of staff has submitted a plan for evacuating the civilian population from the occupied zone of Wakkanai. The governor of Hokkaido refused to take any step until he received instructions from the prime minister. Now it is too late. The military men are furious with the civilians because only the governor has the power to mobilize the reserve forces. The chief of staff foresaw this situation and deserves his nickname, Mr. Computer, because in a few hours the situation has become so bad that not much can be done. Migs have begun machine-gunning columns of refugees. Secret peace negotiations have started at Geneva. . . .

ARTICLE IX

Several hundred thousand copies of this scenario were published in November 1978. Its publication date was surely a matter of chance.

Although I have not been able to talk with the author, this fiction undeniably reflects the reality as the Japanese military perceive it. Certainly, during the seventies, Japan has made big budgetary concessions in favor of the Self-Defense Forces, but it can be safely stated that faced by a superpower like the U.S.S.R., Japan would be defeated in advance. One can also perceive in this war scenario Japan's uncertainty as to immediate armed intervention by the United States. Some people are even convinced that Washington would not intervene with nuclear power if the Soviets landed at Hokkaido. Nobody doubts that they would intervene at Geneva. Therefore, the entire question of the future of the Self-Defense Forces is up to the Japanese themselves; they must first decide what is possible and reasonable.

The possible and reasonable presuppose maintaining the American commitment in Asia at all costs. That is what Deng Xiaoping told the Japanese leaders during his visit to Tokyo in November 1978, and on that assumption an anti-invasion plan was developed, at the end of 1978, that deals with the operational and political aspects of a Japanese parry in case of an invasion of the archipelago. In 1965, the general staff had worked out a plan that provoked a great deal of discussion when it was made public in the Diet by a Socialist deputy, embarrassing Mr. Ikeda's government. It took as its hypothesis the invasion of South Korea by the North and supposed the intervention of Japanese forces outside the archipelago. It even entertained the possibility—and this was what principally generated an outburst of emotion—of a new Japanese occupation of Manchuria. They were very specific about the details, even calling attention to curfew time at Shenyang, the capital of the region, the old Mukden. Such a plan was in total contravention of the spirit of Article IX of the constitution and ran counter to the basic tenets of national defense adopted by the Diet in May 1957: Support of the U.N.'s activities and promotion of international cooperation; stabilization of general prosperity and development of love of country; development of an effective military potential in proportion to the country's resources; and opposition to any foreign aggression in the framework of a treaty of security with the United States.

Starting from these principles, Japan has defined its attitude to nuclear weapons: not to possess them, not to make them, not to import them.

Japan's security is based on the power of the American nuclear deterrent.

Japan has also forsworn medium- or long-range ballistic missiles, long-range bombers, and attack warships. It further refused ever to send troops abroad to exert any sort of military pressure.

These relatively strict rules confine the national forces within limits that make the Japanese per capita expenditure for defense the smallest of any industrialized country. In 1979, the government decided to assume most of the cost of the upkeep of the American forces stationed on the archipelago. These number 48,000 men and 200 planes, and the Japanese subsidy initially came to $591 million a year, to which was subsequently added $100 million. As for the Self-Defense Forces, they number 155,000 men in the land army, 200,000 men in the navy, and 500 planes, which cost about $10 billion, about 1 percent of the gross national product. In comparison, France spends a little less than 5 percent of its gross national product on defense, the United States expenditure goes as high as 8 percent, and the U.S.S.R. spends around 12 percent.

The Japanese army, after its defeat, was not popular with the citizens, and Japanese soldiers got into the habit of leaving their barracks in civilian clothes. There are no bars for soldiers and sailors except on the fringes of the American bases, and then only in well-defined areas, where the Japanese public does not set foot.

Lately this attitude has begun to change. First of all, defense was never mentioned in the press until 1970; it has been discussed a great deal since—too much, in some people's opinion. In this regard, two statistics are significant. In 1972, 71 percent of the Japanese electorate were in favor of a Self-Defense Force. In 1978, 83 percent were in favor. In 1972, barely 40 percent of the electorate supported a combined defense with the Americans, in the framework of the security treaty. In 1978, their numbers rose above 80 percent.

Just before Mr. Ohira's election as prime minister in 1978, *Asahi*, one of the three largest Japanese dailies, published the results of a poll, according to which, 82 percent of the Japanese approved of Article IX of the constitution, which stipulates Japan's total renunciation of war as a means of solving conflicts. Four years earlier, *Asahi* said, only 34 percent of the Japanese considered the Japanese-American Security Treaty beneficial, but at the end of 1978, this percentage had risen to 49 percent. In the same poll, the public was asked to indicate what it considered essential for Japan's defense: 42 percent backed diplomacy; 20 percent, economic power; 15 percent, the constitution; 13 percent, love of country; 2 percent, Self-Defense Forces; 8 percent did not express an opinion.

The results of this poll are substantiated by the 87 percent of the Japanese who approved the treaty of friendship with China, a triumph of diplomacy for peace. And it is certain that Japan has no intention of changing its policy from one day to the next. It believes in being discreet when it comes to defense, whatever the efforts to which it will devote the allotted 1 percent of the gross national product. The fantastic growth of Japan's defense capability should logically lead to her possessing the most powerful, best-equipped armed forces in Asia, after those of China.

THE WHITE BOOK OF DEFENSE

The ideas of the Japanese authorities on defense questions were published in a White Book in 1978. "We must have a realistic approach," a staff officer pointed out to me. "The networks of collective security are determined by the two superpowers, and even the nations outside those networks must take into account the military positions of the United States and the U.S.S.R.

"On the one hand, the U.S.S.R. tries to develop its nuclear armament to attain parity with the United States; on the other hand, this effort is undercut by certain handicaps: its relations with China and with certain Warsaw Pact countries such as Rumania; its internal economic situation, and so on. What is dangerous is Soviet policy in conventional weapons: they give top priority to quantitative superiority and to the value of a surprise attack. Hence the Russians' massive development of a tank corps, airplanes, and navy. We are concerned with North Asia, but we must not forget that a conflict in Europe would lead to one in Asia, or at least would pose a serious threat of such a conflict. No doubt we would also be directly involved if a conflict broke out in Korea."

On October 29, 1978, I was invited to Asaka for the annual review of the troops. About twelve thousand Japanese had gathered to see their army on parade. That day the prime minister summed up the general feeling when he said: "In the absence of all certainty and assurances concerning the security of Japan, we must be ready to repulse resolutely any invader, whoever he might be, and to do that, we must take the necessary measures. The foundation of our security rests on the efforts we make to give our country the capability of self-defense."

THE KURISU AFFAIR

While thinking about Japan's attitudes toward defense, I was struck with admiration for their artfulness in saying without saying while still saying—especially about Japan's being forced to resort to war, if attacked. But it is even more astounding to see them act without acting while still acting—or, to put it another way, to see Japan building up its armed forces within the limits of 1 percent of its gross national product, which theoretically would not enable them to possess armed forces; the explanation, of course, lies in the increase in absolute value of the gross national product. In this regard, the affair of Major General Kurisu is exemplary. When a man is president of the High Council on Defense, he is justified in assuming that he can reply frankly to a journalist's questions, particularly when the questions have already been asked by the entire press and are standard in public discussion. Hence television commentator Kenichi Takemura had no malevolent purpose when interviewing the chief of staff of Japan's armies.

"General, sir, the forces under you could not intervene in an emergency if Japan were to be attacked since you must first of all obtain authorization from the prime minister, who in turn must first consult with parliament. . . ."

"That is so, but I believe that in certain circumstances, which one should not exclude, the Self-Defense Forces could on their own responsibility take the initiative in carrying out certain paralegal actions—for example, if they suddenly found themselves facing invaders. Our first duty is to ensure the protection of the Japanese people."

The next day, General Kurisu was asked to hand in his resignation for having advocated breaking the law. In parliament, a Socialist deputy accused the general of having made this statement in order to open the way to a renaissance of prewar militarism.

"Well, then, what should our forces do in case of a surprise attack, and if the prime minister's order does not arrive in time?" was the question flung at the Socialist from the ranks of the conservatives. The assistant director of the defense agency in charge of administration replied imperturbably: "In that case, our forces must run away."

Takemura, who had interviewed General Kurisu, commented on the minister's reply and said with great feeling: "This is nonsense. There is something here that does not work. . . . They must be really confused to make such a ridiculous statement. Let's suppose that a battleship is attacked. If the sailors decide to run away, what should they do? Jump overboard!" *Asahi* reporter Shiba Kimpei concluded: "The Japanese are, without a doubt, the most illogical people on earth. They order F-15 bombers that carry missiles; they include in the defense budget the cost of three airplane carriers; in this way they spend three or four times what it costs to maintain the armed forces of three or four countries together . . . and they are horrified at the thought of having to modify Article IX of the constitution. . . . But there is more—the Japanese possess another unique character trait: a guilt complex. Never during the war did any person in authority admit that the army or the navy had lost a battle. Even Midway became a Japanese victory. It was the same thing at Okinawa, and later, in 1945, at the moment of the final surrender. . . . But logic now demands that the constitution be amended or that the Self-Defense Forces be disbanded."

THE AFTERMATH OF HIROSHIMA

It should be realized that such logic has little chance of prevailing. The ambiguity that flows from the progressive development of the armed forces suits the Japanese government too much for it to consider logic. Logic in any case is an imported mental attitude and cannot be understood except by a few journalists or a few nostalgic persons wanting to use logic to justify the translation of economic power into power *tout court*. Watching the Japanese army march past at the Asaka camp and comparing it with the armies of powers comparable to Japan, one was forced to conclude that the Japanese army does not exist. One should certainly not condemn Japan's effort to manufacture the arms necessary for its defense, and there is a real Japanese armaments industry, with the potential of building up a formidable army supplied with nuclear weapons. But what is lacking is the political determination and popular consensus to carry through this operation. Two percent of the population believes in the virtue of arms. Foreign observers are sometimes blinded by the freedom of a debate that did not exist five years ago. Now the debate points up a confusion: each Japanese, traumatized by the word "war," searches for other ways to get out of the impasse to which the logic of power leads.

I became aware of this debate as soon as I arrived in Japan. Yukio Mishima was emphatic: "We will become a nuclear nation. . . . Japanese politicians deceive the people. They tell them the things they are only too willing to hear. The nuclear allergy is a matter of circumstances." Soon after this, I went to Hiroshima. I had rented a small plane, and before landing, the pilot undertook on his own to give me a tour of the bay and to cross the city above the ruined dome of the Chamber of Commerce, precisely where the atom bomb had struck. "Now, that's the view the pilot of the *Enola Gay* had just before the fatal moment." Two young Japanese women, waiting for me at the airport, took me to the university campus, where I was surrounded by a group of students.

"My mother's husband was killed in 1945. My mother did not suffer any harm. She had gone into the countryside on her bicycle. . . . After that, she remarried."

"What do you think of the Americans?"

"Nothing."

"And you?"

"Perhaps it was the fault of the Japanese. I don't know anything about it."

"But don't you have it in for them?"

"No, not especially."

"And you? What do you do?"

"I am studying chemistry. . . . I was not born in Hiroshima, I come from Fukuoka. . . . The atomic bomb? It is a terrible weapon. We must do everything we can to ban it—demonstrate, protest, sit down in the middle of the street and not get up until the Japanese government has made a solemn commitment against it."

"But it has done so—there is Article IX of the constitution."

"Article IX is a good thing, but one can easily get around it."

"Do you hate the Americans?"

"No."

"What is your name?"

"Setsuo. I am sixteen. I study foreign languages. The bomb? . . . I don't know. I do not know war, but I have seen the photographs in the museum. It is horrible."

"Do you like Hiroshima?"

"Yes, very much. I come from Tottori. Hiroshima has become an international capital. There are many tourists. The city is rich and the museum attracts a lot of people, especially Americans. Many Americans live in Hiroshima."

"Nobody has a grudge against them?"

"Yes, of course, but in any case, those who are here had nothing to do with it."

"Would you like to go to the United States?"

"Yes, very much, to perfect my English."

I had been invited afterward to ceremonies marking the twentieth anniversary of the atomic attack. The "festivities" were organized by two associations: the Gensuikyo, a group connected with the Communist party, and the Gensuikin, a group supported by the Socialist party and Sohyo, the left-wing trade union. All the hotels in Hiroshima were full and business was great. A memorial zone had been marked off beside the Park of Peace and the museum, but in the small streets nearby, restaurants, bars, nightclubs, striptease joints, and cabarets were, on August 6, 1965, packing them in and making money hand over fist. The event survived thanks to its political sequel: in 1977, a world conference, and the first to be organized by the two rival associations, adopted international and domestic programs of action. The first aimed at a worldwide campaign for signatures on a petition demanding an international treaty prohibiting all nuclear weapons. But the Hiroshima forum remained just that, a forum. It has not to this day succeeded in obtaining more than lip service to its goals—people say how awful, but go right on doing what they feel they have to.

Decisions are made elsewhere. The former minister of defense, Nakasone, who is also the leader of the most conservative faction in the majority party and who lost the November 1978 election for party president, declared, when he was still in charge of defense:

"We will never have recourse to nuclear weapons under the present circumstances." This seems to be the most commonly admitted point of view. But how long will the present circumstances last? General Hashimoto, former commander of the Army of the North, now retired, told me: "If we are attacked with tactical nuclear weapons, we will be obliged to react as if we had been subjected to an all-out nuclear attack. It is therefore necessary for us to rely on the arrangements of the Japanese-American Security Treaty."

THE PROVISIONAL ARMY

Accused on the one hand of being hawks, the Japanese are caught in an ambiguous debate which goes beyond the dilemma. Should we go nuclear or not? At first shoved aside or rejected, the idea of public discussion has finally been accepted, and here, as on other questions, the pragmatic attitude prevails. The Japanese find it paradoxical to find themselves reproached, for a modest effort toward self-defense, by a superpower that devotes more than 12 percent of its GNP to defense. They watch with mistrust the development in Asia of a competitive situation that involves the United States and the U.S.S.R. They are not of a mind to become a pawn in this game, and so they have welcomed with favor China's new contribution to the equilibrium of the region. On the domestic plane, although several courts have confirmed the constitutionality of the Self-Defense Forces, the Japanese still question the compatibility of these forces with the famous Article IX. In 1978, the celebration of an armed forces day was presided over by the prime minister. There still remains a further step: for the emperor himself to preside over such a ceremony. The trauma of defeat has become somewhat less severe, but it is still there. In the old days, the soldiers were called "thieves of the products of taxation" (zekin dorobo). Those times are gone. Yet the soldiers are still shut up in their barracks. It is a provisional situation.

THE OBSESSIVE QUEST FOR INDEPENDENCE

In the West, unfortunately, certain simplistic clichés precipitate passionate convictions regarding Japan. In return, these crudely critical views have reinforced in Japanese their historical and visceral tendency to shut themselves off. In 1868, it was in the name of Japanese independence that the Meiji were brought to power to reinforce a closed-door policy. Later, and again in the name of independence, the decision was made to practice a policy of rapprochement. "Enrich the state, strengthen the army" underlay Japanese political thought, which was dominated by the desire to achieve equality with the great empires at the end of the nineteenth century, while furiously protecting Japan's independence in relation to those all-powerful nations.

That is how Japan entered the twentieth century. It chose, by annexing Korea, to become an imperialist country, and as such it participated in the division of spoils in the Treaty of Versailles, which recognized the legality of its twenty-one demands of 1915. In the name of independence, it fought a war in Manchuria and set up a military government. In 1939, "Enrich the state, strengthen the army" represented a line of conduct that succeeded fairly well. Japan withdrew from the League of Nations, which had insisted on reparations. It was prepared to face the entire world on a footing of equality. Hiroshima disrupted this development, but when Japan was reborn after defeat, the slogan was still operative, at least in regard to its first part: "Enrich the state." Did the fact that the second part, "strengthen the army," was for the moment eclipsed signify a break in the continuity of its political policy?

Its Western partners have accepted Japan as an "economic giant," but do not hesitate, even today, to call it a "political pygmy." By 1980, nothing seemed able to halt the progress of an economic power that had become second in the world after the United States.

It was therefore appropriate at the start of the decade to ask about the political and military translation of this power. Indeed, it is not uninteresting to point out that since the Kurisu affair, matters of defense were debated more and more often in the press, and these debates began to be echoed by the public. Zenko Suzuki, who became prime minister in the mid-seventies, chose the theme of defense as the pivotal question of his first press conference. The Japanese leaders realize that they cannot avoid much longer the more and more shocking contraction between Article IX, which prohibits Japan from having an army, and the continuing growth of the Self-Defense Forces. Even 1 percent of the GNP has made the Japanese army the seventh in the world in respect of weapons. The Japanese also know that they can no longer play on two tables, all the more since this annoys the Americans, who cannot understand how the Japanese can invade the American market to the detriment of U.S. interests, while their productive capacity benefits from United States responsibility for their defense needs. Yet the Japanese are still not comfortable with the idea of ending the separation between economics and politics. No doubt they will come to this, in the name of independence.

In the course of talking with Chinese leaders in Peking in 1965, I became convinced that the Chinese knew their own minds as to the renaissance of Japanese militarism. They feared that "American imperialism" might use Japan as a base for aggression. The changes in

China's attitudes since then have relaxed one of the imperatives that kept Japan in a waiting, very cautious posture. Hua Guofeng has given the green light to a new Japanese army, as a guarantor of regional equilibrium.

Japan's pragmatic government, barring an accident, will go forward only one small step at a time, as it has since June 25, 1950, when John Foster Dulles, then secretary of state, not without some difficulty obtained Prime Minister Yoshida's agreement to the creation of a Self-Defense Force of sixty thousand men. But there was something special about that event—Yoshida yielded under the pressure of the North Korean tanks which were surrounding Seoul.

8: The Japanese and Democracy

THE NEW JAPANESE MAN

The new Japan, born from the ashes of 1945, proves to be, like the old, full of tensions and challenges rooted in the deepest levels of individual behavior. Yet its citizens have in common goals that give modern Japan the appearance of the cohesion and homogeneity that marked traditional Japan: to create a new society, to become the driving force in Asia, to achieve political equality with the superpowers. After thirty years of obstinate and patient revising and then building, the Japanese have produced a country that is the very image of a democracy on the Western model, revealing a new face to the rest of the world. Japan has followed the path of the West so closely that it has succeeded, through economic prosperity, in dispersing the fears it aroused from 1930 to the end of the Second World War. Having rejected fanaticism, it preserved enough of the spirit of its past to escape the Marxist ideologies, while much of Asia succumbed to the temptation of the better worlds being built by forced labor. Japan, preferring capitalism and the "slavery" of a consumer society, was ready to accept in return the inconvenience of the crises that shake the Western democracies. Yet nonetheless Westernization seems more and more a facade battered and weakened increasingly by the "old demons" and the pressure of new challenges.

The *kokutai*, the overall structure of the state, has certainly become a stable democratic whole, but its foundations are still threatened by conflicting emotional forces that have no counterparts in any model known to the Western industrialized countries.

The history of Asia has always evolved through compromises among powerful empires: Russia, France, Britain, Japan, and the United States. Today powerful empires again confront Japan: the U.S., the U.S.S.R., and China. So the Japanese have patiently rebuilt their house, though conscious of two realities: the impossibility of having a dialogue on an equal footing with the two superpowers, who are in a position to guarantee or threaten the security of the

244

archipelago; and the difficulty of defining the cultural identity of the new Japanese society.

Any change, especially a radical one, takes time. Yet clearly the physical aspect of the Japanese citizen is changing. We were accustomed to small yellow men, wearing glasses, dark business suits, nondescript ties, and white shirts. One must now get used to young people, often as tall as their European counterparts, who crowd the platforms of the Shinjuku railroad station or the campuses, wearing jeans and long hair, guitars within reach, and with the customary accessories—a leather jacket and a motorcycle. Before the Second World War, the consumption of meat and wheat was extremely limited and the basic foods were fish and rice. New eating habits have led to quite obvious physical changes.

The traditional approach to housing is regarded as more and more inconvenient by the new Japanese man. The patterns of family life are being transformed, and whereas three or four generations used to live under the same roof, the clan lifestyle is tending toward couples sharing living quarters. Little by little, the disintegration of the family erodes the principle of the father's unchallenged authority, and arranged marriages, which were the rule, have now become the exception.

All these changes are not made without clashes. Many Japanese are still attached to fish and rice, to paternal authority, to wooden houses with paper partitions, tatamis, and low ceilings suitable for people seated in the lotus position, to the absolute submission of the wife, and to individual conformity. For centuries now, the Japanese have been buoyed up by and enclosed in a complicated network of obligations imposed as duly itemized and accounted-for duties toward their family, the family of their spouse, their eventual adoptive family, their company, their neighbors and friends, their government, their emperor and state. All this is still accepted.

To be employed in an important company is considered success in itself, like belonging to an exclusive club, and implies the acceptance of a whole series of debts of gratitude. But if one considers that half the workers in the country are not lucky enough to be employed by an important company, one perceives that several million of them have only a small chance at social success. Thus the system is challenged at the same time by those who do not belong to the club and by some of its members. With the idea of mitigating this situation, Japanese employers during the past twenty years have replaced the old system of promotion by seniority with a system that also takes merit into account. But Japanese capitalists have accepted these compromises only on condition that the basic structure be left intact. For thirty years, Japan has not had a significant strike, despite certain bold attempts, notably on the railroads. In general, the unions are weak. Even when they are not directly controlled by the employers, they are unable to stir up a mass movement. People working for wages have always shown a certain social apathy, but one can expect some change in this situation, keeping in mind the growing feeling of dissatisfaction among the small and medium-sized companies, the "family" companies, the artisans and small merchants, the peasants and the service industries.

In the archipelago, the crisis of 1972 created a disease that was until then unknown: unemployment. Since 1965, bankruptcies in the less favored sectors have varied from three hundred to five hundred a month, leading to mergers and conglomerates and arousing increased bitterness. As for the beneficiaries of prosperity, they are confronted with problems of pollution and of the environment, which are certain to influence the future of the industrial-paternal society. Japanese capitalism dominates the state apparatus through the Federation of Economic Organizations, and the employers can thus manipulate the instruments that permit them to preserve law, order, and their own interests.

In the period following the war, economic growth united the ultraconservative regime and a great number of increasingly prosperous citizens. Political stability resulted from the intelligent opportunism of the Japanese elite, who were able to construct a credible democracy without destroying the mechanisms of the traditional society and the old system of authority. The imperial symbol, which could have been swept away in the tidal wave of defeat and under pressure from the American occupier, has survived and preserved its mystical attributes, even while stripped of all temporal power.

THE DEMOCRATIC COMPROMISE

In 1980, the ruling elite were rewarded for their ability to surmount the economic crisis born from the energy crunch. They were able to engage in a dialogue vital to the nation's interests. The government and the employers consider their interests identical, which makes any attempt to change the system or undermine the position of the ruling elite more difficult.

Closely tied to the business world, the different factions of the party in power have launched a supple policy of accommodation. Inside the Liberal Democratic party, one can meet impassioned partisans of a treaty of friendship with China and intransigent defenders of Taiwan, the headquarters of the "true" China. One can find both friends and adversaries of America, and those for and those against social legislation. The opposition has never been in a position to seize power. Until now, it has sometimes succeeded in influencing the process of decision by making public certain sensitive matters involving security and defense or some politico-financial scandals. However, the radical movement has been unanimously against such tactics ever since they realized they were an open threat to the institution of the state. Public opinion, the press, the trade unions, every Japanese citizen—all are inseparably linked to the structure that is Japan. If it is threatened by the "truth," a national conspiracy will spring up spontaneously to eliminate the threat.

In 1980, the Japanese took a leap forward. After winding up their dispute with the United States on the return of Okinawa, with Southeast Asia on the settlement of the so-called debt of blood— that is, reparations for acts committed during the Second World War—and with China by signing the treaty of friendship, Japan passed, without too much grinding of gears, from the industrial to the postindustrial era. Tokyo, that great department store for the Asian consumer society, no longer exports its finished products but instead sells its technology. The next stage of this not very orthodox progression, if it succeeds in modifying the conditions of national security and transforming Japanese society and mentality, will be a form of political hegemony.

The Japanese have not found a satisfying substitute for their traditional order. Hopes and realities continue to confront each other: the beauty of their gardens is threatened by pollution, urbanization, the abandonment of public services. Artificial flowers are sometimes preferred to *ikebana*. The innate feeling for the aesthetic is systematically destroyed by the ugliness of the environment. Yet the most daring architecture is emerging in Tokyo and Osaka. Medieval cities have to integrate the most sophisticated innovations without transition.

A society that emphasized law and order, by limiting the right to free expression of students opposed to the selection process for university admissions, has widened the gap between the generations. An outdated chauvinism combined with certain social tensions has at times endangered tolerance and freedom. Emotional currents, in a country where it is considered proper to camouflage one's feelings, have precipitated a difficult schism. The emotional reactions in question are contrasted with rational decisions. The decision to go to war with the United States was ascribed to emotion. The decision to surrender was laid to reason. In both cases, the confrontation between the opposing camps was bitter.

Without a doubt, the Japanese are unconvinced that logical thought can help them comprehend reality correctly. They have therefore built an intuitive democracy out of the tensions engendered by conflicting views of the way a modern nation should be governed.

Rational arguments sever the objectives of a privileged oligarchy and provide the state with structures and an institutional setup quite similar to that of Western countries. Within this framework, emotional tides create and develop conflicts—sometimes violent—which only a consensus of compromise can resolve.

The homogeneity of the social structure gives an impression of rational unity, while, underlying this, anarchic and impulsive forces provoke chaos. Activated by the stale smell of fanaticism, these forces sever the cause of progress and freedom. This duality—rationality/emotionalism—constitutes democracy Japanese style.

OHIRA

Prime Minister Masayoshi Ohira, elected at the beginning of December 1978, was a man from the peasant class. He retained the shrewdness of his origins and a bulk that gave him solidity. From Christianity he had learned the value of modesty, and he had weighed the political advantages of this quality. A ready and sonorous laugh was his way of replying to an embarrassing question, expressing an opinion, or giving himself time to reflect. Quick-witted, his brief replies often came at you in the form of another question. That is how Japan's former prime minister seemed to me during our first encounter, in 1963—he was then minister of foreign affairs in the Ikeda cabinet, representing the most liberal wing in his party. He was backed by a solid clan among the other influential clans in the Liberal Democratic party: the clans of Tanka, Miki, and Fukuda, all three former premiers; the clan of Nakasone, former minister of defense; and the clan of Komoto, the youngest but also the most right-wing. The Japanese system of government is, to a great extent, a function of the institutionalized power struggles between rival or allied clans—an undisguised inheritance from feudalism.

For many years, politics was of insignificant concern to the nation, whose affairs were managed by the Liberal Democratic party through a small number of men who held boundless power. The boiling of the Japanese pot, beneath which burns the flame of occasional scandals, demonstrates the danger to the conservatives of losing power. Takeo Miki, prime minister at the time and hence elected president of the party after a deal between the factions, saw the country endangered by a crisis of confidence in democracy. He therefore proposed a new method of electing the party president, of whom custom demands that he first become prime minister. The latter, instead of being elected by the usual party deputies after negotitations between the leaders of the clans, would be chosen by popular vote, achieved by setting up primaries in which all citizens who are members of the party could cast their ballot. The two candidates who got the most votes would participate in a second round, in which the only voters would be the members of Parliament. In December 1978, all forecasts gave Fukuda, the retiring prime minister, a second term. There is no doubt that if the old electoral method had been used, he would have won, but "proposition Miki" had been adopted. In the first balloting, Mr. Fukuda was beaten by the rank-and-file votes, to Mr. Ohira's advantage. Fukuda drew the proper lesson from it and retired immediately. So there was no second balloting.

That same Miki brought about Ohira's fall at the beginning of 1980. By switching the votes of his clan to the opposition, he deprived Ohira of his majority. Ohira did not let him get away with it. He dissolved the assembly, trusting in the trend which the results of the municipal elections seemed to have indicated. Osaka had elected a Liberal Democrat and Tokyo itself had made a clean sweep of the Socialist regime of Minobe, which had lasted for more than twenty years. Behind the scenes, former premier Tanaka, despite having been compromised by the Lockheed scandal, maintained his influence. Then, right in the middle of the election campaign, Ohira died. This was on June 12, 1980. Three candidates immediately stepped forward: the representative of the business world, Komoto, the rather versatile young and hopeful Nakasone, and the young, very competent expert in international affairs, Miyasawa.

Miki then promised to abandon his divisive role and dissolved his clan: a spectacular gesture which left his rivals unmoved. Tanaka tried another solution. In the course of a traditional geisha party, a certain Zenko Suzuki, a virtual unknown, came out of nowhere and wound up achieving unanimity in the name of unity. A member of the Ohira faction, he won an absolute majority on June 22, 1980, and promised to continue the policy of his predecessor.

THE LIBERAL DEMOCRATICS CAMPAIGN

So a Japanese democracy exists today. At least, the politicians behave like democrats, having reached an agreement with their electorate. . . .

My subway train was arriving in the Shibuya station. After having traversed the Ebisu quarter above the rooftops, the train had pulled into the fourth floor of Tokyu, the big department store. I went down through the store into the square, where the statue of the faithful dog who waited until death for the master who had gone to war serves as a gathering place for lovers, lonely people, and during election campaigns, politicians. That day the Liberal party was explaining itself to the voters, and the prime minister himself, perched on top of a truck, was addressing the passersby, many of whom were totally indifferent. Others stopped for a few minutes, laughed, then went about their business. Impassive, the president of the Liberal party continued his harangue in support of his party's candidate for deputy. With him were five or six party officials, each wearing an enormous red rosette pinned on a ribbon hanging from his lapel. They spoke in turn. An imposing group of private guards formed a cordon around the car, which was covered with banners urging the public to vote for their candidate.

"You know me," the prime minister shouted. "I have always kept my promises. If you vote for our candidate you will not regret it. He will be in a good position to help you get a job, to get loans to improve public transportation and create schools. You know him too. Born in this section of town . . ."

An election campaign is essentially a ceremonial consisting of processions, banners and slogans, greetings and speeches. The party's program is not presented—instead the character of the candidate is played up, his local roots validated. During another election campaign, on the peninsula of Chiba, Prime Minister Sato visited a basically agricultural election district. (In the small towns, they stop for several minutes, make a speech that thunders from the roof of a car equipped with powerful loudspeakers, then engage in endless handshaking.) The prime minister personally shook my hand in the French style four times in the same morning. For the Japanese it is not a question of shaking hands but rather a ceremony of touching, to show that one is close to the people, while a flood of more or less Westernized popular music pours from the car's loudspeaker. At lunchtime, the organizers had arranged for a brief snack; the premier and the candidate for deputy were received by the mayor in the large reception room of the city hall, where twenty low tables were lined up, perpendicular to the head table. We were seated on cushions, our legs folded under us. I have always found this posture unbearable after a few minutes, but I consoled myself when I saw my Japanese friends gradually letting their legs stretch out straight, to end the meal with their legs under the table. Some small platters were already set before each of the guests. On a tiny plate some macerated vegetables took the place of hors d'oeuvre; a tempura, composed of two large shrimps, a piece of cuttlefish, and an eggplant, was next to a polished lacquer bowl filled with a very hot clear bouillon. Beer and sake were poured into gray ceramic cups. The prime minister chatted with the future deputy. The mayor read a speech from a rolled-up manuscript he had taken from the inside pocket of his jacket. The future deputy got up in his turn and proposed a *kampai*. Everyone lifted his cup of sake and shouted: *"Kampai."* Then the prime minister took the floor briefly to thank the notables and local officials. He proposed a second *kampai*. He sat down, but almost immediately stood up to leave. At this moment, in the room where at least two hundred people were gathered, a voice began to shout:

"For Japan and the Emperor: *Banzai!*"

Everyone stood up, raised both arms toward heaven, and re-peated: *"Banzai!"* a sonorous *banzai*, evocative of the old demons and no doubt touched off by some nostalgic militant belonging to a right-wing faction of the Liberal Democratic party.

In postwar political life, a form of democracy has been imposed which is very close to that of the United States and of most of the countries of Western Europe. The politicians try to get elected by presenting themselves as resolutely modern, young, sporty. There are not many extreme right-wing parties invoking tradition, Japan's mythical history, its national grandeur. As the journalist and Japa-nese expert Robert Guillain has observed, the extreme right has in fact lost all the battles of the postwar period, at least until now: they demand revision of the constitution, reconstituting the armed forces, conscription, nuclear weapons for the archipelago, the rejec-tion of friendship with China, the return to Shinto as the state reli-gion. Their defeat demonstrates the weak hold of a relatively recent past. Ought one to believe that the Japanese are now converted to democracy?

THE SOCIALISTS PARADE

In 1966, Narita, the leader of the Socialist party, mounted a cam-paign against the American military presence. An imposing proces-sion of ten thousand people walked past the Yokosuka naval base. The loudspeakers on the accompanying cars beat out: "Down with the security pact!" repeated still more vigorously when the proces-sion reached the base's principal entrance, locked iron gates with two impassive sentries, who were no doubt very nervous. "Democracy is freedom for the people to express themselves as they are doing today," said Narita-San, whose tall, thin silhouette dominated the front ranks of the crowd, but he added, for my ears: "In Japan, democracy is stifled. It will be hard for it to survive. It is a question of money. Each time we want to present an idea, we have to bring together all the democrats. That is a day's pay lost, which we must compensate. Buses must be chartered to bring the demonstrators to the site. We must also compensate each participant for his *o'bento* at noon. All this costs a lot, and we do not have the money the bosses have, which the majority party benefits from."

The leader of the Socialist party was profoundly convinced that only a solid alliance with the U.S.S.R., after the signing of a peace treaty and a settlement of the territorial disputes over the southern Kuril islands, can bring Japan peace and security. Ten years later, at the moment when Deng Xiaoping visited Japan and the U.S.A. nor-malized its relations with Peking (to Tokyo's great relief), the new leaders of the Japanese Socialist party went to Moscow, but with little chance of coming up with an agreement. Their international position has not changed. To make it change, the Russians have to agree to negotiate on the four famous southern Kuril islands whose population is Japanese; as Japanese, the Socialists cannot sacrifice their compatriots, even at the risk of losing some of their military supporters. Within the country, the Socialists suffer the consequences of the policy of rapprochement with China suddenly launched in 1972 by conservative Prime Minister Tanaka.

When, in 1978, Deng insisted on meeting with Tanaka, he wanted to pay homage to a courageous political act on behalf of Chinese friendship. But he also remembered another pioneer supporter of this friendship, a Socialist, Secretary General Asanuma, assassinated in 1960 by a militant of the extreme right. Accompanied by the Socialist party leadership, Deng went to visit Asanuma's widow as evidence of his sympathy. The Socialist party, although careful to maintain a balance between Peking and Moscow, has approved the Sino-Japanese treaty despite being unable to hide its chagrin because the initiative for it came from the conservatives. How could they oppose the massive popular support—more than 80 percent—for the policy?

BETWEEN THE SOVIET HAMMER AND THE CHINESE ANVIL

The Communists were just as embarrassed. In November 1978, at the time of the ratification of the friendship treaty, Miyamoto, their secretary general, refused to attend the official banquet in honor of the Chinese guests in Tokyo. Officially, the party once again follows the Moscow line. Under Miyamoto's influence, it had, during the period of industrial expansion, seen its membership increase by many who were excluded from the benefits of progress, notably an urban, underpaid proletariat living in dismal districts on the periphery of Tokyo—localities like Sanya. The Communists also found adherents among railroad and subway workers.

Born in 1921, the Communist party existed illegally until 1945. A Stalinist popular front prevailed until 1953, especially after 1951, when the Communist leaders, openly advocating violence, went underground. Since Stalin's death, the idea of violent action has faded. The party has concentrated on infiltrating associations and organizations of intellectuals, whose most radical elements they want to attract. There is nothing clandestine about it now. However, it has not been able to escape "factionalism" due to the Sino-Soviet quarrel. It became evident after 1960 that the rank-and-file militant was more inclined toward Peking than Moscow; since then the situation has changed somewhat.

The Japanese Communist party, torn by internal contradictions,

despite a well-organized and relatively numerous militant membership—about 300,000—can play only a limited role, largely confined
to social agitation. No large municipality has voted it into office, and
even locally it has not yet succeeded in carrying through any significant action.

THE IMMOBILE "CENTER"

Between the conservatives in power and the Socialist and Communist left, two parties occupy the center. One, the Democratic Socialist party, split off from the right wing of the Socialist party; it includes celebrities and local elected officials. The other party, the
Komeito, is an outgrowth of the new Sokkagakai religion, which has
five million followers.

All the members of Sokkagakai do not vote for the Komeito, I
was told. And the religious hierarchy has steadfastly chosen to disso-
ciate itself from the Komeito's political activity. However, during a
visit to the party's secretary general, I observed that its offices are
located in the Sokkagakai building. The Komeito party has always
worked for rapprochement with Peking. Starting from scratch in
1964, it now has about thirty members in parliament.

THE LIBERAL DEMOCRATIC PARTY

The most representative party in Japanese politics is incontestably
the Liberal Democratic party. First of all, as the majority party, it is
the center of political life. Moreover, in its operations it illustrates
perfectly that Japanese duality which one encounters constantly in
institutions and behavior. Yukio Mishima pointed out to me one day:
"Democracy contains everything that derives from a technical system and can be attributed to a political system." In the Liberal Democratic party, one finds structures and modes of behavior, which can
be called techniques, directly modeled on those of the West, and
political methods directly inherited from feudal power struggles,
giving the party's conduct of affairs a typically Nipponese coloration.
No party escapes this dichotomy, but in the Liberal party its manifestations and consequences are more evident.

Some weeks before the elections for the presidency of the
Liberal party, former Prime Minister Tanaka, victim of Japan's
"Watergate," was going to be arraigned in court. Then came the
Chinese deputy prime minister's unexpected request to meet with
the Japanese politician, which rehabilitated Tanaka's image. The trial postponed, the anti-Tanaka witnesses were less assured than six
months earlier; the charges lost ground. Despite his disgrace, Tana-

ka has retained the benefits of his 1972 trip to Peking and has preserved a certain prestige in suburban and rural milieux. He can muster many political supporters and a solid parliamentary group. He decided to support Ohira in the primaries and so reinforce the most liberal clan in the party.

The young hopeful Nakasone, former minister of defense, then became Fukuda's most dangerous rival rather than Ohira's, since he was ideologically closer. Voting in the primaries is a well-oiled political mechanism in the United States; the agreement between the Tanaka and Ohira factions is an illustration of this procedure as it functions in Japan—shifting support from one politician to another, with negotiations carried on in the secrecy of the geisha houses, involving a whole series of "I give you this, you give me that," ranging from a ministerial portfolio to blue-ribbon stocks. Elected to the post of prime minister, Masayoshi Ohira dutifully began balancing his cabinet between the different factions. A skillful maneuverer, he gave his rival Fukuda four ministerial portfolios, the same number as those allotted his own faction. More bargaining began, however, with the appointment of a secretary general belonging to the same faction as the prime minister, but this appointment ended up being endorsed after a secret conference between Fukuda and Ohira.

The duality of a technical system and a political system appears in all structures and procedures at the parliamentary level. From 1868 to Japan's defeat in 1945, parliament was merely a concession to democracy and had the power only to reject or approve the text of a law or a budget. It could neither decide on the constitutionality of a law nor criticize the government—nor, understandably, could it declare war. All these were the emperor's prerogatives. Since the 1947 constitution, parliament's rejection of an important law is equivalent to a censure; the result is either the cabinet's resignation or the dissolution of the lower chamber. The mechanism functions very well, according to democratic rules, except for the use of obstructive methods on the part of the people in power. In 1970, the renewal of the Japanese-American Security Treaty was achieved only by surprise. The speaker of the chamber, a member of the majority party, suspended the session for a few hours, while they discussed a proposed law of no interest or importance. The deputies went off to have a snack, or to their offices, to a committee meeting, or even outdoors. But then the members belonging to the majority party, who had returned surreptitiously, were given the floor, the speaker reopened the debate, after making sure there was a quorum, and put the disputed treaty to a vote.

To parry such methods, the opposition must be vigilant. When big debates are in prospect, the Socialist and Communist deputies, often joined by the Democratic Socialists and the Komeito, sit themselves down in the corridors and block the entrance to the meeting hall in order to prevent the speaker from starting the proceedings without warning and getting the deputies to vote almost clandestinely. When the opposition has failed to win in the lower chamber, it can try to win in the upper. The system of two chambers gives it a larger field in which to operate.

The Japanese Diet is the oldest parliament in Asia. The United States, through the 1947 constitution, made it an instrument of democratization. However, one should not be led astray; the Liberal Democratic party is assured of power, and the most significant struggles for influence take place between its factions.

LOCAL POWER

Political life does not revolve around Tokyo only. The local candidates have their say and possess a power that is far from negligible. For a long time, the Socialist party has controlled the prefecture of Tokyo, whose elected governor, Minobe, has always demonstrated his independence vis-à-vis the party in power, whether on the question of protecting minorities like the North Koreans, whose schools were threatened, or of imposing antipollution standards on the automobile industry.

When Minobe's term ended, it was evident that he had cleaned up Tokyo by means of a whole legislative arsenal, repressing prostitution in all its forms and regulating the sale of liquor in the nightclubs. This repression not being in the Japanese moral tradition and not helping business, the effects of the laxity of Minobe's Liberal Democratic successor at the beginning of 1980 were soon visible.

Gifu is the seat of a prefecture in the center of Japan, not far from Nagoya. People come there from all over the archipelago to watch the cormorants fishing. I had decided to get myself invited to the fishing display organized for the diplomatic corps by the imperial house. Despite influential connections, I could not swing it; even the French ambassador had intervened without success. Then, on the advice of a member of the emperor's cabinet, I turned for help to the mayor of Gifu. He put a boat with his ensign at my disposal; it was the only boat authorized to sail with the imperial boats and the emperor's guests. Thus was mayoral prestige demonstrated.

In each prefecture, the governor is an elected official, and a local parliament sits whose members number from fifty to one hundred and fifty, according to the size of the population. Municipal councillors number twelve to one hundred and twenty, depending on the number of voters.

Thus, in the "technical sphere," Japan functions like a democracy. In the "political sphere," it's an open question. Democracy is "an imported foreign concept," as Mishima observed. Is the constitution currently in force, the one imposed by General MacArthur in 1946, in conflict with *kokutai*, the concept of the state? Japan's defeat in 1945 caused a psychological rupture: National sovereignty had been exercised by the emperor by divine right; then, from one day to the next, it was transferred to the people by the occupying power. Yet, for the present leaders of Japan, even if a change in the form of government has taken place, the national structure of the state, based on the imperial system, has remained the same. The ambiguity is overwhelming.

If a change has occurred, and Japan is now really embarked on the path of democracy, it means abandoning everything that over the centuries has shaped the fundamental character of the Japanese nation and has embodied (within the imperial dynasty) the heritage of Confucian influences and moral virtues which today continue to be points of reference for individual conduct. But if there has *not* been a change, how can one speak of democracy? *Kokutai* contains the roots of Japanese cultural identity. Yet all responsible circles—political, economic, and intellectual—realize that *kokutai* was first manipulated under the Meiji. The foreigner and everything he produces were admired and imitated, but this also gave rise to a Nipponese ideology, whose mystical elements would surface among the militarists, before and during the Second World War.

For Japanese youth, *kokutai* in its twentieth-century version has brought the country dishonor and collapse in the chaos of defeat, thus proving its lack of substantiality and idological meaning. Yet the fact remains that in 1980, *kokutai* embodies Japan's cultural identity crisis. The distortion of *kokutai* by the militarists represented an effort at clarification. *Kokutai No Hongi*, published in 1937 by the Ministry of Education, reflected the official doctrine: distrust for the West's pernicious influence, primacy of the state over the individual, Bushido values, loyalty, filial piety, harmony. . . .

CONSTITUTIONAL LEGITIMACY

Thus, before the Second World War there had been a distortion of the original Confucian model. According to the late Herman Kahn, today one would find a similar situation. Just as the Japanese in the past absorbed and digested China's contribution, so they have now absorbed and digested Western democracy. Still, according to Kahn, the comparison between Anglo-Saxon and Japanese behavior presents us with two versions of democracy, altogether contradictory. Political sovereignty in the West is the business of the people and is delegated from low to high. In Japan, to the contrary, it is cornered, monopolized, and distributed by the leaders on high to the lower rungs of the hierarchical ladder.

Japanese citizens put themselves under the protection of the establishment. Placing their trust in the authority of the government, they accept the compromise and support the cohesion of the "nation-family," giving priority to harmony within the group and thus to the subordination of the individual, with each person allocated, a position in the hierarchy. They are concerned less with their rights than with their duties and obligations.

This national state of mind has perplexed Americans. They have asked whether the Japan of the past should not be destroyed once and for all and the democratization of existing institutions be pushed ahead. The emperor escaped being judged as a war criminal, only in the realization that he alone, thanks to his moral authority, could make the Japanese accept defeat and the occupation. The imperial system is still alive, but in a form more like the British constitutional monarchy than the absolute monarchy, based on divine right, reestablished by Meiji in 1868.

Emperor Hirohito often goes to his country house on the seashore at Hayama, south of Tokyo Bay. I had rented a weekend house a few miles from the imperial residence, and one spring Sunday, after a long walk on the beach, I came to the boundary of the estate. A few yards away, I could see Hirohito from the back, alone, walking on the empty beach. Some plainclothes detectives signaled me to keep moving.

Hirohito knew this house even before becoming emperor. His father, Emperor Taisho, died there. Leaving this village on December 26, 1926, Hirohito made his first contact with his subjects, who were lined up along the road, their heads bowed; they had come from all over the region for a glimpse of the new sovereign. He waved to them. At his side, in the same automobile, the grand chamberlain of the imperial house carried the sacred treasures—two of them anyway: the sword and the precious stones, the mirror being stored in the Grand Shinto Temple of Ise. Hirohito was the 124th emperor-god, come to a throne burdened with 2,600 years of history.

The emperor had chosen the name Showa to distinguish his reign: Light (Sho) and Peace (Wa). He was twenty-five years old. He knew several foreign countries, especially Europe, having visited, while he was crown prince, Great Britain, France, Belgium, the Low Countries, and Italy. He had married Princess Nagako, daughter of a ruined nobleman.

In 1926, when he mounted the throne, Hirohito, emperor by divine right, could not suspect that the years ahead would bring a procession of sorrows and misfortunes immeasurably greater than those of the first decade of his reign, when Japan was still suffering the consequences of the great Kanto earthquake in 1923. According to the famous phrase of Akutagawa, author of "Rashomon," Japan in this period was afflicted by an "indefinable anxiety." A year later, in 1927, Hirohito heard of the writer's suicide, which the press made into a symbol of the malaise of Japanese society. At this time, a newspaper cost three yen, three hundred times less than today. The banks were in difficulties and the country was dangerously close to a financial catastrophe due to the earthquake-insurance bonds guaranteed by the government, on which investors demanded immediate reimbursement. The incident gave the military a pretext for pursuing their expansion in continental China. Public morality was disintegrating. The newspaper *Mainichi*, reviewing fifty years of the imperial reign, reported that in 1926, three hundred houses in Tokyo were set on fire by their owners, who had more than adequately insured them beforehand. Women and young girls began to wear high heels. The first subway line began operating.

Japan's malaise found its expression in the researches undertaken by Akutagawa in order to choose the method of his own death. Kenji Miyamoto, secretary general of the Japanese Communist party, was twenty-one years old. He was studying economics at the University of Tokyo. He did not hide his sympathy for Akutagawa, but he described his work as the "literature of defeatism." This state of mind would continue to prevail in Japan for several years. Patriotic fanaticism intensified and was manifested in 1933 by Japan's withdrawal from the League of Nations. One afternoon in February, the *Mainichi* article tells us, the police arrested an adolescent girl, a boarding school student, just as she finished descending Mount Mihara, an active volcano in the center of Oshima island, south of Tokyo Bay. The girl admitted that she had accompanied one of her classmates, who had committed suicide by flinging herself into the boiling crater. Questioned further, she insisted on her story and stated that she had accompanied another classmate the month before. Mount Mihara became a pilgrimage site, while the unwilling witness of this wave of suicides died soon after, her nerves shattered.

GUARDIAN OF THE LEGITIMATE DEMOCRACY

The reign of Hirohito thus continued as a long ascent of Calvary, an ascent strewn with suicides, assassinations, a revolution in 1936, right down to the holocaust of the war, with the atomic bomb and defeat. On Tuesday, August 14, 1945, at 11:25 P.M., Hirohito recorded his message announcing to Japan that he had accepted the Potsdam conditions for surrender. Hiroshi Shimomura, director of information, who was present at the recording session, says that he saw tears fill the emperor's eyes. Less than twenty years later, at the beginning of October 1964, on one of those days when autumn dresses Japan in festive garments, the emperor entered the great stadium to declare the Olympic Games open. The entire world followed this on television screens, and it seemed as if the little man with the keen, sparkling eyes was ready to express to the world the profound yearning that each of his subjects, powerful or miserable, bears within him: the need to be loved: *amae*. In 1964, it was almost a supplication.

In March 1970, at Osaka, when the emperor inaugurated the Universal Exposition, his act subsumed all the evidence of a power which was by then second in the Western world. It is therefore an accepted fact that the emperor once again has the force of a symbol, even if not the force of actual power. He is conscious of his role. On April 29, 1971, he was seventy years old. The empress was sixty-seven. When he chose Nagako, he had trampled underfoot a thousand years of tradition which prescribed that the emperor take his wife from among five princely families. Although of aristocratic birth, Nagako did not belong to any of these families. Hirohito and Nagako lead a simple life in a modest, one-story house, Fukiage Palace, in the middle of the Imperial Park. The new Imperial Palace, where official ceremonies are held, such as the issuing of diplomatic credentials, is a ten-minute walk away.

Hirohito had not left Japan since 1921. At that time, writing from London to his younger brother, Prince Chichibu, twenty years old, he said: "It is in England that I have for the first time learned what freedom means to a human being." When thousands of foreigners from all over the world came to Japan on the occasion of Expo '70, Hirohito declared: "It was fifty years ago that I who have always been a bird in a cage had the experience of freedom in Europe."

That long ago first journey, repeated in September 1971 as if it were a pilgrimage, left the young prince with habits he has retained ever since. He always sleeps in a bed and not, like other Japanese, on a mat on the tatami. He eats an English breakfast and wears European clothes. Yet he remains obsessed by memories of the war, and the role the military forced him to play, making him shoulder the responsibility of unconditional surrender. Since 1945, he has led a quiet and simple life, even though surrounded by what journalists have called the "chrysanthemum curtain." But few men have experienced as he has the vicissitudes of history, from the summit of grandeur right down to the depths of a people's misery. It is this view of things that makes his an exceptional history of human adventures. Paradoxically, it is this imperial view that bears witness to democracy in Japan.

Conclusion

I have always been fascinated by sumo wrestling matches. The theater in which the tourneys take place four times a year—twice at Tokyo and twice at Osaka—is dimly lit, arranged like a circus tent, and the floor beneath the seats of honor are covered by the traditional tatami. On entering, you take off your shoes, as if at home, and settle down in the most relaxed position possible. You cannot see all the matches in one day, so you must bring along your *o'bento*. You can come with your family or with friends, and if the wrestlers are second-rate, you can neglect the show and chat.

A social meeting place, the sumo becomes, at certain moments of the day, an entrancing ceremony, setting in motion mythic forces which confront one another in the beyond.

After hours of preparation, the demigods come face to face for a few seconds. The ritual is punctuated by a master of ceremonies. The wrestlers watch each other from under the platform, from time to time tossing salt on the ground—a rite of purification before the *tachai*, the wrestling match. Each of these men generally weighs about 220 pounds. Some champions of the Federation of Sumo Wrestlers, an almost feudal corporation, have gone to Europe and America. The great champions are watched over and coddled. Thus an airline company, in order to obtain the contract to bring one of these demigods to Europe, had to guarantee that he would not get a venereal disease.

Watching the matches, then going to visit the wrestlers backstage, I sought the reason why they are so seductive to the Japanese. One can offer an answer: the wrestlers are equipped with all the virtues; they are stronger and more virile; in their world they can win or lose, but in the eyes of the average citizen they represent invincibility. For the Japanese, surrounded by often malevolent forces, to which he pays tribute, the sumo is a reassuring element in his daily dream, the element supplied in the real world by the police, institutions, or his own group. Europeans and Americans are aware of a new comic-strip hero imported from Japan, whose worldwide success cannot be explained only by fleeting fashion. Goldorak represents something more: again a myth only Japan could make: the

261

myth of security. For all the children of the world, Goldorak is invincible, the strongest, the only guarantee of stability.

To what does the individual Japanese aspire? The Japanese do not reply directly to such a question, but their choice of the forms of daily life is sufficiently eloquent. They want a form of modern life consistent with the traditional context of Japanese space—that is, in coexistence with nature. *Wa*, harmony, seems to be the supreme commandment of social conduct and is linked to the concept of *ma*, the sense of space. Immediately accessible and nearly physical, harmony flows from *ma*, making itself felt on the intellectual plane in a conception of time that is reckoned not in minutes or seconds but in intervals between two sounds or two events. Thus one listens to the rhythm of the water in a small pond at the back of the garden where three carp wave their tails when, by a kind of seesaw motion, a bamboo reservoir overflows, is emptied, and is refilled . . . indefinitely. One could also be in harmony with the familiar noise of fishing boats, whose morning motors announce that it is lovely to sail out into the sea. Everything is a pretext for rhythm: the snow that appears at the summit of Fuji before the coming of winter, the rain that returns in June like a refrain, the red of the maple tree each autumn, or the ephemeral cherry blossoms in the spring.

To what does the individual Japanese aspire?

To preserve the spirit of eternal Japan.

In the words of an eighteenth-century poem by Motoori Norinaga: "If one should ask you to define the spirit of eternal Japan, you should reply: It is like the cherry blossoms in the first rays of the morning sun, pure, clear, and deliciously perfumed."

Index

263